bikeline

What is bikeline?

We are a team of writers, cartographers, geographers and other staff united by our enthusiasm for bicycling and touring. Our project first "got rolling" in 1987, when a group of Vienna cyclists came together to begin producing bicycling maps. Today we are a highly successful publisher that offers a wide range of bikeline® books in five languages covering many European countries.

We need your help to keep our books up-to-date. Please write to us if you find errors or changes. We would also be grateful for experiences and impressions from your own cycling tours.

We look forward to your letters and e-mails (redaktion@esterbauer.com).

Your bikeline team

Preface

In ancient times the Danube bordered the Roman Empire, later the river was the lifeline of the Austro-Hungarian Empire until the Iron Curtain separated countries and ended the economic and cultural connection of the countries till 1989. The changeful history of the countries at the Danube cycle route between Vienna and Bratislava cannot only be seen in cities like Bratislava, Györ or Esztergom, but also right next to the route at the roman excavations at Petronell-Carnuntum. The cycling tourist can look forward to excellent cycling paths on the dykes that line the Danube which leads him through its floodplains. Not less scenic is the Danube's Bend near Visegrád where the river turns south and is headed to Hungarian capital city, Budapest.

This bicycle touring atlas includes detailed maps of the countryside and of many cities and towns, precise route descriptions, information about historic and cultural sites as well as background information and a comprehensive list of overnight accommodations. The one thing this atlas cannot provide is fine cycling weather, but we hope you encounter nothing but sunshine and gentle tailwinds.

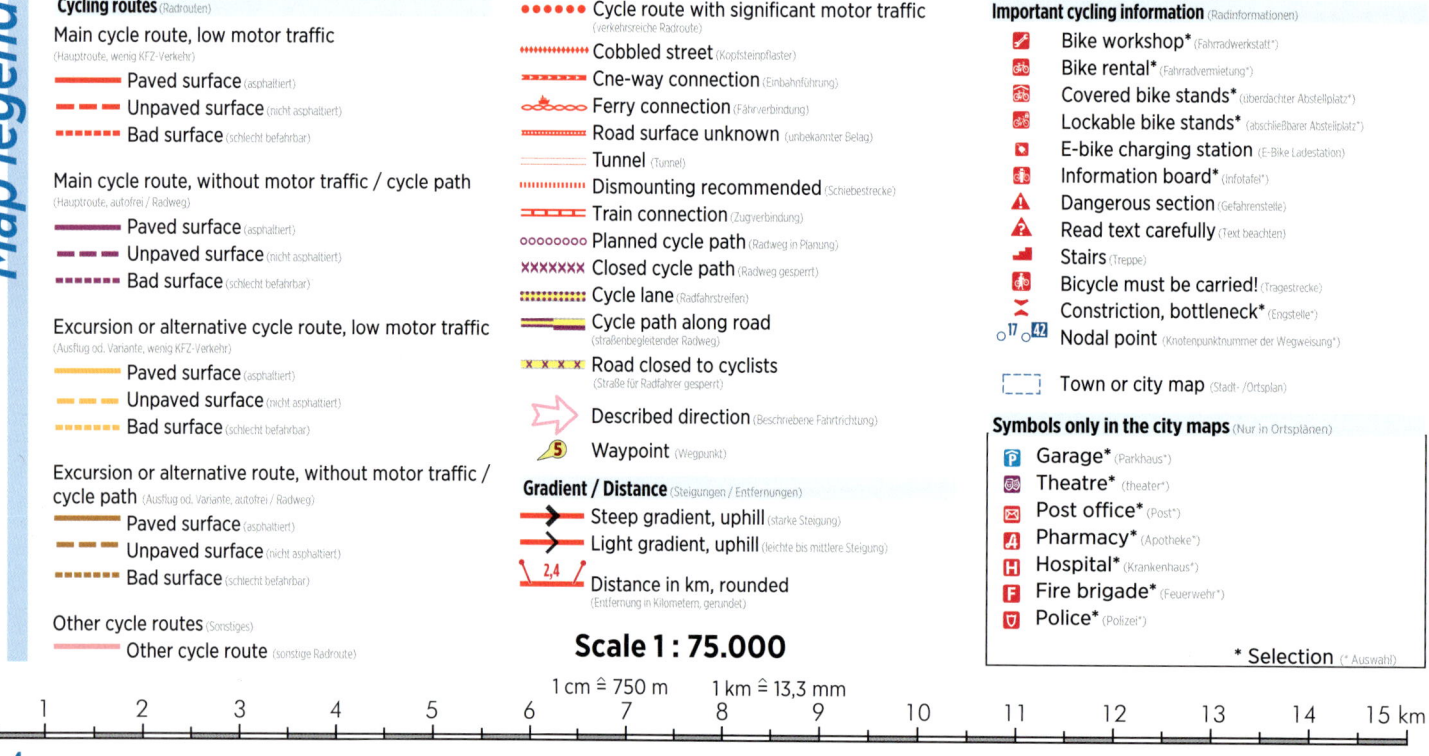

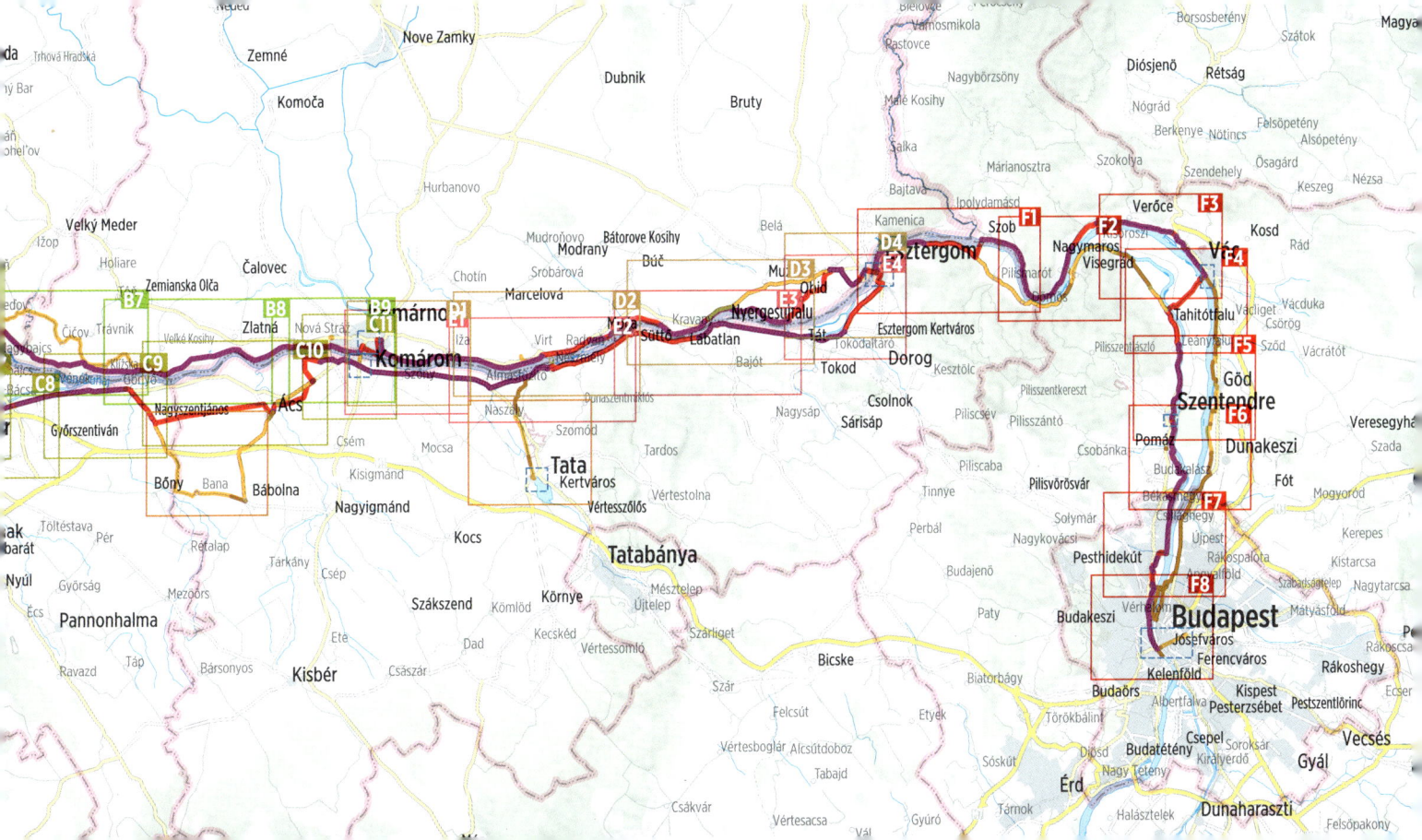

bikeline®-Cycling guide
Danube Bike Trail 3
© 2006-2022, **Verlag Esterbauer GmbH**
A-3751 Rodingersdorf, Hauptstr. 31
Tel.: +43/2983/28982-0, Fax: -500
E-Mail: bikeline@esterbauer.com
www.esterbauer.com
6th. revised edition, Summer 2022
ISBN 978-3-7111-0071-9
Please quote edition and ISBN number in all correspondence!

We wish to thank all the people who contributed to the production of this book

The *bikeline*-Team: Birgit Albrecht-Walzer, Katrin Baumhauer, Beatrix Bauer, Michael Binder, Veronika Bock, Petra Bruckmüller, Roland Esterbauer, Dagmar Güldenpfennig, Martina Kreindl, Gregor Münch, Mario Nakić, Karin Neichsner, Carmen Paradeiser, Amélie Pommier, Manuel Randa, Petra Schartner, Sonja Schleifer, Christina Steinbrecher, Christian Thoren, Isabella Tillich, Martin Trippmacher, Carina Winkelhofer, Martin Wischin, Wolfgang Zangerl

Cover photo: Budapest: © milosk50 - Fotolia; Gloriette: © Jenifoto - fotolia; Orth an der Donau: © Jerzy Bin - Fotolia
Photo credits: anderm - stock.adobe.com: 106; © avirid - Fotolia:11; © Blumesser - stock.adobe.com: 118; © dmpalino - Fotolia:55; dudlajzov stock.adobe.com: 74; Erik Schmidt: 10, 62; Ferenc - stock.adobe.com: 96; Frank Wagner - stock.adobe.com: 19; Gästeinformationsbüro Hainburg: 36; GezaKurkaPhotos - stock.adobe.com: 114; © iza_miszczak - Fotolia:112; Jaroslav Moravcik - stock.adobe.com: 78, 84; © kaycco - Fotolia:34; © kotomiti - Fotolia:45; Mikhail Markovskiy - stock.adobe.com: 90; © mRGB - Fotolia , 23; © Noppasinw - Fotolia:120; Noppasinw - stock.adobe.com: 123; Österr. Bundesforste: 32; Pasztilla aka Attila Terbócs, CC BY-SA 4.0 <https://creativecommons.org/licenses/by-sa/4.0>, via Wikimedia Commons: 68; © PHB.cz - Fotolia:40; photo 5000 - stock.adobe.com: 25; Posztós János - stock.adobe.com: 94; © Renáta Sedmáková - Fotolia:7; rihas - stock.adobe.com: 72; Roland- stock.adobe.com: 61; Roland Esterbauer: 15, 66; SAndor - stock.adobe.com: 100; Sergii Figurnyi - stock.adobe.com: 43; Shchipkova Elena - stock.adobe.com: 52; Sina Ettmer - stock.adobe.com: 124; Stadtverwaltung Györ: 70; Steve - stock.adobe.com: 88; tamas - stock.adobe.com: 80; Tourinform Vác: 108; Ungor - stock.adobe.com: 93; WerbeGrafikDesign Eva Horak: 30; zgphotography - stock.adobe.com: 104

bikeline® are registered trademarks. The cover design is legally protected. While the greatest of care has been taken in researching the contents of this book, it is presented without guarantee. Data and information may change without notification. All rights reserved. No part of this book may be reproduced or electronically altered, reproduced or processed in any form without the publisher's written permission.
Cartography created with axpand (www.axes-systems.com)

Sights of interest / Facilities (Sehenswertes / Einrichtungen)

- Church; Chapel (Kirche, Kapelle)
- Monastery/Convent (Kloster)
- Synagogue; Mosque (Synagoge; Moschee)
- Palace, Castle; Ruin (Schloss, Burg; Ruine)
- Tower; Lighthouse (Turm; Leuchtturm)
- Watermill; Windmill (Wassermühle, Windmühle)
- Power station (Kraftwerk)
- Mine; Cave (Bergwerk; Höhle)
- Airport, Monument (Flughafen, Denkmal)
- Other sight of interest (sonstige Sehenswürdigkeit)
- Museum (Museum)
- Excavations; Roman site (Ausgrabungen; röm. Objekte)
- Zoo; Nature info (Tierpark; Naturpark-Information)
- Nature reserve/Monument (Naturpark, -denkmal)
- Natural sight of interest (sonstige Natursehenswürdigkeit)
- Panoramic view* (Aussichtspunkt*)
- Tourist information; Restaurant (Tourist-Info; Gasthaus)
- Hotel, Guesthouse; Youth hostel (Hotel, Pension; Jugendherberge)
- Campground; Simple tent site* (Camping-; Lagerplatz*)
- Shopping facility*; Kiosk* (Einkaufsmöglichkeit*; Kiosk*)
- Picnic tables*; Covered stand* (Rastplatz*; Unterstand*)
- Outdoor pool; Indoor pool (Freibad; Hallenbad)
- Natural pool; Thermal baths; Waterpark* (Naturbad; Thermal-; Erlebnisbad*)
- Drinking fountain*; Parking lot* (Brunnen*; Parkplatz*)
- **Schönern** Picturesque town (sehenswertes Ortsbild)
- Facilities available (Einrichtung im Ort vorhanden)

Topographic information (Topographische Informationen)

- Church; Chapel (Kirche, Kapelle)
- Monastery/Convent (Kloster)
- Synagogue; Mosque (Synagoge; Moschee)
- Palace, Castle; Ruin (Schloss, Burg; Ruine)
- Tower; Lighthouse (Turm; Leuchtturm)
- Watermill; Windmill (Wassermühle; Windmühle)
- Power station, Solar power station (Kraftwerk)
- Mine; Cave (Bergwerk; Höhle)
- Monument; Burial mound (Denkmal; Hügelgrab)
- Airport; Airfield (Flughafen; Flugplatz)
- Windturbine (Windkraftanlage)
- TV/Radio tower (Funk- und Fernsehanlage)
- Transformer station (Umspannwerk, Trafostation)
- Wayside cross; Boundary stone (Wegkreuz; Grenzstein)
- Playing field, Stadium (Sportplatz, Stadion)
- Golf course; Tennis courts (Golfplatz; Tennisplatz)
- Boat landing; Sluice/lock (Schiffsanleger; Schleuse)
- Natural spring; Wastewater treatment plant (Quelle; Klaranlage)
- International border crossing (Staatsgrenze; Übergang)
- State border (Landesgrenze)
- District border (Kreis-, Bezirksgrenze)
- Nature reserve, National park (Naturschutzgebiet, Naturpark, Nationalpark)
- Prohibited zone (Truppenübungsplatz; Sperrgebiet)
- Contour line 100m/50m (Höhenlinie 100m/50m)

- Motorway/Freeway; Expressway (Autobahn, Schnellstr.)
- Highway (Fernverkehrsstraße)
- Main road (Hauptstraße)
- Secondary main road (untergeordnete Hauptstraße)
- Secondary road; Access road (Nebenstraße; Fahrweg)
- Track; Ferry (Weg; Fähre)
- Road planned/under construction (geplant/in Bau)
- Railway/station; S-train station (Eisenbahn/Bahnhof; S-Bahnhof)
- Railway disused; planned (Eisenbahn stillgelegt; geplant)
- Narrow gauge railway (Schmalspurbahn)
- Mountain railway; Cable car (Bergbahn; Seilbahn)
- Forest; Park (Wald; Parkanlage)
- Marsh/Bog; Heath (Sumpf; Heide)
- Vineyards; Allotment gardens* (Weinbau; Gärten*)
- Quarry; Open cast mine* (Steinbruch; Tagebau*)
- Cemetery; Dunes/Beach (Friedhof; Düne; Strand)
- Tidal flats; Glacier (Watt; Gletscher)
- Rock; Cliff; Scree (Felsen; Geröll)
- Greenhouse; Plantation (Gewächshäuser; Plantage)
- Commercial/Industrial area (Gewerbe-, Industriegebiet)
- Urban area; Public building (Siedlung; öffentl. Gebäude)
- Defensive wall/Wall (Stadtmauer; Mauer)
- Embankment, Dike (Damm, Deich)
- Canal (Kanal)
- River/Dam/Lake (Fluss/Staumauer/See)

Contents

3	Preface	
7	The Danube Bike Trail from Vienna to Budapest	
16	About this book	
18	Vienna to Bratislava	69.1 km
30	South bank alternative	24.1 km
44	Bratislava to Komárno (SK)	100.9 km
50	On the Hungarian side to Győr	17.5 km
56	Bratislava to Komárom (H)	122.5 km
60	Alternative via Szigetköz	34.8 km
70	Alternative route along the Mosoni Duna to Győr	13.2 km
76	Alternative via Bábolna	22.1 km
82	Komárno to Esztergom (SK)	56.5 km
84	Alternative route via Mužla	12 km
92	Komárom to Esztergom (H)	53.2 km
94	Excursion to Tata	10.9 km
102	Esztergom to Budapest	81.4 km
103	Alternative via Visegrád	24.7 km
112	Alternative via Göd	35.8 km
126	Accommodation and service directory	
138	English-Hungarian-Slovak dictionary	
140	Location index	

City maps

Bratislava	41
Budapest	121
Esztergom	91
Győr	73
Hainburg	37
Komárno	54
Komárom	80
Mosonmagyaróvár	64
Szentendre	114
Tata	96
Vác	110
Vienna	21

The Danube Bike Trail from Vienna to Budapest

As most cycling tourists finish their journey along the Danube's bank at Vienna the Danube Bike Trail through Slovakia and into Hungary, to the city of Budapest, is accordingly quieter and more idyllic. The continuation of the one can indulge the senses while cycling through riverside forests, quiet villages and historic towns where the Iron Curtain once divided Europe in two; all this while crossing two borders without even needing to present a passport.

Bratislava, Devin Ruin

LIVE-UPDATES

 On our web page we offer an online-service, that provides updated information and current changes concerning this cycling guide. This information is brought up-to-date regularly and enables you, in combination with the current edition of this book, to plan your trip in the best possible way. The Live-Update for this book is freely available on our web page while looking up the title or under:

https://www.esterbauer.com/danube-bike-trail-3

Have you noticed some changes or mistakes during your journey concerning the itinerary, the overnight accommodation or the tourist information along the route? Then you have the possibility to bring the bikeline-team up-to-date using the Update-section on our web page. We are looking forward to getting your information and say Thank You in the name of all cyclists.

 The latest bikeline GPS-Track for this book is freely available under:

https://www.tracks.world/?dir=at/trk44cj257

Downstream from Vienna, the Danube is lined with game-rich forests, along the edge of which generations of Austrian Monarchs built their summer residences. After the war they were often referred to as "Dying Palaces", but luckily the Austrian state decided to renovate these places of princely hunting pleasure before it was too late.

Traces of the Roman Empire have been found near the right bank of the Danube. Carnuntum was a Roman military base and one of its most important cities. Today it is separated from the Danube by several smaller arms of the river. The last of the large riverside settlements on the Austrian side is the town of Hainburg, where vessels once shipped out the production of the imperial tobacco industry from its harbour. Above the confluence of the March and Danube rivers lie the ruins of the medieval castle of Devín, its earliest history going back into ancient times. From here, the castle of Bratislava can be seen in the distance. A border stone near here marks the end of the western world, but the Danube ignores such categories and merely changes its name: known in German as the „Donau", it becomes the Slovak „Dunaj" and later the Hungarian „Duna". The section of the Danube between Hainburg and Bratislava is known as the „Hainburger Gate", where the Danube divides the Hainburger Mountains from the Little Carpathians. After entering Slovakia the Danube comes to define the border between Slovakia and Hungary as it makes its way through the Small Hungarian Plain. The transition from the lowlands to the mountain ranges in Slovakia seems quite surprising, possibly due the small size of the country. More than half of the country is dominated by the Carpathian mountains. The Danube loses its natural flow shortly after Bratislava, becoming slow and bordered by dykes. The reason is that you are riding towards one of the largest dams in central Europe, the Gabčíkovo dam and hydro-electric scheme. One of the positive results

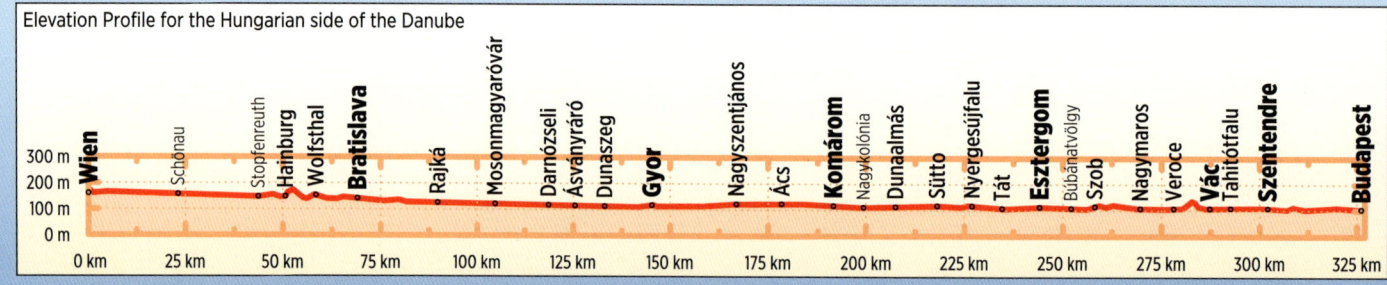

of this massive reconstruction of the natural river landscape is that the area has become a popular recreational area for the people of Bratislava. There was even enough space on the dam at Čunovo for a water sport centre and museum.

After the river regains its natural character by Medved'ov, it flows unhurried past the towns of Komárno and Komárom, where friends of castles, fortifications and culture absolutely need to take their time.

At the eastern end of the Small Hungarian Plain before the river runs into another range of mountains, there appears in the distance a great dome like some optical illusion that blocks light and the river's flow. It is the Esztergom Cathedral, modeled after St. Peter's Cathedral in Rome, and seat of the Hungarian Roman Catholic primate. The classical basilica forms one of the three monumental Hungarian edifices that line the Danube. The other two are the Parliament in Pest and the castle in Buda. Downstream from Esztergom the Danube continues towards the east before the river narrows between Zebegény and Visegrád. The river's flow accelerates, forming dangerous eddies and currents, before it slows again as it passes through Visegrád. The scholar Archbishop of Esztergom wrote in his publication of 1536 „Hungaria", that the royal palace on Visegrád was more beautiful and radiant that words could describe. Already in the 19th century no trace of the palace was to be seen. No wall or stone confirmed the account of the archbishop. It was not until later that the impressive ruins of the palace were excavated. After Visegrád the Danube then curves around steep cliffs, freeing itself of the mountains and making its ways slowly towards the old bishops seat of Vác. This section of the Danube,

Route statistics	
Length of main route: 308 km	
elev. m/km: ↗ 0.5 m (153 m) ↘ 0.7 m (213 m)	
cycle path: 80 % unpaved: 3 % busy road: 5 %	
Sum of all routes: 822 km	

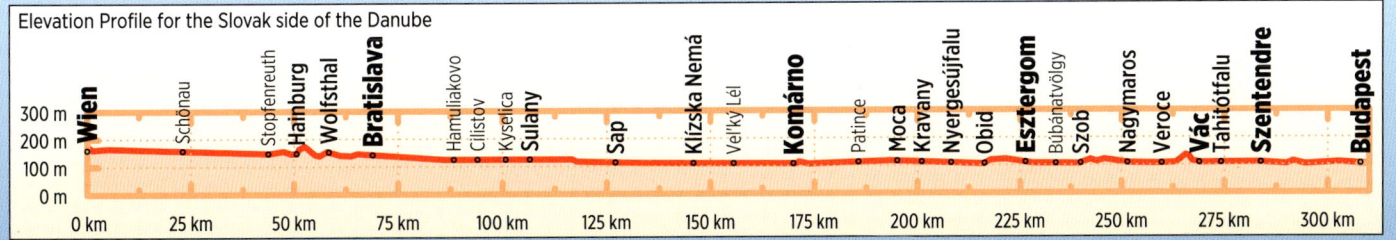

known as the „knee", is among the highlights of a journey along the Danube.

On the right bank, the river flows past the beautiful small town of Szentendre, which still looks much unchanged from how it was built in the 18th century. Szentendre's narrow streets, its many church towers, the wooden staircases, steep alleys, covered walkways and gardens create an inviting atmosphere for romantic walks. The town has a significant Serbian community, which gives it a southerly flair mixed with the smell of garlic from hot "lángos," the delicious Hungarian fried bread.

Just beyond Szentendre lies Budapest. From the Danube's source in the Black Forest to its mouth on the Black Sea, there is no other place where the graceful river is enclosed with greater magnificence, generosity and dignity than in the Hungarian capital. This is where the Danube finds its "golden section" with a city that greets visitors with light and life. Budapest is a worthy end to a journey along the Danube - or an important stop along the way to the Black sea!

Yellow Signage in Hungary

Green Signage in Hungary

Route characteristics

Length

The total length of the Danube Bike Trail from Vienna to Budapest is 308 kilometers on the Slovak side of the river, and 324 kilometers on the Hungarian side. This does not include side trips and alternative routes.

Surface quality and traffic

In **Austria**, all but a very short section is well developed, mostly following a paved path without motorized traffic on the Hubertusdamm. Only in the village of Wolfsthal you have to cycle on the very busy main road. Alternatively you can choose quiet roads through the village.

Completion of the major hydro-electric plant on the Danube in **Slovakia** has also resulted in outstanding paved bicycle paths on the crowns of the dykes on both sides of the river. Partly you also cycle on asphalted paths parallel to the dyke. From Gabčíkovo you continue cycling along the well asphalted cycleway on the dyke until you reach Komárno. Between Komárno and Štúrovo the route alternates between public roads – sometimes with heavier traffic, paved cycleways and paths along the river, some of which are not paved and difficult to negotiate.

Hungary has undertaken significant improvements, the Danube Cycle Route has been and is being continuously developed. You will mostly be riding on quiet roads and newly constructed bicycle paths. Two shorter sections of unpaved paths remain which are quite difficult to negotiate not even in wet weather. Sections which run along roads with heavy traffic are to find between Neszmély and Lábatlan, shortly before Esztergom and around Búbánatvölgy. The heavy city traffic in Budapest is mostly avoided by the bicycle path along the Danube.

Signage

Signage marking the route varies from country to country. In **Austria**, the Danube Bike Trail is uniformly marked with large green rectangular signs. **Slovakia** uses the same signs as far as Medved'ov. The cycle route is also continuously signposted through Slovakia.

The Danube Bike Trail in **Hungary** is now, as part of the EuroVelo-Route 6, completely signposted. The are two signs in use: green signs along completed bicycle paths and yellow signs where the route runs along roads or poor quality paths and temporary routes.

Planning a Tour

Important Telephone Numbers
International telephone codes:
Hungary: 0036
Slovakia: 00421
Austria: 0043

Central Information Offices
Tourist Info Vienna, Albertinaplatz/Maysedergasse, A-1010 Wien ✆ +43/1/24555, www.wien.info/en, info@wien.info

Esztergom, Basilica

Slovak tourist office in Austria, Opernring 1/R/507, 1010 Wien, ☎ +43/1/5139569, https://slovakia.travel/en, office.at@slovakia.travel

Slovak tourist office in Germany, Hildebrandstr. 25, D-10785 Berlin, ☎ +49/30/25942640, office.de@slovakia.travel, https://slovakia.travel/en

Slovak Tourism Board, Lamačská cesta 4256/8, SK-83304 Bratislava, ☎ +42/2/50700801, https://slovakia.travel/en, info@slovakia.travel

Bratislava Tourism Board, Klobčnicka 2, SK-81101 Bratislava, ☎ +42/2/16186 or +42/2/54419310, touristinfo@visitbratislava.com, www.visitbratislava.com

Hungarian Tourism Board Kacsa u. 15-23, H-1525 Budapest, ☎ +36/1/4888700, info@mtu.gov.hu, https://visithungary.com/en

Hungarian Bicycle Tourist Association (MKTSZ), H-1065 Budapest, Pf. 483, ☎ +36/1/311-2467, www.facebook.com/pages/MKTSZ/553072134728576

Arrival & departure by rail

There is a good long-distance connection from Budapest Keleti pu (Central Station) to Vienna Central Station by Railjet (RJ) or Eurocity (EC). Note that you need to book a space for your bike (€ 3,- online or € 3,50 via ticket counter). Due to the constantly changing prices and conditions for transport of a bicycle by rail we suggest that you inform yourself about your personal rail travel at the following addresses.

Information centres

Deutsche Bahn AG (German Rail): Service-Hotline ☎ +49/30/2970, Mon-Sun 0-24 hrs, information on ticket prices and timetables, information on services of the German Railways, www.bahn.com/en

ÖBB Österreichische Bundesbahnen (Austrian Rail): Customer service ☎ 05/1717 (Austria-wide at local rates), Mon-Sun 6-21 hrs, www.oebb.at/en/, www.oebb.at/en/reiseplanung-services/im-zug/fahrrad-mitnahme

Schweizer Bundesbahnen (Swiss Rail): Rail-Service ☎ +41/848/446688 (CHF 0,08/Min.), Mon-Sun 0-24 hrs, www.sbb.ch/en/home.html, www.sbb.ch/en/timetable/travel-advice/bicycles/take-your-bike-with-you.html

MÁV, Hungarian State Railways Ltd., Customer service ☎ +36/(1)3/494949, Mon-Sun 0-24 hrs, www.mavcsoport.hu/en

BKK Centre for Budapest Transport, Rumbach Sebestyén u. 19-21, H-1075 Budapest, ☎ +36/13/255255, bkk@bkk.hu, https://bkk.hu/en/

ZSSK, Železničná spoločnosť Slovensko (Railway Company Slovakia), ☎ +42/124/4858188, info@slovakrail.sk, www.zssk.sk/en/

Arrival & departure by ship

The **Twin City Liner** takes you from Vienna to Bratislava in 75 min. Registration is required for bicycle transport and costs € 5. For more information call ✆ +43/1/9048880, booking@twincityliner.com, www.twincityliner.com.

Bike & Public Transport
In Vienna, bicycles can be taken along at any time on trains marked with a bicycle symbol in the timetable. In the Vienna core zone (zone 100), a half-price ticket must be purchased for this, on all other routes a bicycle ticket.
On the underground, transport is free, access only at doors with a bicycle symbol (not at rush hour). Vienna City Card: 24, 48 or 72 hour-ticket for public transport incl. discounts at many museums and sights in Vienna. Available at the tourist information office, hotels and at the sales points of the larger underground stations. (www.wien.info/en/travel-info/vienna-city-card)

Cycling in Vienna
The bicycle paths and lanes in Vienna have their peculiarities, as you will see. Here are some of the most important rules:
Cyclists must **yield the right of way** at the end of the bicycle path, or when leaving any bicycling facility (bicycle path, bicycle lane, multi-purpose lane or bicycle crossing)! At bicycle crossings (marked on the pavement), the cyclist has the right of way but may not ride faster than 10 km/h! On one-way streets (Einbahnstraße), cyclists may ride against the flow only where this is explicitly permitted. In Vienna's pedestrian zones (Fußgängerzone), cyclists must dismount.

Overnight accommodation
In **Austria** you will find many different accommodation options - from noble hotels to cosy guesthouses and private rooms. Especially in the high season, accommodation can be fully booked quickly, which is why it is advisable to book in advance.
In many of the towns and villages along the route through **Hungary** it is easy to find inexpensive accommodation in private homes. These also often offer a good breakfast for an additional price. Reservations for rooms are usually necessary only in the Main season, and can be made in the local county seat. In

Budapest it is always a good idea to reserve a room in advance. In emergencies, one can rely on the great hospitality of the Hungarian people. Hotels are usually expensive and well-equipped. Guesthouses are considerably more affordable, clean and comfortable. During the summer holidays it is also possible to stay in cheap student accommodation. Information can be found at the tourist information or via the internet.

Overnight accommodations in **Slovakia** are harder to find. Local tourism offices and travel agents have little information about the areas along the Danube.

Travelling with children

The Danube Bike Trail between Vienna and Budapest is in great part not well suited for children. The necessity of riding with considerable traffic in some sections means that this tour should probably not be undertaken with children under the age of 12. This applies, however, only to the route in parts of Hungary. In Austria and in Slovakia as far as Medved'ov the well developed bicycle paths are well suited to riding with children.

Bicycle rentals

Bike & Relax Kft, Madach Imre ut 12, HU-1075 Budapest, ✆ 0036/30/3008003, info@bike-and-relax.com, https://bike-and-relax.com

Bicycle tour operators:

Eurobike Eurofun Touristik GmbH, Mühlstr. 20, A-5162 Obertrum am See, ✆ 06219/60866, Infohotline (free of charge from Germany, Austria and Switzerland) ✆ 0800/0706333, eurobike@eurobike.at, www.eurobike.at

Donau-Touristik GmbH, Ledererg. 4-12, A-4010 Linz, ✆ 0732/2080, Free service telephone number from Germany: ✆ 0800/1001147, office@donautouristik.com, www.donaureisen.at

Rad & Reisen, Schickg. 9, A-1220 Wien, ✆ 0800/0700570 (free from A, D and CH), office@radreisen.at, www.radreisen.at

Austria Radreisen, Joseph-Haydn-Str. 8, A-4780 Schärding, ✆ 07712/55110, office@austria-radreisen.at, www.austria-radreisen.at

Velotours Touristik GmbH, Bücklestr. 13, CH-78467 Konstanz, ✆ 07531/98280, info@velotours.de, www.velotours.de

Oberösterreich Touristik GmbH, Freistädter Str. 119, A-4041 Linz, ✆ 0732/7277-260, info@touristik.at, www.touristik.at

Pedalo, Kickendorf 1a, A-4710 Grieskirchen, ✆ 0800/2400999 (freecall from A, D and

CH) od. ☎ 07248/635840, info@pedalo.com, www.pedalo.com

Velociped Fahrradreisen, Alte Kasseler Str. 43, D-35039 Marburg, ☎ 06421/886890, info@velociped.de, www.velociped.de

Velo-Touring, Elöpatak u. 1, H-1118 Budapest, ☎ 01/3190571; pedal@velo-touring.hu, www.velo-touring.hu

Reisen & Radeln, Carl-Benz-Str. 49, D-73235 Weilheim Teck, ☎ 07023/9570840, info@reisen-radeln.de, www.reisen-radeln.de

Rückenwind Reisen, Am Patentbusch 14, D-26125 Oldenburg, ☎ 0800/5889717 (freecall from D) otherwise ☎ 0441/485970, info@rueckenwind.de, www.rueckenwind.de

Radreiseprofi, Bücklestraße 13, D-78467 Konstanz, ☎ 07531/98280, office radreiseprofi.com, www.radreiseprofi.com

Kunath Reisen, Robert-Blum Str. 9, D-08523 Plauen, ☎ 03741/4060780, mail@kunathreisen.de, www.kunathreisen.de

About this book

This cycling guide contains all the information you need for your cycling vacation along the Danube from Vienna to Budapest: Precise maps, a detailed description of the route, a comprehensive list of overnight accommodation, numerous detail maps of cities and towns, and information about the most significant sights.

And all that information comes with our **bikeline guarantee**: The route described in this book has been tested and evaluated in person by one of our editors! To assure that the book is as up-to-date as possible, we welcome corrections submitted by readers and local officials or businesses. We cannot, however, always check and confirm such changes before deadline.

The maps

The detail maps are produced in a scale of 1:50,000 (1 centimeter = 500 meters). In addition to exactly describing the route, these maps also provide information about roadway quality (paved or unpaved), climbs (gentle or steep), distances, as well as available cultural and culinary highlights.

Even with the most precise map, consulting the written description of the route may be necessary at times. Locations where the route is difficult to follow are shown by the ⚠ symbol on the maps, the same symbol can then be found in the written description where the route is explained in detail.

Note that the recommended main route is always shown in red or purple; alternative and excursion routes in orange. The individual symbols used in the maps are described in the legend on pages 4 and 5.

Height and distance profile

The detailed route altitude profiles at the beginning of each section provide a graphic depiction of elevations along the route, the total length as well as waypoints and the location of towns and cities along the way. The waypoints enable a direct reference to the maps and route description. The altitude profile does not show every individual small hill and dip, but only the major changes in elevation. On the detail maps smaller gradients are shown by arrows that point uphill.

The text

The maps are supplemented by a written text that describes the route starting in Passau and proceeding down the Danube to Vienna. Key phrases about the route description are indicated with the symbol.

Many distinctive or important positions along the route are marked as waypoints with consecutive numbers 1, 2, 3, ... and, to help with navigation, are to be found with the same symbol in the maps.

The description of the main route is also interrupted by passages describing alternative and excursion routes. These are printed in orange color.

TIP: Text printed in purple indicates that you must make a decision about how your tour shall continue. For instance, there may be an alternative route that is not included in the tour description, or a turn-off to another location.

EXCURSION: These also indicate excursion suggestions, interesting sights or recreational facilities that are not directly on the main route.

Furthermore, the names of important **villages**, towns and cities are printed in bold type. If a location or community has important points of interest, addresses, telephone numbers and opening times are listed under the headline with the name of the place.

Descriptions of the larger towns and cities, as well as historic, cultural and natural landmarks help round out the travel experience. These paragraphs are printed in italics to distinguish them from the route description.

Opening hours - Categories
- ⏱ Opening hours
- 24 freely accessible
- 7⃝ daily
- ⊜ frequently (5-6 days/week)
- ⊜ average (3-4 days/week)
- ⊜ rare (up to 2 days/week)
- ℭ after tel. request

This information is valid during the cycling season and serves as a guide. The daily opening hours can be found via the web link.

Weblink
In the location data block at the respective tourist entry there is a six-digit number and a letter combination after the @ symbol (e.g. @ abc123en). Entering this weblink ID on our website www.esterbauer.com will take you directly to the corresponding website and thus replace the tedious entry of long web addresses.

List of overnight accommodation
The last pages of this cycling guide provide a list of convenient hotels and guest houses in virtually every village or town along the route. This list also includes youth hostels and campgrounds.

With the e-bike
More and more cyclists are now riding an e-bike. Basically, the requirements are the same, even if longer sections and more climbs can be covered. Since the performance of non-motorised cyclists also varies greatly, we have not specified section lengths in the past. Narrow passages, stairs or carrying points that are difficult to manage due to the weight of an e-bike are marked on the maps and alternatives are indicated where possible. We deliberately refrain from systematically recording official charging stations, as the "unofficial" charging stations (sockets) are disproportionately more frequent. Do not forget your charging cable.

Vienna to Bratislava

69.1 km

m/km: ↗1.0 (68m) ↘1.3 (87m)   cycle path: 84 %   unpaved: 4 %   busy road: 0 %

The first stage of the bicycle tour takes you along posted bicycle routes through extensive flood-plains. The majestic forests are criss-crossed by forgotten arms of the Danube and riddled with small ponds and lakes. Within the urban area of Vienna you cross through the famous Prater and the Lobau. Between Vienna and the small city Hainburg you ride along the Hubertusdamm through the Stopfenreuther und Hainburger flood-plains and from Hainburg you can take a leisurely side trip to explore the Roman town of Carnuntum. Beyond the Hainburger Gate you leave Austria and arrive in the charming Slovak capital of Bratislava.

In this section you ride along well signposted bicycle paths and dykes of excellent quality. It is only in the city streets in Vienna and along the B 9 road near Wolfsthal that one needs to take special care due to the traffic.

From the central train station to the city centre 2.4 km

If you have not already arrived in Vienna by bicycle, but are starting your journey from the **Hauptbahnhof,** than you can use the metro line U 1 to get to the city centre at **Stephansplatz** but you can also ride by bike.

TIP The central train station was opened in 2014. 1.100 trains and 145.000 passengers depart and arrive here. You can use a centre map and a map of the surrounding area to navigate through the train station.

It's best if you start your journey at the main entrance of the station at **Wiedner Gürtel/ Südtiroler Platz** ~ cross the **Wiedner Gürtel** and cycle along the **Favoritenstraße** ~ turn right at the first opportunity, **Schelleingasse** ~ at the end of the street turn left into the **Argentinierstraße** ~ cycle down the road and around the church and you will eventually end up at the **Karlsplatz** which is named after the striking St. Charles church ~ turn left and ride alongside the park ~ at the end turn slightly right into the **Operngasse** ~ soon you will reach the tram lines and the opera house at the **Opernring**.

TIP From here you can connect with the Ring-Rund-Radweg (Ring-Round Cycle Route), a bicycle route that encircles the old city and connects some of the most important sights in Vienna. You will find many of Vienna's major sights right along the **Ringstraße**: the Opera House, the Art History Museum, the Natural History Museum, the Hofburg, the parliament, Town Hall, Burgtheater (Court Theatre), University, Votiv church and many more. It is tradition to undertake a sightseeing tour of Vienna in a horse drawn coach, a Fiaker. But the major sights along the Ringstraße can, thanks to the bicycle path, easily be explored with the bicycle. It doesn't matter if you ride along the Ringstraße in a clockwise or anti-clockwise direction, you will eventually reach the start of the Danube Bike Trail by the Urania, at the Donaukanal.

If you are looking to get to the **St. Stephen's Cathedral**, you need to ride through the historic town centre. If coming from Opernring you need to cross **Herbert-von-Karajan-Platz**, which was named after the famous maestro. Right behind the square you will find the **Kärntner Straße**. From here you must push your bicycle through the busy shopping street to the Stephansplatz. Afterwards you ride along the **Rotenturmstraße** to **Schwedenplatz**, where you ride to the right and along the **Donaukanal** to Urania.

TIP After a sightseeing tour, the best thing to do in Vienna is to seek out one of it's famous coffee houses to relax and enjoy a

Vienna, Danube Canal at the Urania

pedalpower bike

Sightseeing
3 hrs **Guided Bike Tours**
March thru November
also with own bike

Classic Vienna
Vienna's Inner City and most
of the beautiful sights

Radverleih
quality bikes in top condition
Service & Repairs
bike transfer to train station

+43 1 729 72 34 vienna

www.pedalpower.at
office@pedalpower.at
1., Bösendorferstrasse 5

"Melange", or get out to a "Heurigen" in Grinzing, Stammersdorf or Nussdorf.

Wien (Vienna) Ⓐ
prefix: 01

Tourist-Information (Tourist information), Albertinapl./Mayonna Maysederg., 1. Bezirk (Wien), ✆ 24555, @ yjw785en

Tourist-Information Hauptbahnhof (Tourist information main station), Am Hauptbahnhof 1, at the infopoint of ÖBB Austrian railways, ✆ 24555, @ vnr853en

DDSG Blue Danube, Handelskai 265, ✆ 58880 Sightseeing Cruises in Vienna. Locations: Schwedenplatz, Marina Wien, Reichsbrücke, @ qyb267en

Albertina, Albertinapl. 1, ✆ 53483540 One of the world's most important art museums. Artists represented range from Michelangelo to Rubens, Dürer to Picasso. Significant special exhibitions about various artists and photographers. Archives include more than 60,000 drawings and about 1 million printed pages from the late Gothic period to the present. @ wpa636en

Heeresgeschichtliches Museum (Military history museum), Ghegastr., ✆ 05020/11060301 Occupies an oriental-classical building from 1857, which was Vienna's first building planned as a museum. Contains valuable Austrian military items from the 30 Years War to World War I. Among other things, the car is exhibited in which Archduke Franz Ferdinand and his wife Sophie Chotek were shot by Gavrilo Princip on June 28, 1914 in Sarajevo. The assassination triggered a European crisis that led to the First World War. @ ksl841en

Kunsthistorisches Museum (Art history museum), Burgring 5, ✆ 525240 One of the most renowned art collections in the world. The core collection includes works by Dürer, Rubens, Titian and Bruegel the older (largest Bruegel collection in the world). Also noteworthy: the Egyptian/Oriental collection, antiquity collections and numismatics collection. @ jbg576en

MAK - Museum für angewandte Kunst (Museum of Applied Arts), Stubenring 5, ✆ 711360 Furniture, textiles or glass and ceramics - how art influences everyday life and how everyday life influences art can be explored in the MAK. The exhibits range from East Asian and Islamic art, art prints, metalwork and works by the Wiener Werkstätte to a collection of carpets and the works of modern artists. @ mlt288en

Mozarthaus Vienna (Mozart House), Domg. 5, ✆ 5121791 Wolfgang Amadeus Mozart lived in this house for three years, from 1784 to 1787. The exhibition deals with his work and life. @ ewy774en

Naturhistorisches Museum (Natural History Museum), Burgring 7, ✆ 521770 The museum displays minerals, rare uncut diamonds and meteorites, a fossil collection and 15,000 skeletons (including dinosaurs). Prehistoric items include the original "Willendorf Venus" and anthropological items from the early-Paleolithic period to the present. @ umu572en

Oberes Belvedere (Upper Belvedere), Prinz-Eugen-Str. 27, ✆ 795570 A survey of Austrian painting from Biedermeier through the Ringstraße Period to art nouveau. Large collections of works by Klimt, Schiele and Kokoschka, plus Waldmüller, Romako, Makart, Wotruba and others. @ cpu853en

Österreichische Nationalbibliothek (Austrian National Library), Josefspl. 1, ✆ 53410 The

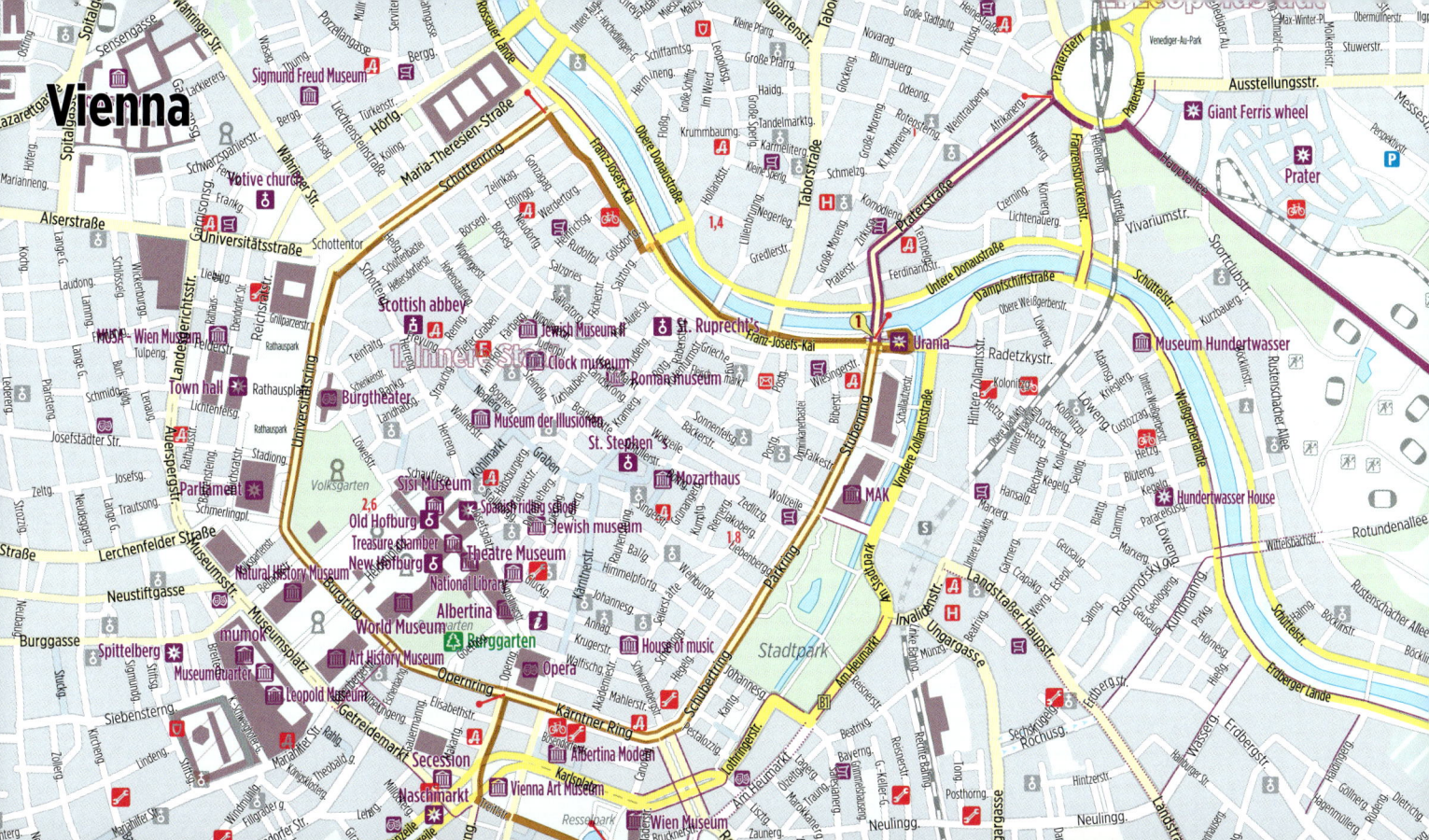

baroque main hall was created by Fischer von Erlach and son 1723-37. Ceiling painting by Daniel Gran. Holds the 15,000 gold-printed volumes collected by Prince Eugene of Savoy. Also worth seeing: State Hall, Literature Museum, Globe Museum, Papyrus Museum and Esperanto Museum. @ xhe814en

Kaiserliche Schatzkammer (Imperial Treasury), Hofburg-Schweizerhof, ✆ 525240 🌐 One of the world's great treasures, includes the Holy Roman Emperor's crown (ca. 962), the Austrian Emperor's crown, the Burgundy treasure and the treasures of the Order of the Golden Fleece. @ ytp216en

Albertina Modern, Karlspl. 5, ✆ 53483540 🌐 The Museum of Modern and Contemporary Art shows Austrian art history of the last 80 years, with a focus on the Essl Collection. Additionally, an insight into collections of international art is provided. @ kbl828en

Belvedere 21, Arsenalstr. 1, ✆ 795370 🌐 The museum shows Austrian art from the 20th and 21st cs. and is housed in a remarkable building designed by star architect Karl Schwanzer as an Austrian pavilion for the 1958 World Exhibition. @ eje228en

Dritte Mann Museum (Third Man museum), Pressg. 25, ✆ 5864872 🌐 Here everything revolves around the film classic "The third man" and post-war Vienna. @ isf382en

Haus der Musik (House of music), Seilerstätte 30, ✆ 5134850 🌐 All about music, with many interactive exhibits that visitors can try. @ gtx815en

Haydnhaus (Haydn house), Haydng. 19, ✆ 5961307 🌐 Information about the last years of the composer's life. @ okk657en

Jüdisches Museum (Jewish museum), Dorotheerg. 11, ✆ 5350431 🌐 Opened 50 years after the end of World War II. Changing exhibitions illustrate Jewish cultural history, art, literature and photography. Another location: 1., Judenpl. 8. @ erc481en

Kaffeemuseum (Coffee Museum), Vogelsangg. 36, 5. Bezirk (Wien), ✆ 0664/1441406 od. 0676/4068728 🌐 The collection highlights everything about coffee, from coffee beans to antique coffee machines and Viennese coffeehouse culture. @ xvr684en

Klimt Villa, Feldmühlg. 11, 13. Bezirk (Wien), ✆ 8761125 🌐 Gustav Klimt created many influential works in the largely neo-baroque villa from 1911 until his death in 1918. The exhibition shows exhibits from Klimt's studio. @ ghf743en

Kunst Haus Wien (Museum Hundertwasser), Untere Weißgerberstr. 13, ✆ 7120491 🌐 Paintings, architecture, sculptures by Friedensreich Hundertwasser, plus exhibitions featuring other 20th c. artists. @ puh754en

Kunsthalle Wien (Vienna Art Hall), Treitlstr. 2, ✆ 521890 🌐 Changing exhibitions featuring contemporary art and masterpieces of classic modernism. @ jxq341en

Leopold Museum, Museumspl. 1, ✆ 525701584 🌐 Houses the art collection of Rudolf und Elisabeth Leopold, one of the world's most important collections of modern Austrian art, including Schiele, Klimt, Moser, Gerstl, Kokoschka and Waldmüller. @ njb763en

Madame Tussauds, Riesenradpl. 5-6, ✆ 8903661 🌐 The world-famous wax museum in Vienna's Prater features more than 80 wax figures and an interactive Sisi experience. @ dgv245en

mumok - Museum moderner Kunst (Museum of modern Art), Museumspl. 1, ✆ 525000 🌐 Modern and contemporary art. Extraordinary collection with works of classical modern art, pop art, Viennese actionism, contemporary film and media art. @ tel748en

Museum der Illusionen (Museum of Illusions), Wallnerstr. 4, ✆ 5322255 🌐 The small museum displays a remarkable collection of optical illusions, holograms and stereograms. @ wyb146en

MuseumsQuartier (MuseumQuarter), Museumspl. 1, ✆ 5235881 🌐 Spectacular cultural area on the edge of Vienna's Old Town and the eighth largest museum district in the world. @ xfd527en

Narrenturm (Fool's Tower), Spitalg. 2, ✆ 52177606 🌐 The so-called Narrenturm (Fool's Tower) was built 250 years ago as the first psychiatric clinic under Emperor Joseph II., it houses the world's largest pathological-anatomical collection. @ rrq563en

Römermuseum (Roman museum), Hoher Markt 3, ✆ 5355606 🌐 Interactive exhibition about the history of the legionary camp Vindobona. @ pka174en

Sigmund-Freud-Museum, Bergg. 19, ✆ 3191596 🌐 The founder of psychoanalysis lived here from 1891 until he was forced to leave in 1938. Freuds former ordination is now a museum. @ eua627en

🏛 **Sisi Museum**, Michaelerkuppel, ✆ 5337570 ⓘ Central themes in the impressively and sensitively designed Sisi Museum are the carefree girlhood in Bavaria, the surprising engagement to the emperor and her official role as Austrian empress. @ sxb461en

🏛 **Theatermuseum (Theatre museum)**, Lobkowitzpl. 2, ✆ 525242729 ⓘ The museum includes mainly stage settings, costumes and props as well as photos and drawings. @ kea186en

🏛 **Time Travel**, Habsburgerg. 10A, ✆ 5321514 ⓘ In the vaults of the St. Michael monastery, visitors can embark on a virtual journey through the history of Vienna. @ oxl671en

🏛 **Uhrenmuseum (Clock Museum)**, Schulhof 3, ✆ 5332265 ⓘ Exhibition of 3,000 watches, with all sorts of curiosities, such as the "Zappler", the smallest of which fits under a thimble. @ cse558en

🏛 **Verkehrsmuseum Remise (Transport Museum Remise)**, Ludwig-Koeßler-Pl. 109, ✆ 790946203 ⓘ More than 80 historical vehicles since 1871 as well as buses and cars of the former Vienna light rail system. @ ysc885en

🏛 **Waschsalon Nr. 2 (Washhouse No. 2)**, Halteraug. 7, ✆ 0664/6587745 ⓘ In the historical Karl-Marx-Hof four thematic areas show the history of the Red Vienna of the First Republic. Waschsalon means laundrette and describes the exhibition space. Here the early inhabitants of the Karl-Marx-Hof,

built in 1926, did their laundry in round 30 washingspaces, there were also bathes and showers for the hygienic cleaning. @ tsr184en

🏛 **Weltmuseum Wien (World Museum)**, Heldenpl., ✆ 534305052 ⓘ Ethnographic museum with unique cultural treasures from all over the world and exciting stories to go with them. @ bkd354en

🏛 **Wien Museum MUSA**, Felderstr. 6-8, ✆ 400085169 ⓘ Historical Museum of the City of Vienna. A fascinating mixture of art and history from the Neolithic to the middle of the 20th century. The Wien Museum can be experienced in the MUSA until about 2022. @ uam287en

🏛 **Wiener Secession**, Friedrichstr. 12, ✆ 5875307 ⓘ Built 1897-98 according to plans by Joseph Olbrich for the "Viennese Secession" group of progressive artists. Rotating exhibitions of modern art plus the 34-meter Beethoven frieze by Gustav Klimt. @ tyg288en

🏛 **Pfadfindermuseum (Scout museum)**, Löschenkohlg. 25, ✆ 0664/4777117 ⓘ The museum provides insights into the history of the scout movement in today's Austria and countries of the former Austro-Hungarian Empire from its beginning In the year 1909. @ fnl218en

⛪ **Stephansdom (St. Stephen's Cathedral)**, Stephanspl. 3, ✆ 5137648 ⓘ Austria's most important Gothic structure and, along with the Prater Ferris-wheel, a Vienna landmark. Noteworthy: the red marble gravestone for Kaiser Frederick III,

Vienna, St. Charles' Church

Anton Pilgram's pulpit (1514/1515), the Viennese "Neustädter Altar" (1447). Guided tours of the extensive catacombs under the cathedral. Below the cathedral there is an extensive system of catacombs with valuable historical testimonies. @ usi533en

⛪ **Votivkirche (Votive Church)**, Rooseveltpl., ✆ 4061192 ⓘ The church was built 1856-79 by the architect Heinrich Ferstel, it is one of the most important Neo-Gothic religious buildings in the world. With a height of 99 m it is the second tallest church in Vienna. @ lwi661en

⛪🏛 **Schottenstift (Schottenstift abbey)**, Freyung 6, ✆ 53498600 ⓘ In the year 1155, when Duke Heinrich II. Jasomirgott moved his residence from Klosterneuburg to Vienna, he summoned

Irish monks to found a monastery in Vienna. In the same year, construction of the Schottenkirche began. In 1418 Duke Albrecht V. withdrew the monastery from the Irish in the course of the Melk Reform and handed it over to German-speaking Benedictines, but the name "Schotten" was retained. The former abbot's flat of the Schottenstift houses a museum. @ wqf356en

- **Hofburg**, Michaelerkuppel, ✆ 5337570 Until 1918 the magnificent castle complex in the centre of Vienna was the centre of the former monarchy, today it fulfils the same function for the Republic of Austria. The Hofburg also houses the Spanish Riding School, the Austrian National Library, the Sisi Museum and the Imperial Apartments. @ cai462en
- **Schloss Belvedere (Belvedere palace)**, Prinz-Eugen-Str. 27, ✆ 79557134 The palace is regarded as one of the most beautiful baroque structures. Built 1700 by Lukas von Hildebrandt as a summer residence for Prince Eugene of Savoy. Includes an elegant terraced garden with cascades and sculptures. @ jeh616en
- **Schloss Schönbrunn (Schönbrunn Palace)**, Schönbrunner Schlossstr. 47, ✆ 811130 Original plans by Fischer von Erlach proposed a palace that would be larger and more magnificent than Versailles. Built 1696-1730, with 1.441 rooms and chambers. Served as Habsburg summer residence and venue of the congress of Vienna. @ spo121en
- **Hermesvilla**, Hermesvillaweg, in the Lainzer Tiergarten, 13. Bezirk (Wien), ✆ 505/874785173 Emperor Franz Joseph gave his wife Elisabeth the "Palace of Dreams" (1882-1886) in the middle of the former imperial hunting grounds as a gift to keep her in Vienna more often. An exhibition on the first floor shows the history of the house. @ yyj734en
- **Palais Liechtenstein**, Fürsteng. 1, ✆ 31957670 In the Garten- und Townpalais, works and furniture from five centuries from the collection of the Princes von Liechtenstein are shown. @ odi284en
- **Burgtheater**, Universitätsring 2, ✆ 514444545. The Austrian National Theatre with its excellent theatre performances is also Europe's largest acting theatre. @ lie188en
- **Wiener Staatsoper (Vienna State Opera)**, Opernring 2, ✆ 514442250. Today's Vienna State Opera evolved from the Vienna Court Opera founded by the Habsburgs. It was ceremoniously opened in 1869 in the presence of Emperor Franz Joseph and Empress Elisabeth. Today, the Vienna State Opera is one of the leading opera houses in the world. The members of the orchestra of the Wiener Staatsoper make up the Vienna Philharmonic Orchestra. @ kgq385en
- **Marionettentheater (Marionette Theatre)**, Schloss Schönbrunn, ✆ 8173247. The award-winning puppet theatre cultivates the tradition of artistic play with hand crafted puppets and, together with Mozart's music, provides princely entertainment. @ wry273en
- **Naschmarkt**, Wienzeile, ✆ 400005430 The largest fruit and vegetable market in Vienna, full of individuality and atmosphere, shows the lively antithesis to supermarkets and the encounter of many cultures. Saturday large flea market. @ lnh758en
- **Hundertwasserhaus (Hundertwasser House)**, Kegelg. 37-39 The building attracts visitors from all over the world because it bears the unmistakable signature of the Austrian artist Friedensreich Hundertwasser, who was known for his imaginative liveliness and individuality. @ gfn835en
- **Margaretenhof**, Margaretenpl., 5. Bezirk (Wien). The architects Ferdinand Fellner and Hermann Helmer built this palace-like complex from 1884-1885, it is an early example of urban housing. @ dwk782en
- **Parlament (Parliament)**, Dr.-Karl-Renner-Ring 3, ✆ 401102400. In 1883, the Austrian Parliament was opened on Vienna's Ringstrasse. The construction under the direction of Theophil Hansen took 10 years and is in the style of Greek classicism. Until the outbreak of the First World War, the deputies of all countries and kingdoms of the Austrian half of the dual monarchy of Austria-Hungary met here. Today, the National Council and the Federal Council hold their sessions here. @ oyn148en
- **Prater**, Riesenradpl. 2, ✆ 7292000 Entertainment park with nostalgic rides, roller coasters, ghost trains, the Prater museum as well as the famous Ferris wheel from 1897. Recreation is offered by the Green Prater with its extensive meadows and forests as well as water areas. @ duk863en
- **Spanische Hofreitschule (Spanish Riding School)**, Michaelerpl. 1, ✆ 53390310 Visitors can gain an insight into the enchanting

world of the Lipizzaners at a wide variety of events. One can regularly watch the morning work, take part in guided tours of the facility or enjoy the official presentations. @ ack331en

✱ **Spittelberg**, in the 7th district. The district between Breite Gasse and Stiftgasse has model character for a revitalization with preservation of the historical (in this case Biedermeier) building substance and presents itself today as a "Beisl" and art district with flair. @ kni465en

✱ **Urania**, Uraniastr. 1, ✆ 89174150000 ⌲, @ fnn776en

✱ **Wiener Ringstraße**. After the former city fortification was removed in 1857-58, one of the most beautiful boulevards with buildings such as the Burgtheater, Kunsthistorisches Museum and Parliament was built on the site of Glacis. The liberal bourgeoisie with its palaces also set a monument here. @ mtu365en

✱ **Tiergarten Schönbrunn (Schönbrunn Zoo)**, Maxingstr. 13b, palace park, ✆ 87792940 ⌲ One of the oldest zoos in the world with new ideas for animal husbandry is located in a baroque park environment. @ fqv153en

✱ **Haus des Meeres (Aqua Terra Zoo)**, Fritz-Grünbaum-Pl. 1, ✆ 5871417 ⌲ The World War II flak tower now houses sharks, turtles, crocodiles, snakes and even monkeys. @ rtt675en

✱ **Lainzer Tiergarten**, Hermesstr., 13. Bezirk (Wien), ✆ 400049200 ⌲ The extensive forest and nature reserve is home to numerous free-ranging wild animals such as deer, mouflon and wild boar. @ fhu454en

✱ **Wüstenhaus Schönbrunn (Desert House)**, opposite the Palm House ⌲ Flora and fauna native to desert areas from Central America to Madagascar. @ wmr514en

✱ **Waldseilpark Kahlenberg (Kahlenberg Forest Rope Park)**, Josefsdorf 47, ✆ 3200476 ⌲ With obstacles such as rope bridges, wobbly nets, flying foxes, gnome courses and 150 exercises, the forest rope park offers the right challenge for every age and size. @ nar681en

📧 **Therme Wien**, Kurbadstr. 14, 10. Bezirk (Wien), ✆ 680099600, @ lpy738en

Vienna! Monarchs called the city on the Danube their capital for more than seven centuries. It was the centre of an empire and today remains one of Europe's most important cultural centres. How can one briefly describe such a city without resorting to stilted clichés or omitting something important? One way, perhaps, is to look at the city's relationship to the river that feeds it.

Although Vienna lies on the banks of the Danube, which may even have been blue long ago, the city has no historic riverfront, no pleasant promenades along the water and little of a river city's character. Merely the Little Danube, a canal really, flows through the centre of the Austrian capital. In the 19th century Vienna sacrificed its direct links to the Danube by digging a ruler-straight canal to bypass the river's winding course and help regulate its flow. Officials at the official opening of the canal in 1875 called it an Austrian engineering marvel. The small Wien River was also banished to a featureless man-made channel.

Are the city and the river irreconcilable opposites? The most recent attempt to manipulate the river and its landscape has, at least, brought the city's residents closer to the Danube. The broad flood plain along the straightened Danube, which for years had been a barren urban wasteland, was excavated for a new channel. The excavated material was piled in the centre, creating the long slim Donauinsel (Danube island) which has since become one of Vienna's most popular recreation areas.

Vienna to Schönau a. d. Donau — 23.1 km

1 When you have seen enough of the city, then you begin your journey by the Urania on the Donaukanal ⁓ cross the **Aspernbrücke** on the bicycle path along the **Praterstraße** ⁓ when you reach the Praterstern, a large traffic node, turn into the **Praterhauptallee** ⁓ motorised traffic is here forbidden ⁓ you ride between shady chestnut trees.

> **TIP:** The **Praterhauptallee** passes through the amusement paradise of the Viennese, the **Prater**. Its attractions such as the giant Ferris wheel or the "Schweizerhaus" where you can enjoy crispy "Schweinshaxe" (Pork Knuckles) or a cool "G'mischtes" (mixed beer) are famous far beyond Vienna.

Viennese Prater

The ancient trees, tranquil waters, game reserves and the Lusthaus at the end of the main avenue have characterized Vienna's Prater for centuries. "The Vienna Prado", as the royal hunting grounds were known, stretched more than 10 kilometres along the Danube. The Wurstelprater, or People's Prater, dates to Apr. 7, 1766 when the enlightened Kaiser Joseph II for the first time opened the Prateraüen (flood-plains) to the public. The first refreshment stands, or Wurstelbuden, soon opened and were quickly followed by restaurants and beer gardens, bowling lanes, carousels and a puppet-theatre. The first fireworks display came in 1771 and 20 years later Jean-Pierre Blanchard launched a gas-filled balloon from the Prater.

Coffee-houses established along the main avenue quickly became a famous part of the Prater's attractions and were especially popular before the first world war. In 1945 the Wurstelprater was almost completely destroyed by fire

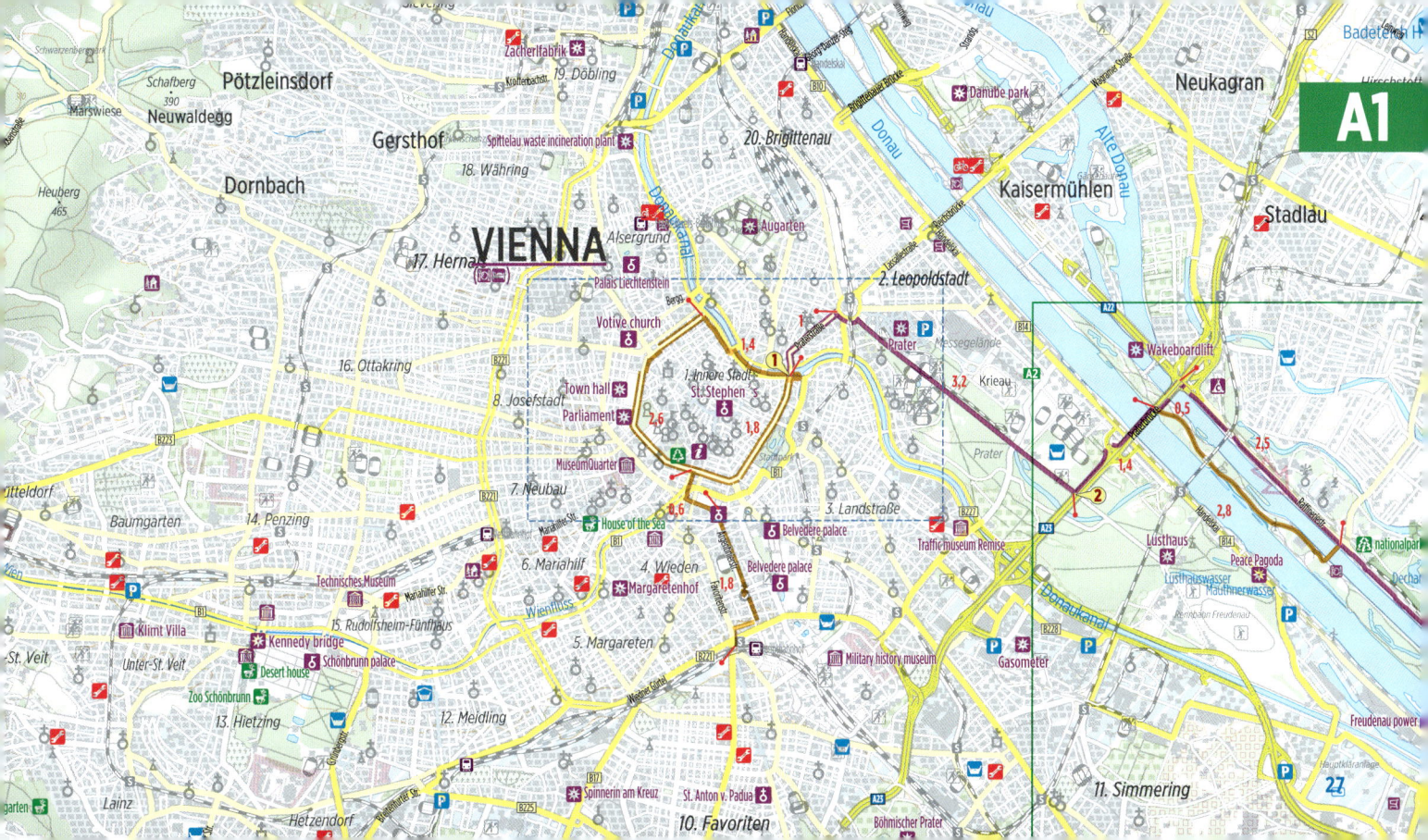

during the battle for Vienna. Only 18 objects survived, and the Wurstelprater has never been the same since. Today it is a collection of carousels, casinos and snack-bars. What little is left of the old Wurstelprater, like the Calafati Carousel and the "Big Chinaman", can be found in the less gaudy areas to the rear of the park. The Viennese always distinguished between the People's Prater and the "Nobelprater" which, with the exception of the race-track in Freudenau, had no carnival atmosphere. An extensive park with long lanes and paths, carefully tended landscapes as well as areas of wild growth that recalled its origins as a royal hunting grounds this was where the city's young lovers would come to find some privacy, where retirees came to stroll and where governesses brought their charges to play. It was, of course, also where high society gathered to see and be seen, mounted or in coaches, especially on the first of May for the traditional "Praterfahrt" to celebrate arrival of the spring. People without horse or buggy came out as well to watch the colorful spectacle, criticise the moneyed classes or review the latest summer fashion being shown for the first time. Starting in 1886, the Hauptallee served as the venue for a flower parade with horse-drawn carriages. Eleven years later a flower parade for cyclists was introduced, as was one for automobiles after World War I.

Those who seek the "old" prater will not find it. It is a part of history just like the visitors of old. Today the Prater serves Viennese and tourists as an amusement park, a place to eat and drink, a vast garden for long walks and quiet picnics. For the Viennese in particular, the "green lungs", as the Prater is often referred to, is increasingly important as a place of rest and recreation. For a first-time visitor no day at the Prater could be complete without a ride on the giant Ferris wheel which affords a spectacular view across the city.

Continue straight ahead to the freeway bridge **2** turn left by the bridge and follow the path beside the freeway ~ after reaching the allotment garden houses take the first turn to the right and ride through the tunnel ~ follow the bicycle path onto the Praterbrücke.

TIP: Cross the Danube onto the Donauinsel, which is a weekend paradise for Vienna's cyclists.

Danube Island

Not only for cycling: the Donauinsel is a popular place to go swimming, windsurfing, boating, skating, dancing, eating and drinking, eating icecream and relaxing.

This recreational paradise was created in 1969 as part of a massive project to regulate the flow of the Danube and make Vienna once and for all floodproof. Although, at first not planned to be a recreational area, the good water quality soon led to the idea of a 21 km long beach and it was not long before the Donauinsel became the most popular recreational area in and around Vienna.

TIP: At the intersection Kaisermühlen (weir number 1) you have the chance to try out the wakeboardlift.

22. Bezirk (Wien) Ⓐ
prefix: 01

- **Donaupark**, Arbeiterstrandbadstr. ㉔
- **Wakeboardlift**, Am Wehr 1, ✆ 0676/5182711 ㊆, @ wud362en
- **nationalparkhaus wien-lobAU**, Dechantweg 8, ✆ 400049495 ㊂, @ tdp823en

Take the bicycle path below the road bridge across the **Neue Donau (New Danube)** to the other bank of the river ⟿ turn right and follow the path beside the river 5 km to the oil refinery ⟿ **3** turn left after the restaurant and cross the **Raffineriestraße** and ride into the **Lobgrundstraße** ⟿ follow the road between the ÖMV oil storage tanks ⟿ continue straight ahead, staying left of the harbour ⟿ you come to follow the paved lane along the dyke past the old forest of the Lobau.

> **TIP** The forest is swarming with water-birds, wild animals and rare creatures that thrive on the forest's natural ecosystem. During flooding the route may be closed, in which case riders face a longer detour.

The **Hubertusdamm** (the dyke also known as the **Marchfelddamm**) is about 30 km long ⟿ the dyke path is almost entirely paved ⟿ just before Schönau you turn left across a bridge over an old arm of the Danube ⟿ continue to the next dyke, where you turn right.

Schönau an der Donau (Groß-Enzersdorf) Ⓐ

Schönau an der Donau to Hainburg   27.7 km
4 Continue straight ahead along the cycle path that will take you to Orth an der Donau.

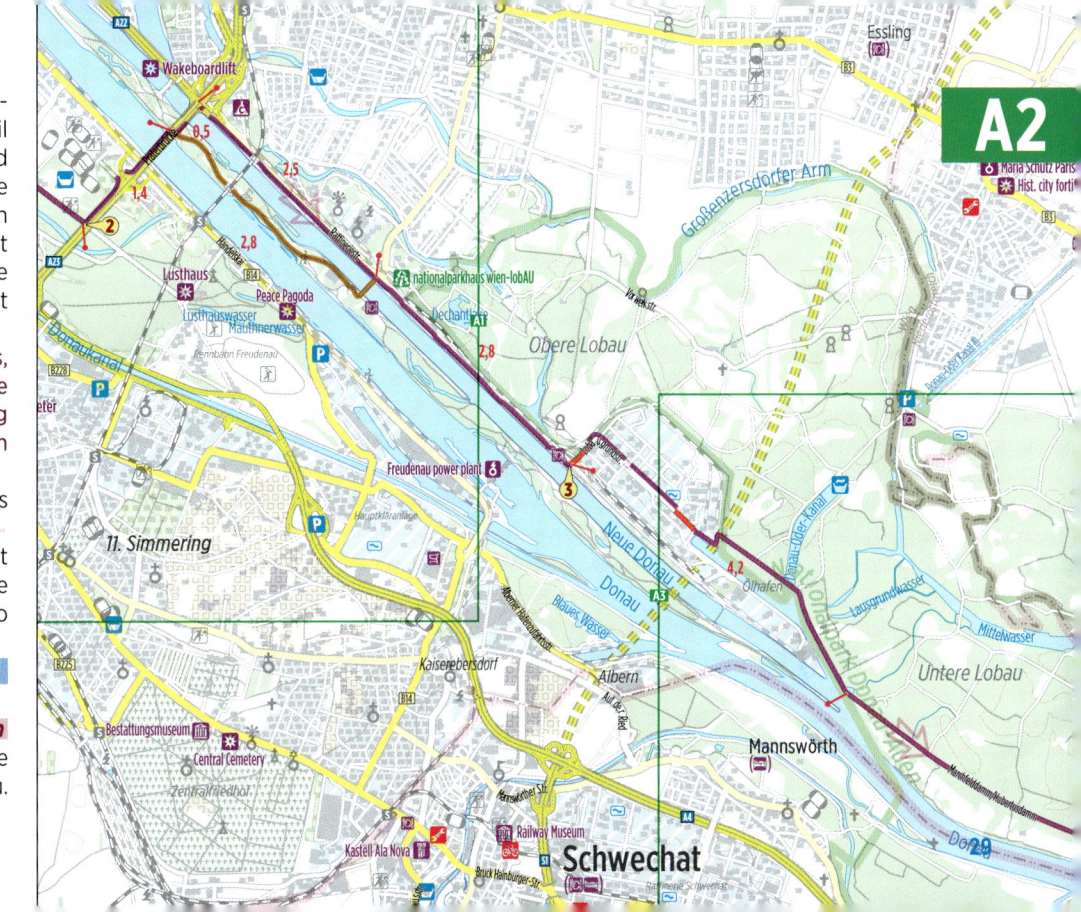

5 To drive into Orth, turn left at the crossroads. Here, lovers of fish dishes will get their money's worth.

Orth an der Donau Ⓐ
prefix: 02212

- **Tourismusinformation**, Schlosspl. 1, ☏ 3555, @ ixn374en
- **Gemeindeamt**, Am Markt 26, ☏ 2208, @ oab841en
- **Fähre Orth - Haslau (Ferry Orth - Haslau)**, Uferstr. 17, ☏ 0664/4210058, @ dnv633en
- **museumORTH**, Schlosspl. 1, ☏ 0676/5642767. Oversized photo albums reveal the history of the town, the life at the Danube's bank and the works of famous inhabitants. @ iku528en
- **Schloss Orth (Castle Orth)**, Schlosspl. 1, ☏ 3555. The moated castle is considered the oldest of the Marchfeld castles. It was first mentioned in a document in 865 and was once the hunting seat of the Habsburg family. @ csk725en
- **Schiffmühle und Tschaikenfahrten (Ship Mill)**, Uferstr., ☏ 0664/3341422. The ship-mill (Schiffsmühle) floats on the river and uses the current as a power source. The Tschaike is an accurate replica of a river ship from 1530, which can also be rowed. Starting point is the landing "Zur Schiffmühle" by the Uferhaus. @ dqb784en
- **schlossORTH Nationalpark-Zentrum (schlossORTH National Park Centre)**, Sclosspl. 1, ☏ 3555. The castle houses the museumORTH and the visitor centre of the Danube wetlands National Park with a multimedia exhibition and the outdoor area "Castle Island" with an underwater observation station; there is also a café, a shop and a tournament courtyard with an observation tower. @ tub466en

5 Here is a good opportunity to visit the Danube and the ship mill - just follow the **Uferstraße**.

After visiting the ship mill, you can transfer to the south shore by ferry. ⚠ The first few metres from the anchorage to Haslau are a little more difficult to ride.

Orth Palace

South bank alternative   24.1 km

After crossing the Danube, turn right onto the more impassable path ~ turn left between the water plains, partly on chunky cobblestones ~ up into the village, following the signs for the Nationalparktour Donau-Auen ~ at the top, turn right into the **Hauptstraße**.

Haslau-Maria Ellend Ⓐ
prefix: 02232

- **Gemeindeamt Maria Ellend**, Wienerstr. 11, ☏ 80250, @ txy166en
- **Fähre Orth - Haslau (Ferry Orth - Haslau)**, Uferstr. 17, Orth an der Donau, ☏ 0664/4210058, @ dnv633en
- **Themenweg Haslau**. Over a length of 3.5 km, the round-trail leads through the national park with interactive stations. @ xdc761en

Keep left at the chapel ~ straight ahead, **Bahnstraße** ~ cross the B 9 and the railway tracks and immediately turn left ~ at the T-junction at **Regelsbrunn** turn right ~ at the next T-junction turn left and continue through the fields ~ in Scharndorf turn left, **Waldweg** ~ turn right, **Hauptstraße**.

Scharndorf Ⓐ

- **Gemeindeamt**, Bodenzeile 1b, ☏ 02163/2303, @ qdq388en

Turn left diagonally ~ at the four-way intersection turn left and left again after the church

Eckartsau baroque palace

↝ straight ahead into the fields ↝ turn left at the windmill ↝ turn right at the second opportunity ↝ follow the path ↝ follow the bend to the right ↝ at the five-way intersection turn left to the Heidentor ↝ continue straight ahead to Petronell ↝ turn left, **Bruckerstraße**.

Petronell-Carnuntum

prefix: 02163

- **Donau Niederösterreich Tourismus**, Hauptstr. 3, ☎ 355510, @ wyc452en
- **Gemeindeamt**, Kirchenpl. 1, ☎ 2228, @ smg466en
- **Museum Auxiliarkastell**, Hauptstr. 78, ☎ 0664/73674493 od. 0650/8901010 ↻ Subject: Types of graves, burial objects, an underground water conduit, special exhibitions. @ tcn872en
- **Schloss Petronell (Petronell castle)**, Schlossallee 1, ☎ 0664/88337904. Rebuilt 1660 to 1667 by the baroque master Dominico Carlone. It was owned by the Abensperg-Traun over 17 generations. @ xdj848en
- **Heidentor (Heathen's Gate)**, ca. 1,5 km south of the Roman City, ☎ 33770 ⓘ The Heathen's Gate was probably built as a triumphal arch under Emperor Constantine. @ ooi512en
- **Römerstadt Carnuntum (Roman City of Carnuntum)**, Hauptstr. 1A, ☎ 33770 ⓘ The largest archaeological park in Austria, divided into three main areas: a museum district, the legion camp, and the civilian town. @ ykb457en
- **Trainingsarena der Gladiatorenschule (Training Arena for the Gladiators)**, ca. 800 m away from the city ⓘ The building structures are similar to the Ludus Magnus school in Rome. @ iui586en

The origins of the provincial Roman capital go back much further. In the times of the Illyrians and Celts two ancient trading roads intersected here – the Danube from west to east and the Amber Road, which connected the Mediterranean and the Baltic seas. During the reign of Caesar Tiberius the city Carnuntum (which means city on the stone) was incorporated into the province of Pannonia. The camp's strategic importance triggered a period of great prosperity.

In 171 AD the Marcomans invaded the Roman empire and besieged the city – without success. The military camp was abandoned in 395 AD. In the ensuing dark periods of migrations the city slowly died. The Huns were followed by the Eastgoths and the Avars. No one recorded the city's final downfall, perhaps because the enemy left no survivors living. In one oven archaeologists found the remains of half-finished bread, as if the Roman baker did not even have time to remove the bread from the oven.

What the Germanic tribes and forces of natural decay did not destroy was dismantled and carried away by humans. Left standing were the massive pillars of the Heidentor (Heathen's Gate). Extensive research appears to have finally revealed its secret: it is neither a gate nor of heathen origin, but one of four entrances to a monumental victory monument erected for Caesar Constantine II around 354-361 AD. At that time Christianity had been the official Roman religion for several decades and was gaining recognition around the Empire. After extensive repairs the gate today is the best-known attraction in the archaeological park.

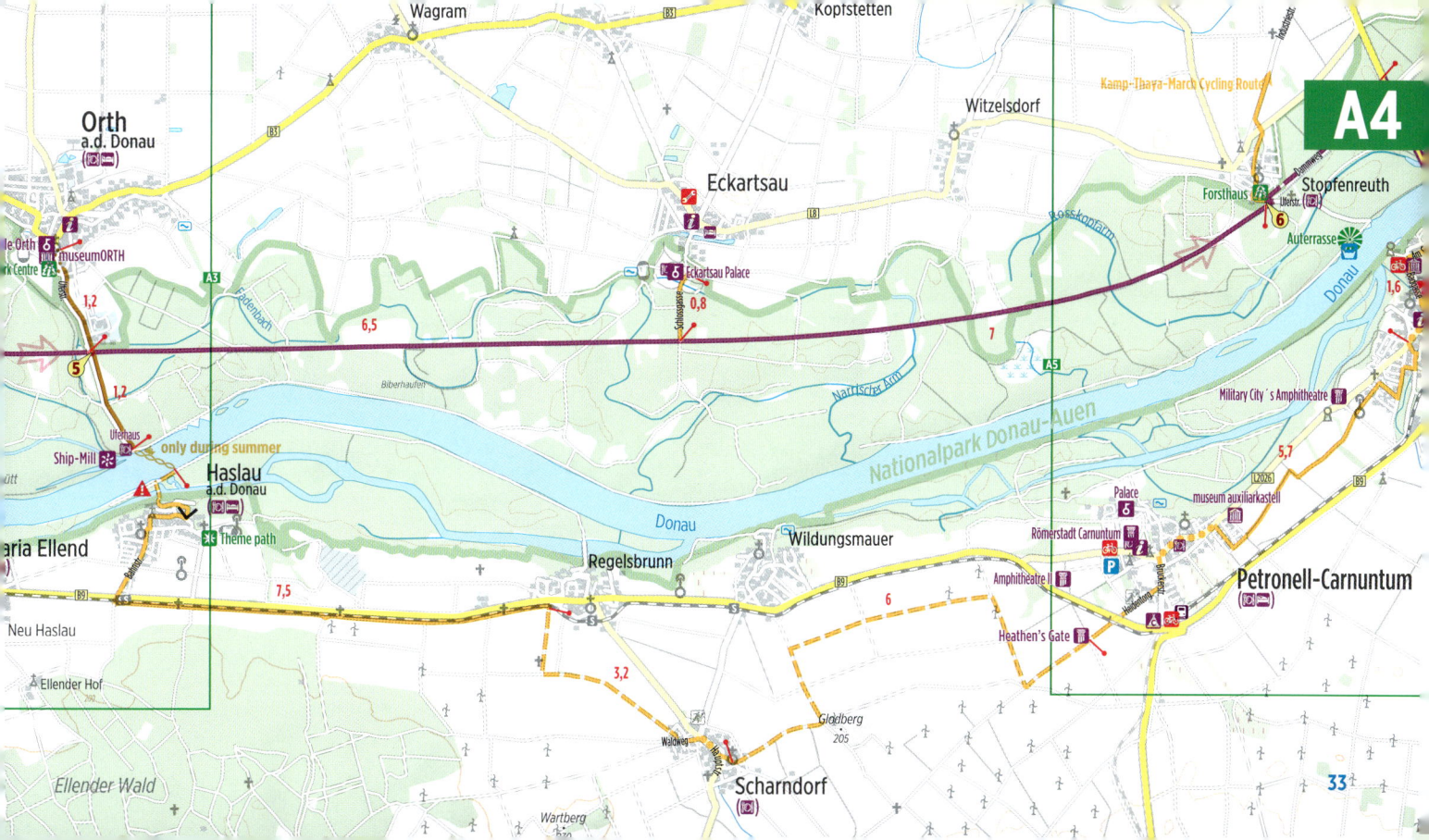

Danube and Hainburg seen from Braunsberg

Turn right at the priority road ~ after a good 700 m turn right, **Dr. Karl-Renner-Straße** ~ at the T-junction left ~ straight ahead into the fields ~ follow the path to **Bad Deutsch-Altenburg** ~ at the T-junction turn right .left, **Roseggergasse** ~ before the one-way right, **Erbstadtgasse** ~ left, **Steinabrunngasse** ~ turn right at the priority road ~ after the clock tower turn left, **Badgasse** ~ at the **Museum Carnuntium** right ~ turn left before the Danube bridge and back onto the main route.

5 The main route continues straight ahead along the dam path.

CENTRE To get into Eckartsau and visit the castle, which is well worth seeing, turn left into the **Schlossgasse**.

Eckartsau Ⓐ
prefix: 02214

- **Gemeindeamt**, Obere Hauptstr. 1, ✆ 22020, @ ldm774en
- **Schloss Eckartsau (Eckartsau Castle)**, Schloss 1, ✆ 2240 Learn more about the history of the end of the Danube monarchy in the baroque palace and stroll through the 27 ha idyllic palace park. Viewing of the palace only as part of a guided tour. @ waw248en

The baroque palace is closely associated with the last chapter of the Austro-Hungarian Empire: On November 11th, 1918 Emperor Charles relinquished his participation in the administration of the empire. He moved to Eckartsau with his family and they were exiled shortly after. The diaries of his wife, Empress Zita, grant deep insights in the last day of the royal family in Austria.

The former water castle was converted to a hunting lodge by Count Kinsky in 1722. It includes statues and reliefs by Lorenzo Matielli as well as frescoes by Daniel Gran. The idyllic, 27-hectare garden combines the wilderness of the wetlands and the cultivated vastness of the Marchfeld.

The cycle path continues straight ahead to Stopfenreuth **6**.

CONNECTION 6 At Stopfenreuth there is a connection to the Kamp-Thaya-March cycle route. More detailed information you'll find in our *bikeline*-Radtourenbuch Fluss-Radwege Niederösterreich.

Stopfenreuth (Engelhartstetten) Ⓐ
prefix: 02214

- **Pranger (Pillory)**. At the village green with bullet and buckle iron from the 16th c.

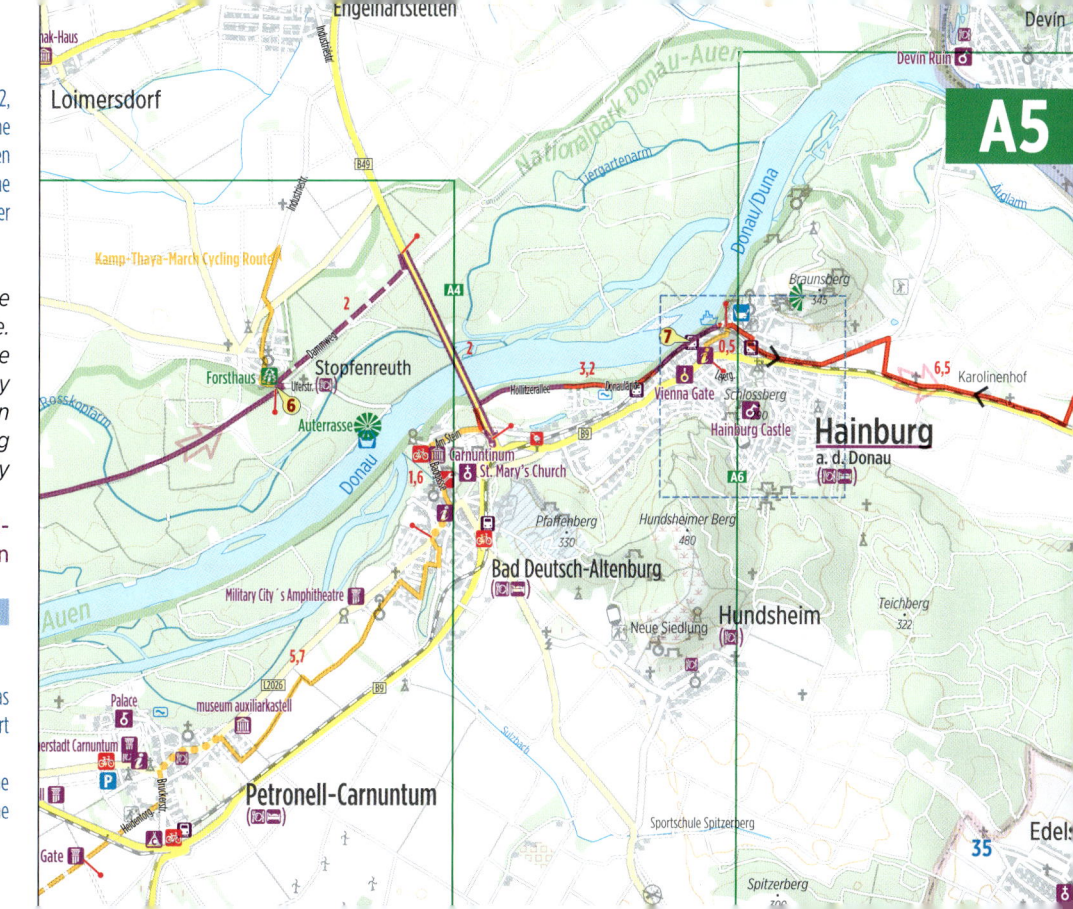

- **Forsthaus Stopfenreuth (Forester's house)**, Uferstr. 1, ✆ 2232, ✆ 0650/2600000. Wetland information centre with wine taverns, canoe hire and cycle information point. @ mwd623en
- **Auterrasse (Wetland Terrace)**, Uferstr., ✆ 02212/3555. The two-storey platform on the Danube offers views of the river and serves as a rest area. @ sgm172en
- **Naturbadeplatz**

Stopfenreuth and Bad Deutsch-Altenburg are connected by an imposing suspension bridge. From the bridge one gets a view of the site of the occupation of the Danube wetlands by environmental activists in 1984. The campaign managed to stop the building of the Hainburg hydro-electric scheme and one can still clearly see traces of the clearfelling operations.

CENTRE To reach the centre of Bad Deutsch-Altenburg just follow the street **Am Stein** on the left.

Bad Deutsch-Altenburg

prefix: 02165

- **Marktgemeinde**, Erhardg. 2, ✆ 62900, @ vig212en
- **Carnuntinum**, Badg. 40-46, ✆ 33770. The museum was opened by Emperor Franz Joseph I. in 1904. It shows a large part of the collections on ancient Carnuntum. @ kcu415en
- **Marienkirche (St. Mary's church)**, Kirchenberg 3, ✆ 62243. One of the oldest churches in lower Austria stands on a hill in the

town. The main building probably dates to about 1000. The church was expanded in the Romanesque style at a later date. In the 14th century the tower and a Gothic choir were added. @ ytc166en

- **Amphitheater (Amphitheatre)**, Wienerstr. 52, ✆ 02163/33570 🕖 The amphitheater was built of stone in the 2nd century A.D., it accommodated crowds of up to 8,000 people. @ bof238en

Bad Deutsch Altenburg is a resort town with modern facilities and the strongest iodine-sulfur baths in Austria. The town lies in the Pannonic region of Austria and is one of the sunniest parts of the country. Two-thousand years ago the Romans built thermal baths at the same site.

EXCURSION Hobby archaeologists will especially relish a visit to the Archaeological Park Carnuntum, which has some of the most important Roman excavations in Austria. Therefore follow the orange alternative route to Petronell-Carnuntum (see p. 32).

For your onward journey follow the signs towards the Danube ~ to the right under the bridge ~ straight ahead on the **Hollitzerallee** ~ you come to ride along the elevated railway tracks and pass the Hainburg train station **7** ~ 600 m after the station go to the right around the water tower ~ pass below the railway tracks ~ by the intersection go left and once again pass under the railway tracks.

CENTRE Turning right brings you via the **Oppitzstraße** and the **Klosterplatz** into the centre of Hainburg.

Hainburg - Vienna Gate

Hainburg a.d. Donau Ⓐ
prefix: 02165

- ℹ **Gästeinformation**, Ungarstr. 3, ✆ 62111400, @ oxu624en
- ℹ **Gemeindeamt**, Hauptpl. 23, ✆ 621110, @ tcc614en
- 🏛 **Stadtmuseum Wienertor (Town Museum)**, Hauptpl. 23, ✆ 0664/2261630 🕖 City history and prehistory as well as the history of tobacco from Hainburg. @ jwd476en
- 🏰 **Heimoburg (Hainburg Castle)**, Schlossbergstr., atop a steep hill south of the centre, ✆ 62111400 🕖 Every year there is a medieval pageant at the castle. Three footpaths lead up to the castle (11th c.), starting point is the car park at the sports field. The breathtaking view makes the breathtaking climb worthwhile! @ dca114en
- 🚪 **Wienertor (Vienna Gate)**, Wienerstr. Built in the 13th century, it is regarded as one of the most artistically-significant city gates in central Europe.
- ✴ **Altstadt (Historic centre)**. With numerous historic city houses, city museum, 11th century and 13th century fortifications, the oldest and best preserved in Europe.
- ✉ **Bergbad**, Braunsberger Str., ✆ 62111577, @ mfm775en

The medieval city of Hainburg lies above the Danube surrounded by wooded hills in the middle of the Donauauen national park. The 2.5 km of walls, 3 city gates and 15 city towers dating to the 13th century are unrivalled in central Europe, and hint that this is one of the most strategic points along the Danube. The earliest recorded mention of Hainburg dates to 1042, and for a long time the city was the main eastern outpost of the Holy Roman Empire.

This is where the Danube winds between the Braunsberg, on the Austrian side, and the Thebener Kogel that looms over the confluence of the March on the Slovakian side. Before 1918 it was called Upper Hungary. At end of World War I the border moved, making the former Hungarian coronation city the capital of Slovakia. Even so, when one leaves Hainburg towards the east one still does so through the Hungarian Gate, built in 1260.

The imposing 31 metres tall Vienna Gate impresses upon the viewer that these city gates were designed to keep invaders from passing. The gate's opening is small and inconspicuous, weighty is that which solidly surrounds it. The fortified gate was built in 1270 and financed in part with the 100,000 Cologne Marks (about 23,000 kg of silver) ransom that was paid for the release of Richard the Lionhearted. It ranks as one of the most handsome gates of the period, a gate for crusaders and against Hungarian armies – a gate which makes the Dark Ages seem romantic instead of gloomy.

Above the town, on the Schlossberg, can be seen the ruins of an extensive castle which is so ancient that it was already considered old when the Song of the Nibelungen was written.

The walls of Hainburg were repeatedly attacked – although between 1270 and 1481 no enemies tried to conquer the city – but its fortifications remain almost entirely preserved. They stretch from the castle down to the Danube. The narrow Blutgässchen in front of the Fischertor, which opens down

to the Danube, hints at the gruesomeness of Hainburg's darkest hours.

When the Turks made their second attempt to push through to Vienna, on July 12, 1683, the walls of Hainburg, which were in poor condition, could not withstand the onslaught. After a short siege, the Turkish armies stormed the walls. The city's population hoped to escape to the Danube's flood plain, but the doors to the Fischer Gate, which opened inwards, could not be opened in time. Trapped in the narrow passage in front of the gate they were either crushed to death in the panic or fell to the Turks' scimitars. The history of that day reports that 8,432 Hainburgers were killed or taken away by the Turks, and just 100 people escaped. One of them was a young cartwright named Thomas Haydn – a lucky stroke for the world of music: He grew up to become the grandfather of Joseph Haydn.

Today the Fischer Gate no longer blocks the way to the Danube. Instead there is a high embankment on which the railway line passes safe from floodwaters. The line once went as far as Bratislava (or Pressburg in German), but today it stops in the Austrian border village of Wolfsthal.

Hainburg to Bratislava — 18.7 km

After passing under the railway tracks follow the right bend and ride along the **Nibelungengasse** right into **Krüklstraße** turn left into **Kriemhildengasse** just before the railway crossing parallel to the railway tracks keep left into **Thebnerstraße** and ride out of Hainburg after 800 m turn right into the paved side road turn left before the railway tracks and proceed straight next to the railway line turn left towards the Danube then, at the crossroads, follow the cycle path signs to the right turn right over a small stone bridge into Wolfsthal **8** up to the main road **B 9**.

ALTERNATIVE: Here the official Danube cycle path leads in the village on the busy main road. You can avoid this unpleasant stretch by taking a diversion on local roads through Wolfsthal. In the book this route is marked as the main route, the official cycle route is marked as orange alternative.

Straight ahead, **Obere Gasse** left, **Triftgasse**, left, **Edelhofgasse** turn right before the tracks, **Leopold Reinweg**, you'll see the train station on your left.

Wolfsthal

prefix: 02165

- **Gemeindeamt**, Hauptstr. 42, ✆ 62676, @ mcd228en
- **Maria am Birnbaum**, Hauptstr. 32, ✆ 02143/2849. The pilgrimage church was originally built as a Romanesque, single-nave church and was extended and redesigned in the baroque style in 1744-49. @ eut436en
- **Schloss Walterskirchen (Walterskirchen Castle)**, Hauptstr. 5. The moats of the former water castle were filled up in the 18th c. The castle was given its present appearance in the style of romantic neo-Gothic towards the end of the 19th c. With its striking towers and entrance area, it has proved to be a sought-after film location. The castle is privately owned and can only be viewed from the outside. @ wwx337en
- **Ruine Pottenburg (Pottenburg ruin)**, on the street towards Berg. The former castle was named after Graf Poto, a son of Count Palatine Hartwig von Regensburg.
- **Mariensäule**, Hauptstr., opposite No. 10. Pillar of the "Immaculate Conception" from 1680.
- **Pranger**, Hauptstr. 34. Pillory from 1747.

Left, **Josef-Ressel-Gasse** near the tracks, but stay to the right of them right-left bend, **Obere Siedlungsstraße** at the cemetery turn left after the left bend turn right in a sharp angle, this is a footpath at the busy main road turn left and at the next oppor-

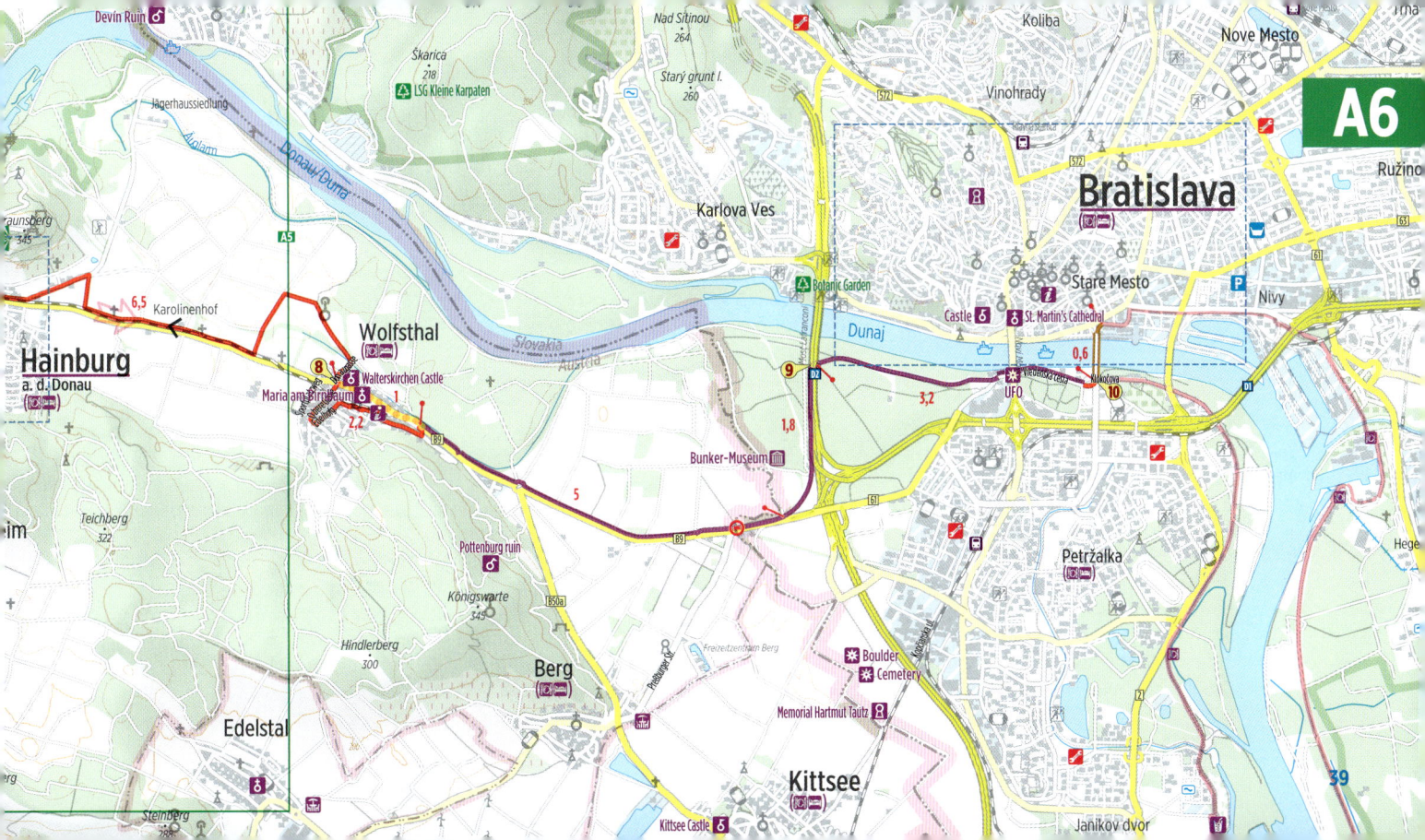

Bratislava, Novy Most

tunity right again into the cycle path ⌇ this leads to the former customs office and on to Bratislava ⌇ after the border crossing, follow the left-hand bend ⌇ **9** after passing under the freeway bridge you continue along the top of the dyke through a forested area ⌇ you now see the bridge Nový Most.

▌**VIEW** The bridge has a viewing platform which can be reached by elevator. It offers a fine birds' eye view of the Slovakian capital.

You reach a street, where you ride straight ahead and pass below the Nový Most bridge ⌇ continue on the two-lane cycle path to the next bridge ⌇ at the cross road straight on onto the bridge **10**.

▌**CENTRE** A bicycle and pedestrian ramp leads up onto the bridge, which can take you directly into the historic centre of Bratislava on the other bank of the Danube.

Bratislava
prefix: 02

- **Bratislava Information Service**, Klobučnícka 2, ☎ 16186, ☎ 54419410, @ gpa638en
- **Galéria mesta Bratislavy - Mirbach Palace**, Františkánske nám. 11, ☎ 54431556 The exhibitions are located in two historic buildings in the centre of Bratislava - the Mirbach Palace opposite the Franciscan Church and the Pálffy Palace in Panská Street 19, opposite the British Embassy. Themes: Medieval painting and sculpture, 20th century art and contemporary artists. @ esj578en
- **Historické múzeum (Museum of History)**, Bratislavský hrad, Bratislava Castle, ☎ 20483104 Part of the Slovak National Museum. History of Slovakia form the middle ages till today. @ aio727en
- **Michalská brána - Múzeom zbraní (Museum of Arms at the Michael's Gate)**, Michalská ul. 22, ☎ 0940/511639 Located in the last remaining gate from the original city fortifications. Originally a Gothic construction from the 14th century, today home of a weapons museum. History of the town defences, bladed arms and firearms, as well as the resistance 1914-1918. The museum ist closed until 2023 due to renovation!, @ yms721en
- **Múzeum Hodín (Clock Museum)**, Židovská 4716/3, ☎ 54411940 History of clockmaking from the end of the 17th to the 19th c. The exhibition is located at the "House of the Good Shepard", a Rococo-style building. @ oxa882en
- **Múzeum mesta Bratislavy (Bratislava City Museum)**, Radničná ul. č. 1, ☎ 59100812 The museum was founded in 1868 and is today the oldest museum still in existence in Slovakia. The museum runs permanent exhibitions at eight different locations. The main exhibition is located in the Old Town Hall. @ hui255en
- **Slov. národná galéria (Slovak National Gallery)**, Námestie Ľudovíta Štúra, ☎ 20476111 The collection includes numerous paintings and sculptures from various periods. Guided tours available by appointment. @ twy735en
- **SNM-Prírodovedné múzeum (Natural History Museum)**, Vajanského nábrežie 2, ☎ 20469122 With its collection of around 3.8 million objects, this museum is one of the most important natural history museums in Europe. It documents and presents the natural environment with a focus on Slovakia. @ qyi523en
- **Františkánsky kostol (Franciscan Church)**, Františkánska 439/2. Consecrated in 1297, remodeled in the baroque style in the 17th and 18th c.
- **Katedrály sv. Martina (St. Martin's Cathedral)**, Rudnayovo námestie 1, ☎ 54431359 The triple-nave Gothic building from the 14-15th c. served as the coronation church for Hungarian kings between 1563 and 1830. It was once

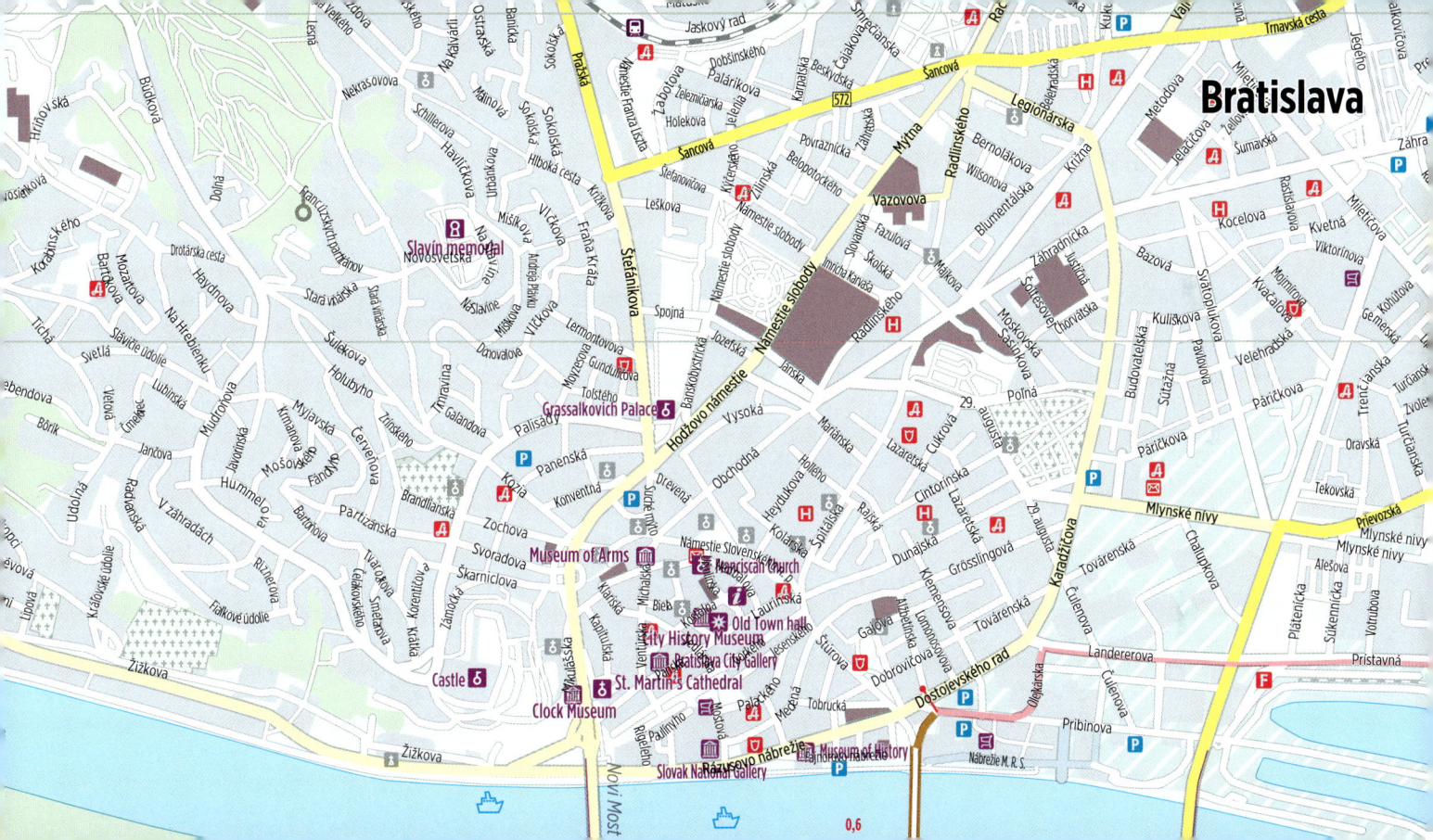

remodeled in the baroque style, then returned to its Gothic style in the 19th c. Opulent interior decoration. @ tti736en

- **Grasalkovičov palác (Grassalkovich Palace)**, Hodžovo námestie 2978/1, ✆ 57888155 🚌 The palace (1760) is the residence of the Slovakian president. The palace is not open for public but you can go for a stroll through the park. Bicycles are not permitted in the park. @ fjg752en

- **Hrad (Castle)**, ✆ 20483110, ✆ 0915/993301 🚌 The 12th century castle was rebuilt in 1430 in the Gothic style and became Hungary's most important fortress. At the time of Maria Theresa a formal palace was added. When Budapest became the Hungarian capital, the castle lost its significance. Today it is the seat of the Slovak national assembly. @ isd557en

- **Hrad Devín (Devín Castle)**, Muránska ulica 1, Located above the confluence of the Danube and March, west of the city, Devín (Bratislava), ✆ 6570105 🚌 During the reawakening of the Slovak national identity in the 19th c. the ruins were a key symbol of the country's "glorious Slavic past". The fortress played an important military role in the 16th c., during the Turkish sieges of Bratislava and Vienna. @ jqe328en

- **Na Slavíne (Slavín memorial)**, Pažického 3, north-west of the city. Originally built as memorial to Soviet soldiers who died taking the city in 1945, today a monument to the communist period. Excellent views. @ udq576en

- **Stará radnica (Old town hall)**, Hlavné námestie, ✆ 59100847 🚌 Gothic building redone in Renaissance style, with pretty interior courtyard and tower. @ pdo582en

- **UFO**, Nový Most, ✆ 62520300 🚌 The 432 m long Nový Most (New Bridge) was opened in 1972 to commemorate the Slovak resistance against the German invasion. There is a circular UFO observation deck on the only pylon, 95 m above the ground, which offers a spectacular panoramic view of the old town. There is also a restaurant on the UFO deck. @ xjg652en

- **Botanická záhrada**, Botanická 3, ✆ 65421311 🚌, @ hub137en

he only capital city in the world which borders on two nations, Bratislava is the political, industrial and cultural centre of Slovakia, and with a population of approximately 430.000, the nation's largest city.

The city had been under Hungarian rule since the 10th century and came to be capital of Royal Hungary between 1536 and 1848, when the Ottomans held much of the Hungarian territory. The city flourished during this period, the marks of which are still clearly visible in its layout and architecture. After the transfer of the seat of political administration to Budapest, the city became the centre of the Slovak national movement. Since 1918 it was the main city of the part-state of Slovakia and part of the greater Czechoslovakia, and in 1993 became the capital of the independent state of Slovakia. The region profited from its proximity to western European markets. Bratislava is part of the Twin City concept, which was developed in cooperation with the only 60 kilometre distant city of Vienna, and now manages to produce 25% of the Slovakian GDP. The city has also attracted numerous multinational companies, thanks in part to the large number of universities and research centres.

Those who want to do this city's most important historical and architectural attractions justice will find a single day not nearly enough. To familiarise the first time visitor with some of these attractions we begin a small introduction at the Hlavné námestie (main square) in the heritage listed historic centre. The most prominent building here is the old town hall, which is comprised of three of the city's oldest surviving buildings and crowned with a baroque tower. Today it houses the City Museum. On the opposite side, in front of the Sedlárska ulica, stands the Maximilian Fountain and the striking, gilded Roland Palace. The street corner on the right is occupied by the white Rokoko

Bratislava

Esterházy-Palace and the left by the architecturally similar, but more neo-classical, Café Maier. The square is often used for concerts, celebrations and markets.

The Sedlárska to the right (NW) leads to the Michalská ulica, a street lined with street-cafés, where the Michalská brána (St. Michael's Gate), the only surviving medieval gate, rises at the end of the street like a baroque church tower. A great view of the historic centre is afforded from a viewing gallery on the 6th floor. Right next to the gate stands Europe's narrowest house, with a width of only 1.3 metres. Going to the south you reach the intersection with the Panská ulica just before the end of the street opens into the promenade-like Hviezdoslavovo námestie, where the National Theatre stands. If you turn right into the Panská ulica you reach the Gothic St. Martin's Cathedral. The importance of this church to the national identity can be seen in its tower, whose tip is literally crowned with a copy of the Hungarian Crown of Saint Stephen instead of a cross. The coronation of the Hungarian kings, who were also Emperor of Germany and Austria, took place in this church between 1563 and 1830.

On the other side of the main road, which passes by the church tower, is the Židovská ulica at the base of the Castle Hill. The name is a reference to the Jewish community which settled here in the protection of the castle. A part of the Jewish cemetery has been restored and, curiously, lies below ground near the subway tunnel. But the name of the street is also a testament to the Jews, who, after the alignment of Austria and the annexation of Bohemia and Moravia in 1939, were given over to the Nazi German state on the south side of the Danube.

Steep streets and steps make their way up the idyllic castle hill. The original Gothic 4-winged fortification that crowned the cliffs 85 metres above the Danube was no less important than that at Devín. But it was rebuilt numerous times before being burnt to the ground in 1811 by the French, not to be rebuilt until after WWII in baroque style. Its appearance is less impressive though, than the location and the spectacular view.

The city at your feet is characterised by its numerous baroque palaces, but one can also find bold and interesting buildings from recent decades. A noteworthy building which spans the bridge between tradition and modern is the Kostol svätej Alžbety (St. Elisabeth Church), whose distinctive Hungarian Art Nouveau style is dominated by the pink and blue pastel tones. You find the church in the Bezručova ulica just east of the historic centre.

Bratislava to Komárno (SK)

100.9 km

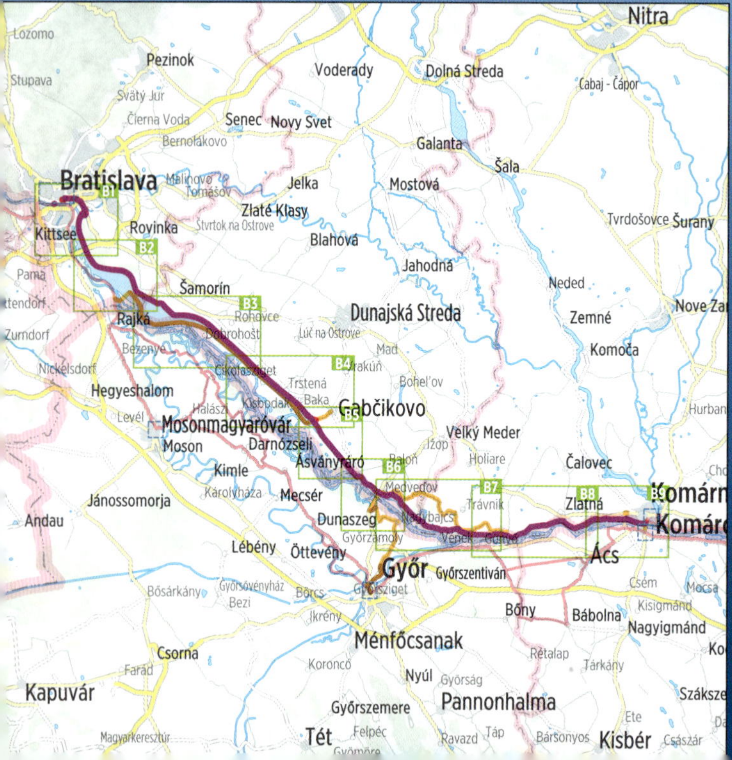

m/km: ⌇ 0.0 (1m) ⌇ 0.3 (34m)   cycle path: 98 %   unpaved: 0 %   busy road: 0 %

Construction of the hydro-electric power plant on the Danube turned this part of the river into a large reservoir and destroyed major portions of a previously undisturbed natural landscape. The man-made canal extends as far as Medved'ov. At Klížka Nemá the Mosoni Duna from Hungary converges with the Main Danube. Because the infrastructure for tourists between Bratislava and Komárno is not yet well-developed, we recommend planning this stage of the trip carefully.

Many kilometres of straight, paved roads along the crowns of the man-made dykes along the Danube are open to cyclists and other recreation-seekers. Your route follows the left side of the reservoir to Gabčíkovo and further on to the town of Komárno.

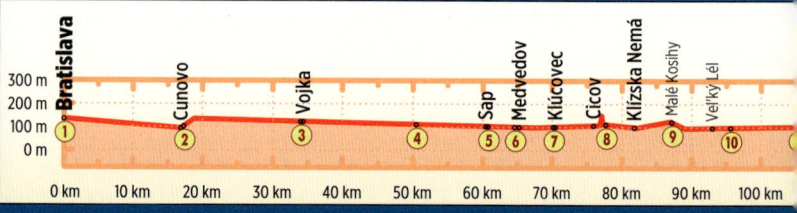

Bratislava to Gabčíkovo 49 km

1 The main route on the north bank in Slovakia starts at the end of the cycle path at the junction with **Pribinova** street ⌁ here, right onto the bus lane ⌁ past the new shopping centre.

TIP There is a lot of construction going on on the upcoming stretch of the road. Currently, a large yellow cycle detour sign indicates that you must follow the left-hand bend in the road. Pass the car park and at the four-lane road turn right onto the pavement, which may also be used by cyclists ⌁ on the pavement cycle path keep following the major road.

TIP When the ground signs point to the right at the large shopping centre, then continue straight ahead.

Bratislava palace

After the next major intersection, a two-lane cycle path begins ~ **2** before entering the business grounds, follow the green-banded cycle path on the left ~ straight on into the park ~ keep left under the bridge.

TIP Here a spiral cycle- and footpath leads up to the bridge. You could switch to the south bank again here.

Alternatively, keep left and turn right at the cycle path junction shortly afterwards ~ now keep following the two-lane cycle path, which has a few unclear but well-marked narrow sections ~ over a branch of water and a narrow cycle passage ~ then turn left ~ directly behind the restaurant kiosk, turn right into the cycle path ~ straight ahead onto the road ~ then a cycle path begins again ~ at its end onto the road ~ **3** right after the Relax restaurant, turn left and immediately right onto the asphalted dam road ~ you will now cycle for many kilometres along the embanked Danube ~ you pass the villages **4 Hamuliakovo** and Čilistov..

5 Čilistov ⓢⓀ
prefix: 031

✱ ✉ **X-Bionic Sphere**, Dubová 33/A, ☎ 3262000. Sports centre with training facilities and equipment for 26 Olympic disciplines,

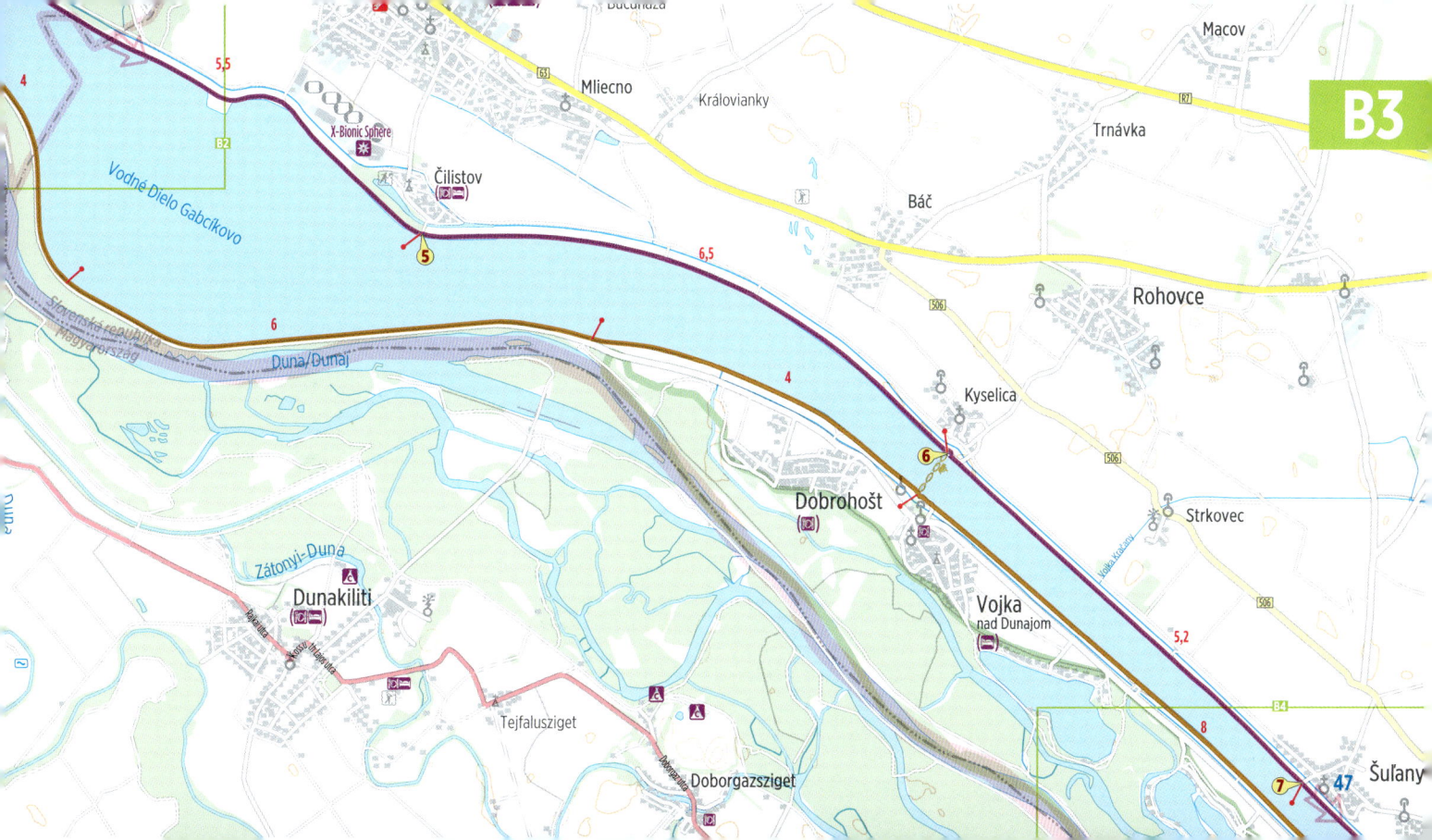

equestrian centre, indoor and outdoor pools, bowling, billard, hotel and restaurants. @ kup541en

6 In Kyselica you can take a ferry to Vojka and ride along the other bank of the Danube to the Gabčíkovo barrage.

Kyselica ⓢ

🚢 **Kompa Kyselica - Vojka,** Kyselica 103, ☏ 031/559 4336, ☏ 0906312219 🕘 Hourly between 5.10 a.m. and 23.10 p.m. @ hsp155en

Continue along the riverside past **Šuľany 7**, **Trstená na Ostrove** and Baka.

Baka ⓢ

8 Shortly before you reach the Gabčíkovo dam, turn left at an acute angle up the dyke — immediately right at the top — turn left at a crossroads and to the main road.

9 On your right is the Gabčíkovo dam. However, to continue, turn left. At the next opportunity, the route branches off to the right at an acute angle. The village of Gabčíkovo is about 2 km ahead of you.

The Gabčíkovo Dam

Despite the strongest protests against the dam project, the construction of the power plant has been completed. The Gabčíkovo-Nagymaros barrage project, which dates back to the Stalin era, means the destruction of the floodplain landscape and the destruction of a sensitive ecosystem between Dunakiliti in Hungary and Palkovicovo in Slovakia. Instead, a huge reservoir has been created that amazes visitors with its masses of water.

The project consists of three dams, the first of which is a barrage on Hungarian territory. It channels 80 percent of the Danube's waters into the man-made reservoir formed by two 17-kilometre dykes that lead to the main dam across the river near the Slovak town of Gabčíkovo. A to-

tal of 150 million cubic metres of fill material were moved in the course of the project and about 4,600 hectares of flood-plain woods and meadows were cleared.

The power station at Gabčíkovo has eight turbines. Twice a day the sluices are opened to feed the turbines and satisfy peak power demand.

Gabčíkovo ⓈⓀ

🛈 **Sv. Margity (St. Margaret)**, Námestie svätej Trojice. The largest church in the region was built in the 14th century and modified in the Baroque style in the 18th century. @ okk786en

🛈 **Amadeovský kaštieľ (Amadeus Manor)**, Športová 568. Renaissance Palace with gardens from the 17th c., redesigned in baroque-classicist style at the end of the 18th c..

Gabčíkovo to Medveď'ov 13 km

9 Turn sharply to the right at the first opportunity after the sluices 〰 ride to the dyke and turn left 〰 follow the path along the top of the dyke to **Sap 10** and further on to **Medved'ov 11**.

ALTERNATIVE This is your last chance to visit the beautiful town of Győr on the Hungarian side of the Danube. From there you can follow the main route in Hungary.

On the Hungarian side to Győr 17.5 km

CONNECTION The description of the main route on the Hungarian side of the Danube begins on **Map C 7**. Follow the main road across the border into Hungary 〰 immediately after the border crossing turn sharply to the left back towards Slovakia 〰 at the first opportunity turn right into the unpaved road 〰 ride towards **Vámosszabadi** 〰 turn left towards **Nagybajcs** 〰 in the village turn right at the inn towards **Kisbajcs** 〰 cross the federal road and continue to the first houses of **Győr-Bácsa** 〰 continue on this road through the suburbs of Győr 〰 in **Kisbácsa** keep following the

Komárno, Europe square

roadside cycle path of the federal road ⁓ cross the state road and turn left at the T-junction into the centre of Györ.

11 The main route continues straight ahead across the road and further along the dyke at Medved'ov.

Medved'ov ⓢⓚ

The countryside between Medved'ov and Kl'úovec is especially pretty. Most of the creeks and canals here are lined with ancient willows, from which the local residents harvest rods in winter and which sustain an active tradition in basket-making. The route also passes directly by a number of inviting lakes, for example in Čičov or in Klížska Nemá, where sweaty cyclists can go for a refreshing swim on hot summers days.

Medved'ov to Malé Kosihy   19.4 km

ALTERNATIVE If you continue along the Slovakian riverbank, you can choose between an alternative on old country lanes lined with shady trees through villages (marked in orange) or the main route along the dyke.

From the cycle path turn left and in the village keep right ⁓ at a crossroads turn half right and leave the village ⁓ cross two canals and ride into Kl'účovec.

Kl'účovec (Medved'ov) ⓢⓚ

Reformovaná kresťanská cirkev (Reformed Christian Church), Kl'účovec 54. Classicist church from 1885 with an onion-top steeple, which is not common in this region.

Follow the road to Čičov and ride on the main street through the village.

Čičov ⓢⓚ

You soon reach Trávnik, where you turn right into the first side road towards Klížska Nemá.

Klížska Nemá ⓢⓚ

In the village follow the road to the left ⁓ continue to **Malé Kosihy** ⁓ in the village turn right and back to the main route **13**.

The main route takes you through meadows and alluvial forests past **Klížska Nemá 12** to Malé Kosihy.

13 Malé Kosihy ⓢⓚ

Malé Kosihy to Komárno   20.3 km

Continue on the dyke along the Danube.

The next few kilometres take you through a nature reserve that was once home to a population of European bustards. They were rare even before the power station was completed, and are now almost completely gone. There are, nevertheless, other birds, including grey herons.

On the dyke you pass **Vel'ký Lél**, **Zlatná Na Ostrove 14** and **Nová Stráž** ⁓ first cross under the road bridge with the distinctive green coloured cyclist ramps ⁓ with a turn cross below the railway bridge and then turn right back to the Danube ⁓ continue along the bank to the end of the cycle path ⁓ here turn left and soon right to the main road **15** ⁓ turn left onto the busy road and into the centre of Komárno.

TIP If you turn right here, you will reach Komárom on the Hungarian side of the Danube.

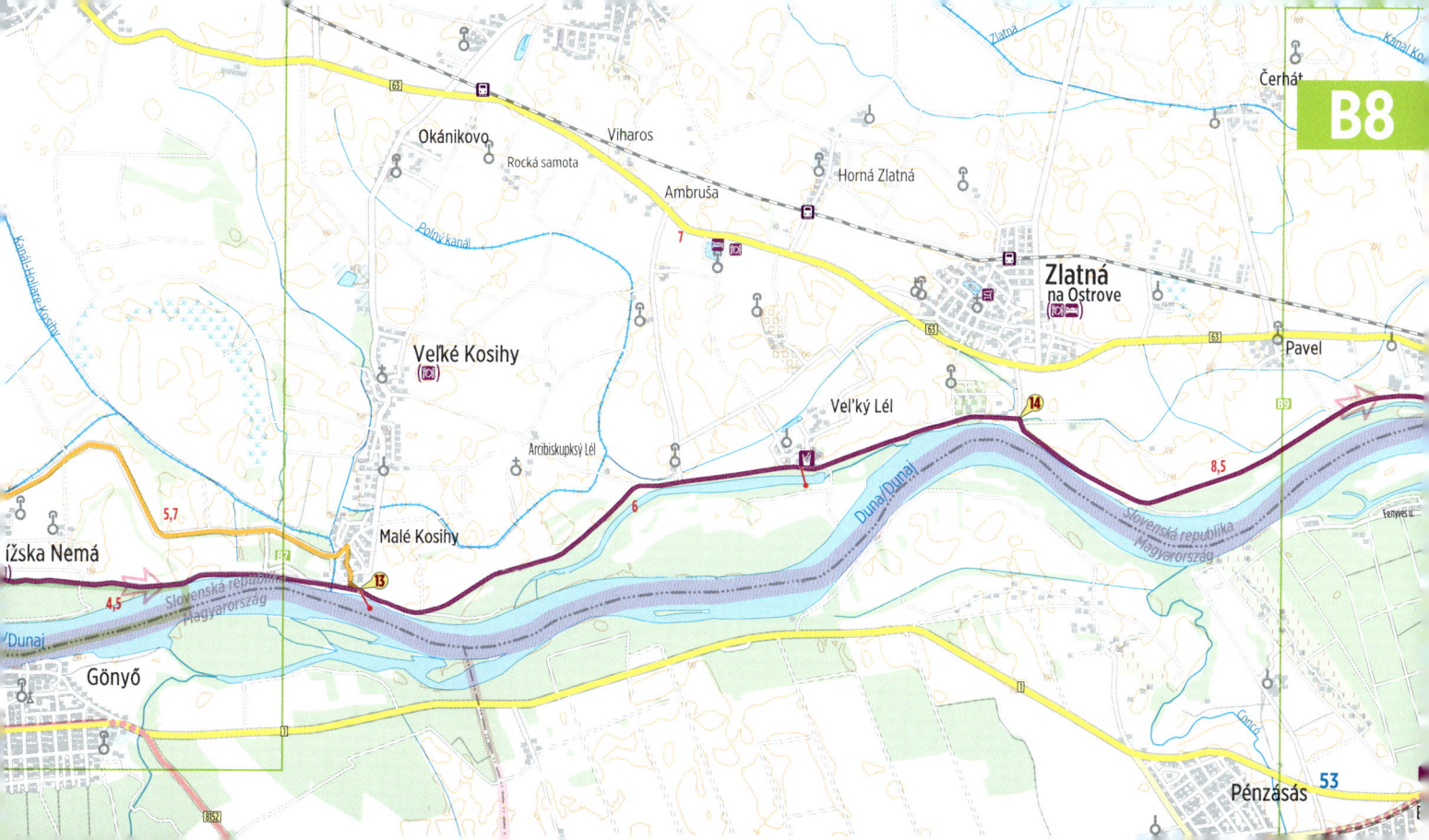

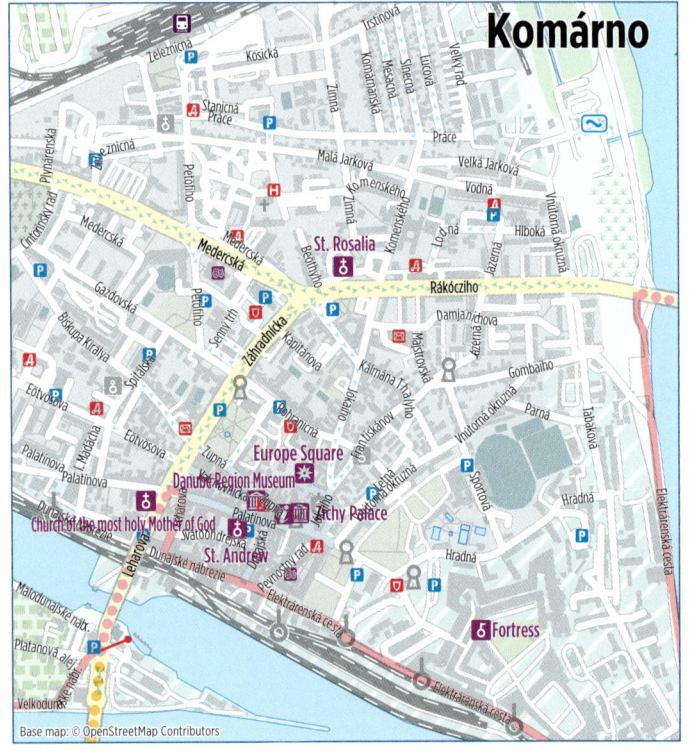

Komárno 🇸🇰

prefix: 035

- **Tourist Info**, nám. Gen. Klapku 1, ☎ 2851205, ☎ 0948/830202, @ raf212en
- **Podunajské múzeum (Danube Region Museum)**, Palatínova 13, ☎ 7731476. Archaeological artefacts, folklore and history, plus 18th and 19th c. paintings. @ dxa817en
- **Zichy Palota (Zichy Palace)**, Nám. gen. Klapku 9, ☎ 7730054. Historic exhibition. The Hungarian writer Jókai (1825-1904) and Franz Lehár are two famous sons of the city. @ gmn777en
- **Presvätej Bohorodičky (Church of the Most Holy Mother of God)**, Palatínova ul. 32, ☎ 7731173. The Orthodox church was built in 1754-70 in late Baroque style. @ vve151en
- **Sv. Ondreja (St. Andreas)**, Palatínova 9, ☎ 7730036. The basilica was built in the 18th c. in late baroque style with classicist elements. @ xaa348en
- **Sv. Rozália (St. Rosalia)**, Nám. Sv. Rozálie 878/2, ☎ 7730036. The church was built in the 19th c. in neoclassical style, next to the church there is a small Calvary with 14 stations. @ itq448en
- **Pevnosti (Fortress)**, Hradná, ☎ 2851250, ☎ 0910/366659. The 16th c. renaissance fortress, built to defend against the Turks, and the new fortress from the late 17th c., were the two largest of their kind in the Austro-Hungarian empire. Remains of the town defences can also be seen in the north and west of the city. @ xeq714en
- **Bašta VI. – Rímske lapidárium (Bastion VI - Roman Lapidary)**, Okružná cesta 42, ☎ 7710066. Fortification building from the 19th c. where Roman carved stone monuments from 2nd to 4th c. AD are exhibited. @ wrb773en
- **Nádvorie Európy (Europe Square)**. A complex of 45 buildings representing the individual nations of Europe, constructed 1999/2000 under the direction of the architects Litomericzky and Varga. @ mcw381en

Komárno is the Slovak half of a city that once occupied both sides of the river. After World War I, when European maps were redrawn, the Danube became the border between Hungary and Czechoslovakia. The city on the Hungarian

Komárno, air plane show at the fortress

side of the river is today called Komárom. In the late Stone Age, small settlements formed in the area where the Vah meets the Danube. Later the Romans arrived and built the Clementia military camp. In the 16th century, a Renaissance fortress was built to protect the area from the Turks. It and the new fortress were among the largest the monarchy held. Today it is regarded a national memorial.

Today Komárno is a growing industrial town and an important centre of Slovakia's shipbuilding industry. The city's large shipyards produce vessels that ply the Danube as well as ocean-going ships.

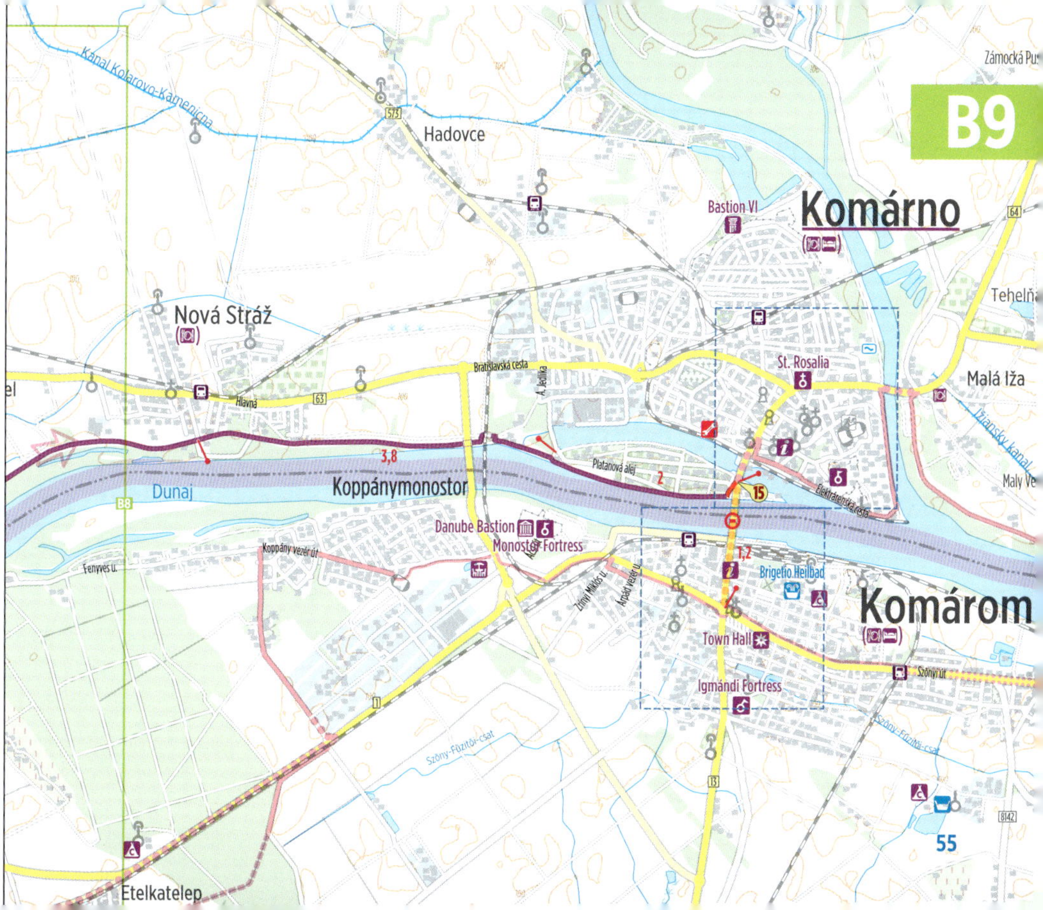

Bratislava to Komárom (H)

122.5 km

m/km: ⬈ 0.2 (19m) ⬊ 0.4 (46m)   cycle path: 76 %   unpaved: 5 %   busy road: 4 %

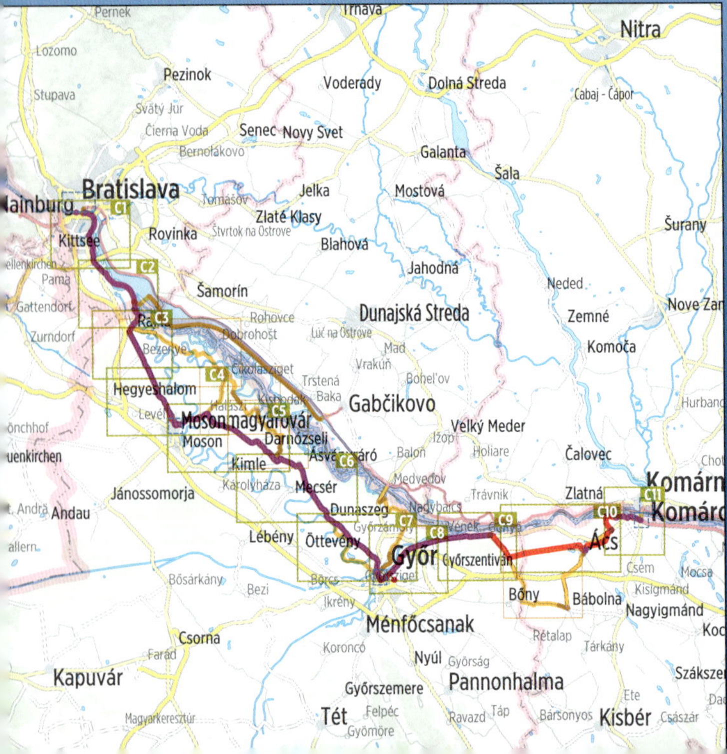

It is a short distance from Bratislava to the Hungarian border at Rajka. The first section in Hungary has a very rural character, with numerous small villages in which you can still find thatched-roof farm houses. Discover Mosonmagyaróvár, the charming old "city of 17 bridges", or the provincial capital Györ with its many sights. Between the two centres the route takes you along the "Szigetköz", an island between the Danube and the Mosoni Duna (Small Danube). Finally, in Komárom you will be able to relax and treat yourself to a thermal spa visit.

The flat landscape between Bratislava and Györ makes for outstanding cycling and you will be riding mostly on bicycle paths. After Györ the route mostly follows secondary roads and takes you through a gently rolling landscape to Komárom.

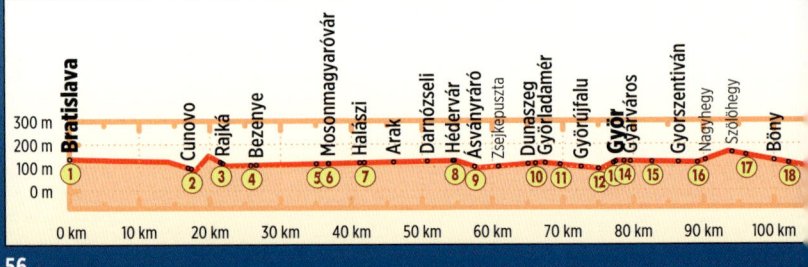

56

Bratislava to Čunovo — 16.7 km

1 For the route on the right bank of the Danube, ride down from the bridge on the long cycle path ramp on the other side ⇢ straight ahead on top of the dyke ⇢ you now cycle for many kilometres on the asphalted two-lane cycle path, partly on the dyke, partly alongside it ⇢ after the sewerage treatment plant the bicycle path comes to a street ⇢ turn right and then immediately left onto the bicycle path, which runs parallel to the dyke along a paved road ⇢ a canal begins here between the dyke and the bicycle path ⇢ simply follow this bicycle path until it ends at a road by Čunovo ⇢ to the right is the village, on the left the route continues.

Čunovo ⓢ

Danubiana, Vodné dielo, on the dam, ✆ 02/62528501 ⓔ The Danubiana Meulensteen Art Museum in the middle of a park filled with futuristic sculptures was opened in 2000. On display are works from artists' private

collections as well as the Meulensteen Foundation collection, @ vfd277en

2 Here you can once again cross over to the north bank into Slovakia. To do so, turn left onto the road and cross the dam. Afterwards, between the dam lake and the Danube, continue along the dyke past the villages **Dobrohošt**, **Vojka** and **Bodíky** (maps in section B). To continue into Hungary, cross the road to the right at this point.

Čunovo to Mosonmagyaróvár   19.3 km

2 Follow the canal on an asphalted bicycle path shortly after the border turn right over the bridge after the bridge turn left and then turn right into the next road towards Rajka pass a little pond on the street **Szent István utca** into the small town **3**.

Rajká (Ragendorf)

Rajkai Kerékpárüzlet, Piac tér, ✆ 30/9374009

In Rajka you have the opportunity to cycle across Szigetköz, the island alley. In the floodplains, you cycle on country roads through small villages and you can marvel at the diverse fauna and flora.

Alternative via Szigetköz   34.8 km

3 Turn left into the street **Kossuth Lajos utca** ~ follow the street ~ your destination is Dunakiliti ~ along the quiet country road you cross the **Mosoni Duna** (Little Danube).

Szigetköz

Szigetköz, the "island alley", refers to the wetlands that runs along the Danube between Rajka and Győr. The area is bounded by the Danube, or Duna in Hungarian, to the north and the Little Danube, or Mosoni Duna, to the south. After breaking through the mountains at Bratislava, the Danube forms a delta as it spreads into the Small Hungarian Plain. This flood plain makes the Austrian March plains seem small in comparison. North of Rajka one stream, the Mosoni Danu, branches southward from the main river. It winds its way slowly through many villages and towns like Dunakiliti and Feketeerdö on its way to Győr.

At Mosonmagyaróvár the Mosoni Duna merges with the Leitha (Hungarian Lajta). In Győr the stream is joined by the Rábca and the Rába before it returns to the main Danube at Vének. The flat and fertile lands of the Szigetköz are

Szigetköz

Alternative Szigetköz 3

covered with grain, pastures and sunflowers. At harvest the huge piles of straw seem to be the tallest objects in sight. The Szigetköz – a quiet and pleasant landscape ideal for relaxed bicycle touring.

Riding along the country road you reach Dunakiliti.

Dunakiliti

Turn left just before the church and follow the main street out of Dunakiliti ～ past the playing fields ～ after 1.5 km you reach the tiny village of **Tejfalusziget** ～ follow the left bend in the street ～ down the tree-lined avenue towards the next village ～ the road turns to the right ～ follow the paved country road through **Doborgazsziget** and continue towards Dunasziget.

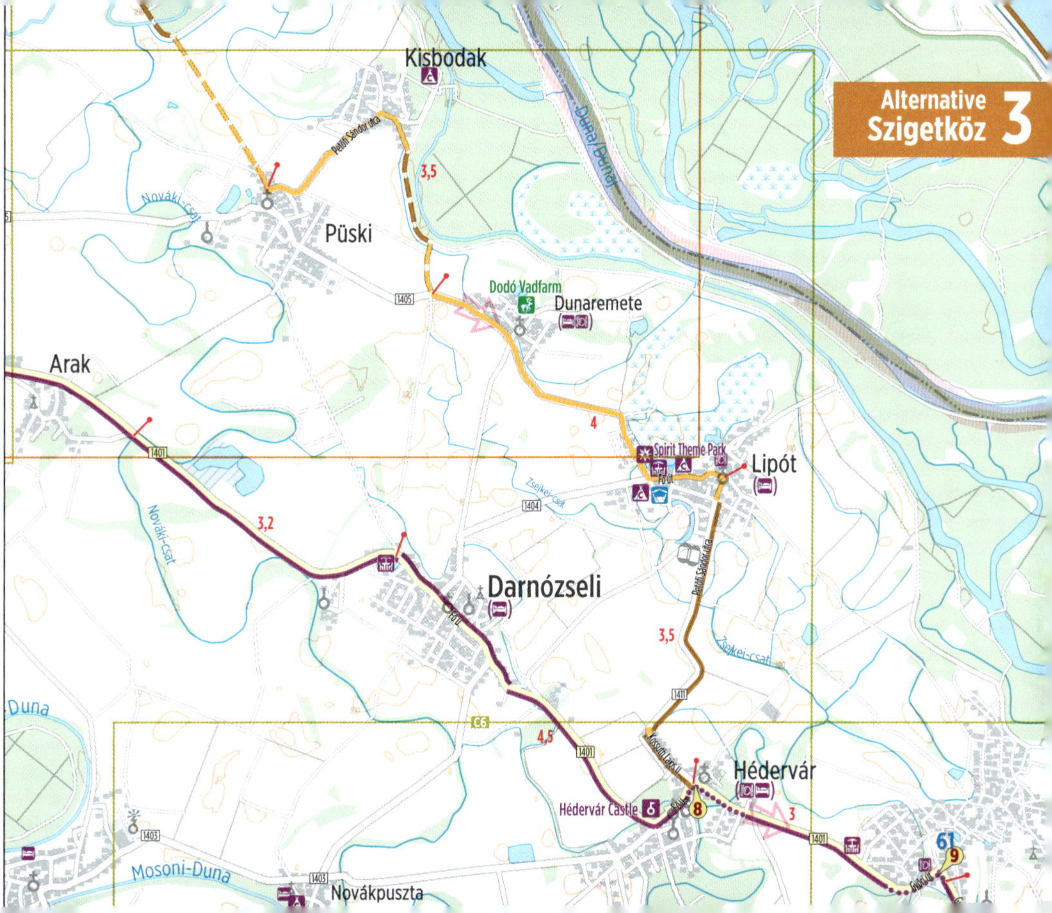

Mosonmagyaróvár, Óvár castle

Dunasziget
✼ **Pisztráng Kör Egyesület (Trout Circle Association)**, Sérfenyő u. 2, ✆ Sérfenyő u. 2. Educational and research centre; Bicycle, kayak and hiking tours. Reservation is requested. @ koo753en

In Dunasziget turn left in the direction of Halászi ⤳ just before reaching the bridge turn left into the road towards Cikolasziget.

ALTERNATIVE If you wish to avoid the unpaved stretches ahead, then simply ride straight over the bridge and follow the road to Halászi, where you can rejoin the main route.

Continue along the road ⤳ you quickly reach the houses of the next village.

Cikolasziget (Dunasziget)
The main road curves to the right as you come into the village ⤳ continue on the main road ⤳ which takes you through a left and right turn ⤳ at the fork at the end of town keep left ⤳ you cross an idyllic watercourse ⤳ at the T-intersection turn right ⤳ the unpaved road makes a left and right curve ⤳ then continue straight for about 1 km ⤳ at which point you ride up onto the dyke ⤳ ride to the right and follow the track along the top of the dyke ⤳ as the dyke curves to the left, leave the dyke and continue straight along the somewhat rough road that leads into Püski.

Püski
As you come into Püski turn left at the intersection in the direction of Kisbodak ⤳ the road curves to the left as you leave Püski ⤳ after less than one kilometre you entre **Kisbodak** ⤳ continue straight to the small roundabout ⤳ turn right ⤳ you come to a fork in the road with a crucifix ⤳ stay right at this fork ⤳ at the end of the village cross a small bridge and ride up onto the dyke ⤳ follow the unpaved track to the right ⤳ after about one kilometre turn right ⤳ you reach the road that leads from Püski to Dunaremete ⤳ turn left and follow the country road past Dunaremete.

Dunaremete
Postal code: H-9235; Dialling code: 96

✼ **Dodó Vadfarm** (wildlife farm), Kossuth Lajos u. 1/A, ✆ 020/4164904. Deer, sheep and boars can be observed. Also: petting zoo, carrigan- and sleigh-rides on appointment. www.platan-dunaremete.hu

Follow the country road to Lipót.

Lipót
prefix: 096

🛁 **Lipóti Therme**, Fő u. 84, ✆ 96215723, @ lap743en
Continue until you reach an intersection with the main road ⤳ turn left ⤳ follow the road until you reach the church ⤳ turn right here in the direction of Hérdervár.

Hédervár   see p. 68
3 At the end of **Szent István utca** cross the main road and turn left onto the bicycle path ⤳ between the street and the train tracks continue to the village Bezenye.

Bezenye
4 Straight towards Mosonmagyaróvár ⤳ the bicycle path ends 100 m after the first houses of Mosonmagyaróvár **5** ⤳ turn right into the side street ⤳ then left into the next side street ⤳ and left again at the T-intersection in front of the canal ⤳ follow the canal ⤳ at the next intersection turn right and ride across the bridge over the canal ⤳ continue straight out into the street ⤳ shortly before reaching the main street, just in front of the chapel, you take the cycle path on the right side ⤳ change to the left side of the street just in front of a bridge ⤳ follow the path between the castle moat

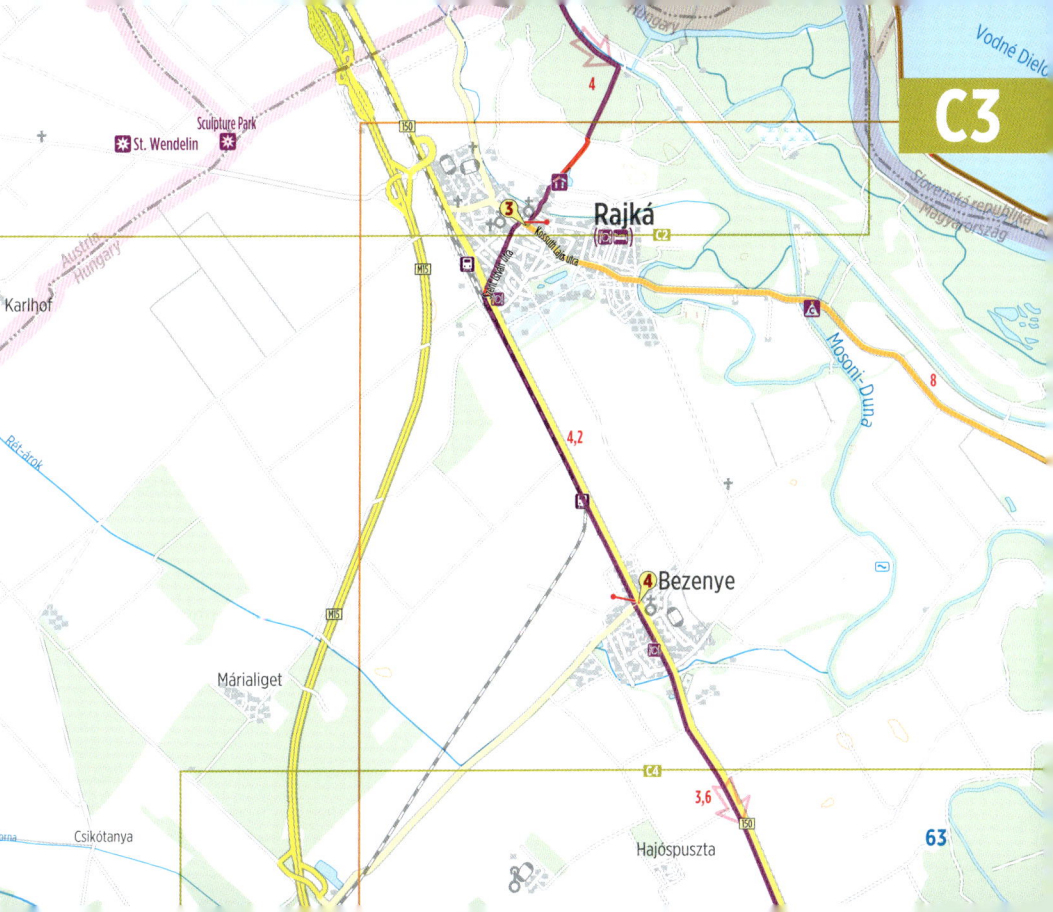

C3

63

and a building and out to another street. To your left lies the impressive palatial castle and to the right begins the beautiful historic centre of Mosonmagyaróvár 6.

Mosonmagyaróvár
prefix: 096

- **Ciklámen Tourist**, Fö út 8., ✆ 555526, @ twf754en
- **Tourinform**, Magyar u. 9, ✆ 206304, @ nrl145en
- **Cselley-ház (Cselley House)**, Fő utca 19, ✆ 212094 ⊟ Collection of paintings and porcelain. Roman lapidary. @ dyh744en
- **Futura**, Szent István király út 142, ✆ 566280 ⊟, @ nmq681en
- **Mosonvármegyei Múzeum (County Museum)**, Szent István király út 1, ✆ 212094 ⊟ Founded in 1802, the museum houses archaeological, historic and ethnographic collections about the nearby Hanság nature reserve. @ mhe658en
- **Tűzoltó Múzeum (Fire Brigade Museum)**, Alkotmány u. 16, ✆ 215633 ⊟ History of the fire brigade of the Győr-Moson-Sopron district from the second half of the last century until today. @ vlf641en
- **Szent Gotthárd (Saint Gotthard)**, Szent László tér 1, ✆ 205050. With grave monument to the Archduke Friedrich and Archduchess Isabella. @ yym433en
- **Óvári Vár (Óvár Castle)**, Pozsonyi út 86, ✆ 566665 ⊟ Built in the 13th c. Today it houses a university of agricultural sciences. The tunnel vault of the entrance has four Gothic sitting niches (15th c.). Also surviving are two towers, the moats, casemates, prison cells and outer walls. @ xsj776en
- **Lucsony utca**. A row of old houses built in a provincial baroque style.
- **Szigetköz Kalandpark**, Soproni út 94, ✆ 0630/2303340 ⊟ Adventure and climbing park in Rudolf-liget with various courses and a flying fox over the Mosoni-Duna. @ dwt586en
- **Bio Flexum Thermalbad**, Kolbai Károly u. 10, ✆ 211533 ⊟, @ ljx284en

The "Door to Hungary", as the oldest town of the Comitatus is also known, was settled by the Romans in the 1st century BC. In 1939 the two settlements of Moson and Magyaróvár were merged,

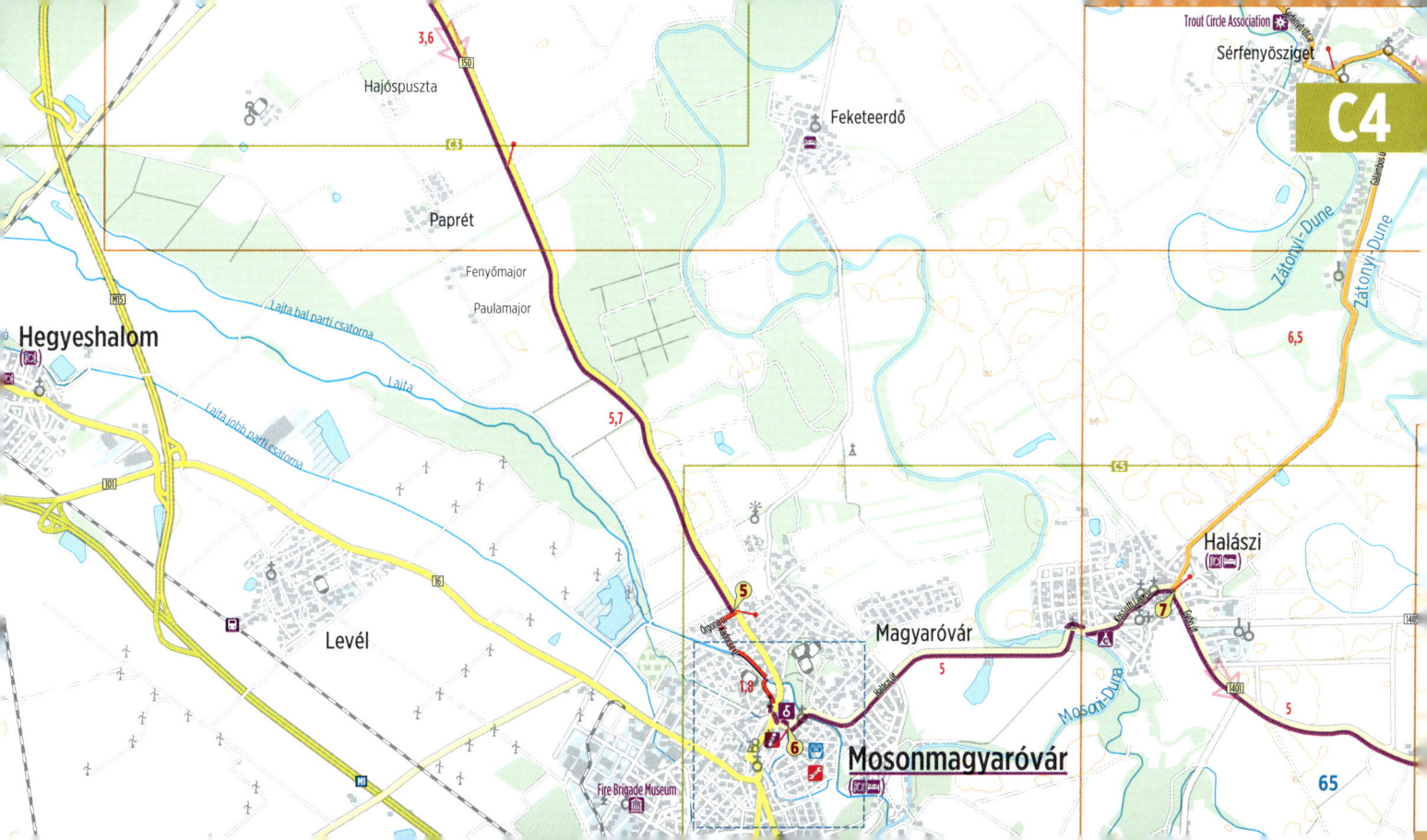

which is how its tongue-twisting name came into being. Mosonmagyaróvár has been an important centre of trade and industry since the middle ages. In the past, cattle in particluar were exportet to Vienna from here.

The historic city centre is noteworthy for its impressive collection of baroque buildings. The river Leitha (Hungarian Lajta) curves through the centre before it converges with the Mosoni Duna. The one-time swamplands were drained with numerous channels, which today contribute to the city's charm. A total of 17 bridges cross these various streams.

The city's well-preserved castle, Ovár Castle, with its massive defensive walls and extensive system of moats, now lies in the middle of a park. When one enters the castle through the main gate, one passes several Gothic seating niches. A fortification was erected here as early as in 1009, at the time of the first crusades. It was rebuilt in 1260. Under Duke Albert Kasimir the castle was to receive a second story in 1798 and in 1810 was remodelled to the appearance that we see today. The duke set up a private business school in the castle in 1818, which today houses a University of Agricultural Sciences. Today the castle and part of the city centre have been placed under heritage protection and have been exquisitely restored. A generously laid-out pedestrian area is being installed in parts of the centre and along the Magyar utca. The low buildings give the town a very hospitable atmosphere, which is reinforced by the many outdoor restaurants and gardens along the streets. In the middle of Magyar utca one can find Szent László tér with a small church. There is a bicycle path along the entire Magyar utca.

Mosonmagyaróvár to Hédervár   17.7 km

6 Just after a left bend the two lane bicycle path changes to the right side of the street simply follow the bicycle path after crossing the canal again you pass a park with large trees you ride past houses and a petrol station as you leave Mosonmagyaróvár the bicycle

Hédervár castle

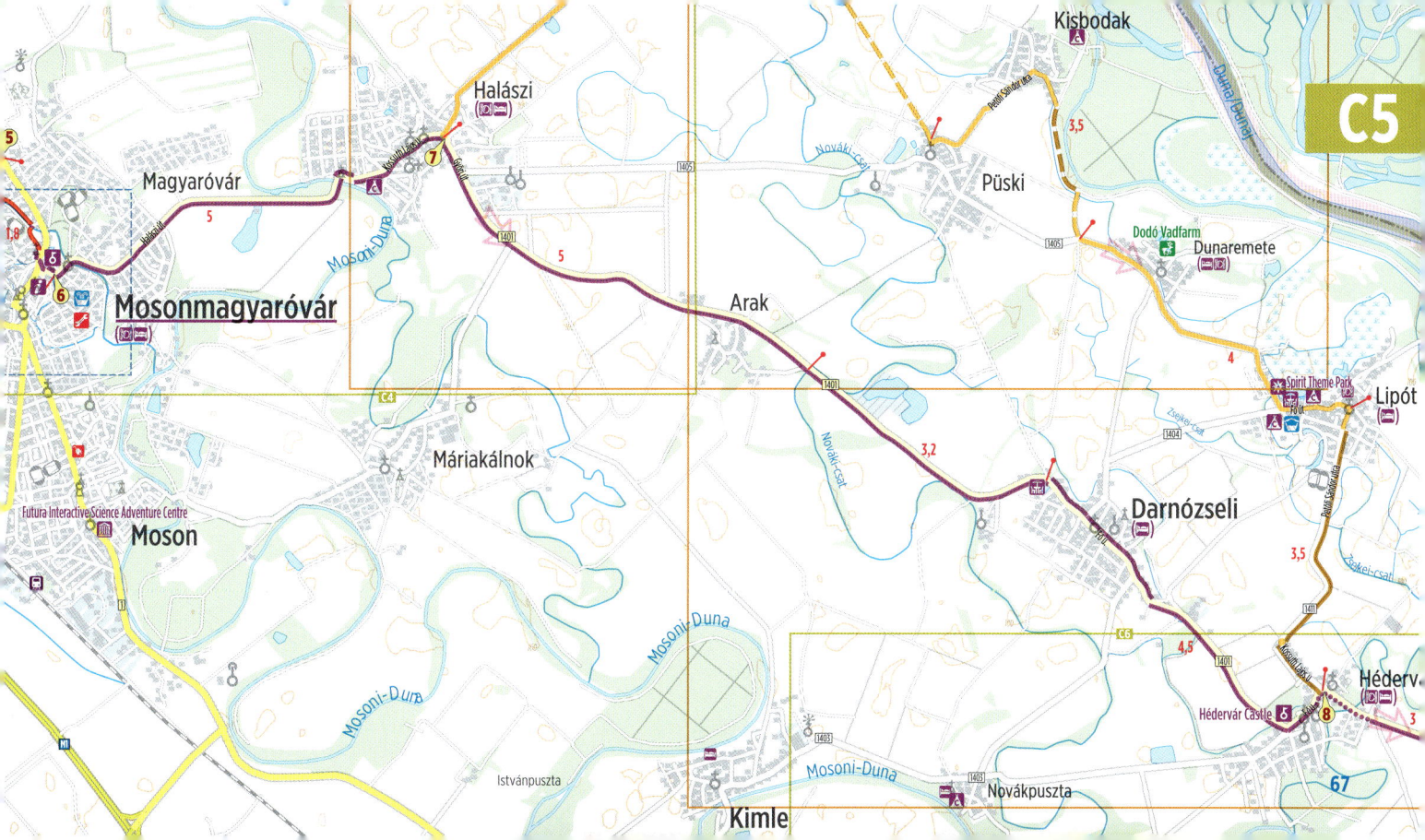

Mosoni Duna near Győr

path takes you along the right side of the road to the village of Halászi.

Halászi
After crossing the bridge over the Mosoni Duna the bicycle path changes to the left side for a short distance, before continuing on the right side ~ simply follow the wide, paved, red bicycle path as it follows the main road through the village ~ you soon leave the village after a sharp right hand bend **7** ~ you move past information boards which have been erected along the bicycle path ~ you pass on the left side of the village of **Arak** ~ a small park with picnic tables lies beside the route as you enter the village of **Darnózseli**,

where the bicycle path changes to the left side of the road ~ follow the bicycle path through the village ~ at the end of which the bicycle path once more changes to the right side of the road ~ after only a short distance you reach Hédervár.

On the left as you enter the village is the large castle park with its impressive palace ~ the bicycle path leaves the road for a short distance through the left bend in the road ~ then ends just before the right bend in the road in front of the church **8**.

Hédervár

6 **Hédervár kastél (Hédervár Castle)**, Fő út 47. Large manor house, originally Gothic, later expanded in the renaissance style, now stands in the middle of a protected parkland. According to local legend, the massive oak tree in front of the Gothic chapel is at least 1,000 years old. @ yth185en

The Hédervár Castle, a magnificent fortified palace that grew out of a medieval fortress, stands in the middle of a fine park. The entrance is guarded by two stone sphinxes. Diagonally across from the church stands a small straw-roofed house. The straw roofs of the region were not only cute to look at, but said to be more weather resistant than shingled roofs.

Hédervár to Győr   22.7 km
8 Continue along the marked bicycle lane until you reach the end of the village ~ where the two lane bicycle path begins again on the right side of the road ~ after only 3 km you reach Asványráró.

Ásványráró
The fishery is the oldest surviving industry in this town, where other trades like towing ships, milling grain, and washing gold have all disappeared. The last gold-panner in Asványráró died in 1944. Some hobbyists still try their luck panning for gold, however, with modest success.

Entering town there is a bicycle lane on the side of the road ~ **9** turn right at the roundabout by the church ~ follow the sign towards Győr ~ at the edge of the town a paved bicycle path begins ~ follow the path beside the road the entire 7 km to Dunaszeg.

Dunaszeg
10 Here you have two alternative routes for reaching Győr: Continue on the bicycle path next to the country road to Győr or cycle along the idyllic dyke for 13 km along the Mosoni Duna (Little Danube). This alternative is

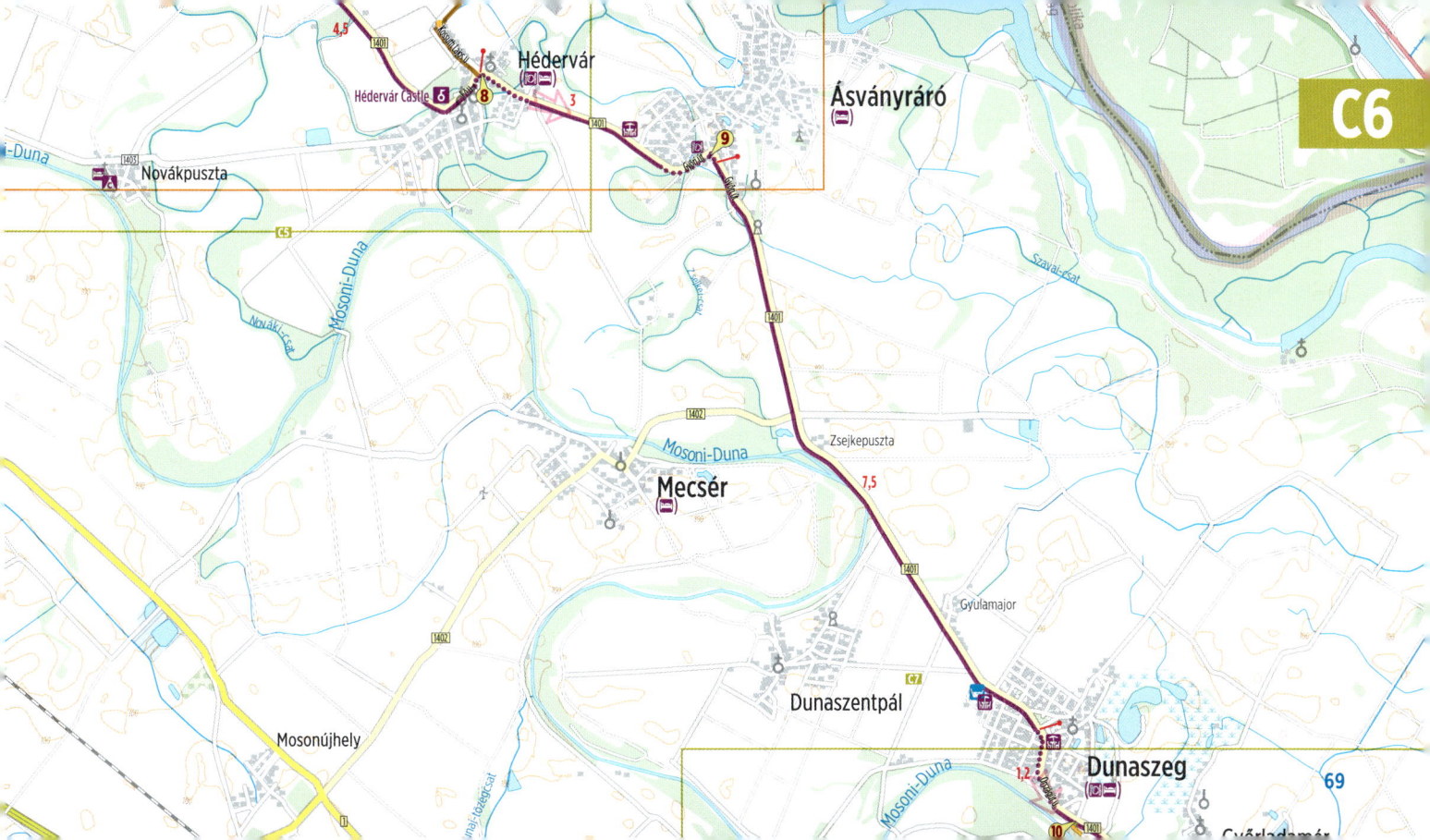

Győr

not asphalted for the first 4 km, but after that the path has been paved and is easy to ride on.

Alternative route along the Mosoni Duna to Győr   13.2 km

To get to the dyke, turn into **Kossuth Lajos utca** in Dunaszeg 200 m after the bend at the supermarket ~ when you reach the dyke, turn left and head towards Győr ~ an idyllic floodplain spreads out on your right ~ the dyke splits ~ go straight ahead on the cycle path into Győr.

Mosoni Duna

The little Danube is actually just a branch of the river. Both currents flow around the Szigetköz island.

To continue along the main route from Dunaszeg, ride along the bicycle path next to the main road ~ you ride through the villages of **Győrladamér** and **Győrzámoly** **11** ~ then come to the village of **Győrújfalu** ~ near the end of the village you come to a square with two small churches ~ follow the bicycle path to the right by the church ~ cross the street into the small side street.

> **TIP** The cycling route here is marked with a small blue sign.

You once again come to follow the bicycle path beside the main road to Győr ~ you soon reach the Győr city boundary ~ follow the bicycle path, **12** which takes you to the right away from the main road ~ the path now follows the street **Hédervári ut.** ~ into the centre of the city ~ straight ahead over the roundabout into the street **Rónay Jácint ut.** ~ change sides of the road ~ follow the bicycle path along the street to **Kossuth híd**, an imposing steel bridge **13**.

> **TIP** From the bridge one can look to the right to see the grounds of the thermal baths on the "Sziget".

Take the left-hand cycle path over the bridge and straight ahead into the pedestrian zone, where cycling is permitted.

Győr
prefix: 096

- **Tourinform Győr**, Árpád u. 32, ✆ 311771, ✆ 336817, @ ovi224en
- **Borsos Miklós Állandó Kiállítás (Permanent exhibition Miklós Borsos)**, Apor Vilmos püspök tere 2, ✆ 316329, ✆ 0620/3125920 ~ Collection of sculptures, illustrations, etc. of Miklós Borsos. @ yma283en
- **Egyházmegyei Könyvtár és Kiállítótér (Diocesan treasure and library)**, Káptalandomb 26, ✆ 525090, ✆ 0630/2551363 ~ Church art from western Hungary from the gothic period to the 19th c. @ fxv337en
- **Patkó Imre Gyűjtemény (Imre Patkó Collection)**, Széchenyi tér 4, ✆ 310588 ~ Housed in the early baroque Eisenklotz House (17th c.), presents Hungarian and European artworks of the 20th

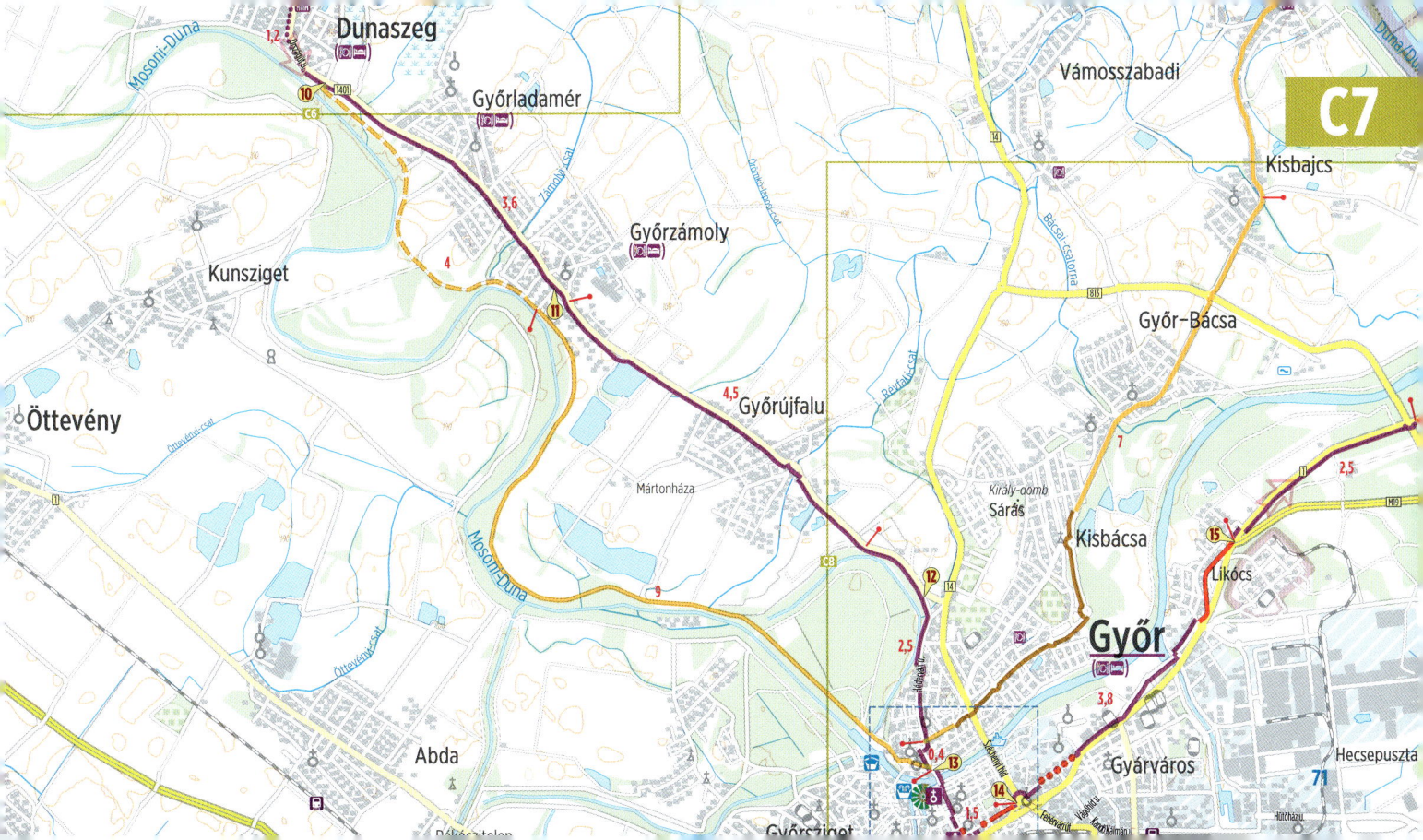

Győr, Szechenyi square

c., Asian arts and crafts from the 18th to 20th c., and an ethnographic collection from Africa.

🏛 **Széchenyi Patikamúzeum (Széchenyi Pharmacy museum)**, Széchenyi tér 9, ✆ 320954 ⊜ The pharmacy's (1654) ceiling is decorated with stucco and paintings. It is the only one in Hungary that is still used as a pharmacy.

🏛 **Váczy Péter Gyűjteménye (Péter Váczy Collection)**, Nefelejcs köz 3, ✆ 318141, ✆ 0620/4520691 ⊜ Private art collection of the historian Dr. Péter Váczy.

🏛 **Városi Művészeti Múzeum (City museum of art)**, Király u. 17, ✆ 322695, ✆ 0620/4252572 ⊜ The museum is housed in the Esterházy palace, an architectural monument from the 18th c. @ ylq675en

🏛 **Xantus János Múzeum (János-Xántus-Museum)**, Széchenyi tér 5, ✆ 322695, ✆ 524888 ⊜ Ethnology collections dedicated to Hungarian naturalist and explorer János Xántus (1825-1894) on display in an abbots house dating from 1741-43. @ ovm424en

🏛 **Apor Emlékkiállítás (Apor Memorial Exhibition)**, Káptalandomb 1, ✆ 0630/2551363 ⓘ The exhibition is a memorial to the work of the martyr Bishop Vilmos Apor. @ ldg373en

⛪ **Karmelita templom (Carmelite church)**, Aradi vértanúk u. 2 ⊜ Baroque facade and interior of the church (1721-25) by Martin Witwer. @ suw248en

⛪ **Nagyboldogasszony-székesegyház (Assumption Cathedral)**, Káptalandomb 12, ✆ 618304 ⓘ Only the apse from the original Romanesque church (11th c.) remains today. From the 13th to the 15th c. it was rebuilt in Gothic style. 1634-45, the interior was reconstructed in early Baroque style by the Italian master Giovanni Battista Rana. The tower was built in 1680. @ msh386en

⛪ **Szent Mór (St. Mór)**, Széchenyi tér 9, ✆ 513020 ⓘ The Benedictine church was built 1635-41 according to plans by Baccio del Biancho. @ gvl173en

⛪ **Püspökvár (Bishop's Castle)**, Káptalandomb 1, ✆ 0630/2551363 ⓘ The former bishops seat with its old residential tower dates to the 12th c. From the observation terrace of the tower visitors have a unique panorama of the city and its surroundings. @ kwk257en

🎭 **Nemzeti Színház (National Theatre)**, Czuczor Gergely u. 7, ✆ 520600. The facade decoration on the modern theatre building was done by Victor Vasarely, a Hungarian painter born in 1908. Home of one of the best dance ensembles in central Europe, the Győr Ballet. @ rsx551en

✤ **Dunakapu tér**. Legend has it that the weather vane on the fountain announced the end of the Ottoman occupation.

✤ **Frigyláda-szobor (Arc of the Covenant-monument)**, Gutenberg tér. The monument is one of the most impressive examples of the Győr Baroque. It was built on the orders of Emperor Charles VI. and is the work of Fischer von Erlach.

✤ **Jedlik-csobogó (Jedlik-drinking fountain)**, Apáca u. 1., in front of the Kreszta House ㉔ The fountain was built to honour the inventor of soda-water and the soda-siphon, Benedictine priest István Ányos Jedlik.

✤ **Széchenyi tér**. Main square with impressive baroque façades. @ fid566en

✤ **Vastuskós-ház (Vastuskós house)**, Széchenyi tér 4. The early baroque Eisenklotz House's (Iron Trunk House, 17th c.) name derives from the log at the house's corner, which was a trade-sign. Travelling journeyman drove a nail into the trump as a memento.

▭ **Achilles Park**, Gyirmóti Tájvédelmi Körzet, ✆ 556011, ✆ 0620/9943577. Boat rental, @ gds812en

▭ **Aranypart**, Vásárhelyi Pál u. 26., ✆ 524297

▭ **Aqua Sportzentrum**, Olimpia u. 1, ✆ 0620/3964839, @ sfu257en

▭ **Magyar Vilmos Uszoda**, Töltésszer 24, ✆ 528306, @ btq766en

▭ **Rába Quelle**, Fürdő tér 1, ✆ 514900, @ gph825en

Győr is one of the largest and most important cities in northwestern Hungary. It lies at the confluence of the Mosoni Duna, the Rábca and the Rába rivers, which then empty into the Danube. The city's origins were in the Bronze Age. It was almost completely destroyed on two occasions: once by the Turks, a second time in WWII when aerial bombardment reduced a quarter of the baroque city to ash and ruin. Today Győr is an important industrial city. It gained its economic importance with the Danube river port built in the 18th century.

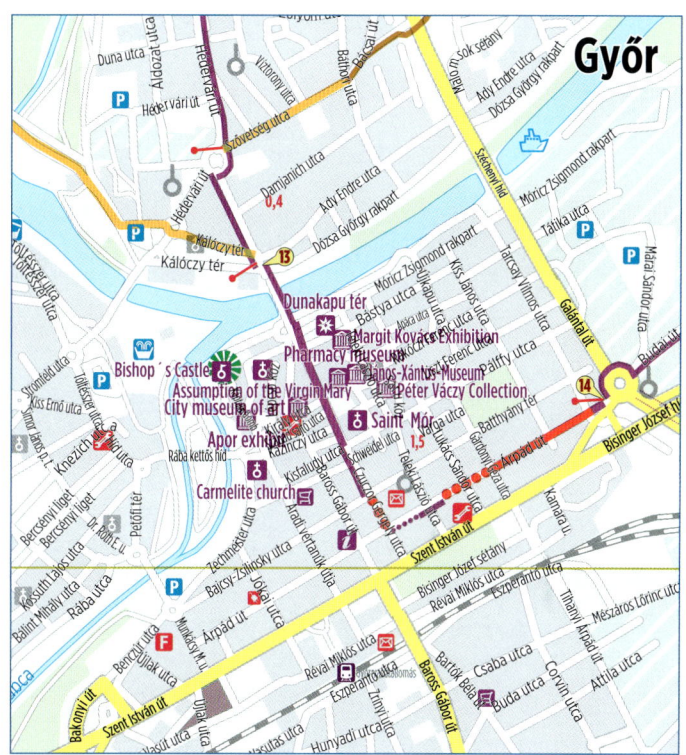

Győr, town hall

The Celts were the first to settle in this fertile area. In the first century AD, the Romans built a town they called Arrabona. It became one of the most important border fortifications of Pannonia province. Hungarians began moving into the area at the end of the 9th century. When you cross the Mosoni Duna along the Kossuth híd, then you are standing before the historic centre of Győr. The motor traffic is restricted here by the generously laid out pedestrian area. Going along the Jedlik Anyos you arrive at the Széchenyi tér. In the middle of this imposing square, which is dominated by a double towered Benedictine Church, stands a column with the Virgin Mary. Hungary's most modern theatre building, the Győr National Theatre, resembles a ski jump and stands nearby. The facades with their black and white tiles and geometric forms were done by the world-famous Hungarian painter, Victor Vasarely. Take Arany János út to reach the flower market and the Raab River. The Carmelite church on Bécsi kapu tér, the Vienna Gate Square, was built between 1721 and 1725. The magnificent baroque facade is done up in a powerful yellow tone. Rising above the square is the central point of this part of the city, the Káptalandomb (capital hill), upon which stand the Bishops castle and the basilica. The 12th century castle contains the baroque bishops almshouse.

The castle has been repeatedly rebuilt and expanded over the ages. In the 14th century, for instance, an addition was built onto the residential tower, and there were further additions in the 16th century as the invading Turks posed an ever greater threat to the city. The result was Hungary's largest fortress. As it lost its value as a defensive edifice in the 19th century, the citizens began using its massive walls as a quarry for their own construction projects. The practice was ended in time to save the castle.

The Basilika, whose foundation stone was laid in the 11th century, is a composite from different eras. The gothic apse is from the 13th century. The dome was rebuilt in the baroque style during the 17th and 18th centuries, after it had been destroyed during Ottoman attacks. In 1823 it received its neo-classical facade. The Ladislaus chapel was completed in 1404. It contains the Hermes, a gold-plated silver bust holding the skull of King Ladislaus the holy.

Visitors who wish to learn more about these stories and the city's history may wish to visit "János Xantus Museum." In addition to exhibits about Győr and the surrounding area, the museum also contains an ethnographic section. You should not miss the healing power of the water in the thermal baths in Győr.

Győr to Komárom — 46.1 km

Through the centre past the Kreszta House on **Jedlik Ányos utca** ~ the pedestrian zone ends at **Kisfaludy utca**, cross it straight on ~ continue on **Czuczor Gergely utca** ~ turn left into **Àrpád út** ~ continue to the large roundabout at the end of the street ~ **14** keep left and cycle around the large roundabout on its left side ~ after the second road crossing, turn left into the **Budai út** roadside cycle path ~ keep right at the next fork ~ then follow the cycle path along **Mártírok útja** ~ the now two-lane cycle path then accompanies **Pesti út** street on the right ~ after a band of water, the path changes to the left side of the road ~ when the cycle path crosses the road to the right again, continue straight on the road on **Pesti út** through **Likócs** ~ **15** continue on a cycle path along the main road ~ until you reach **Gönyű** always ride either to the right or to the left of the main road no. 1 ~ **16** at the end of Gönyű there's a short distance on a

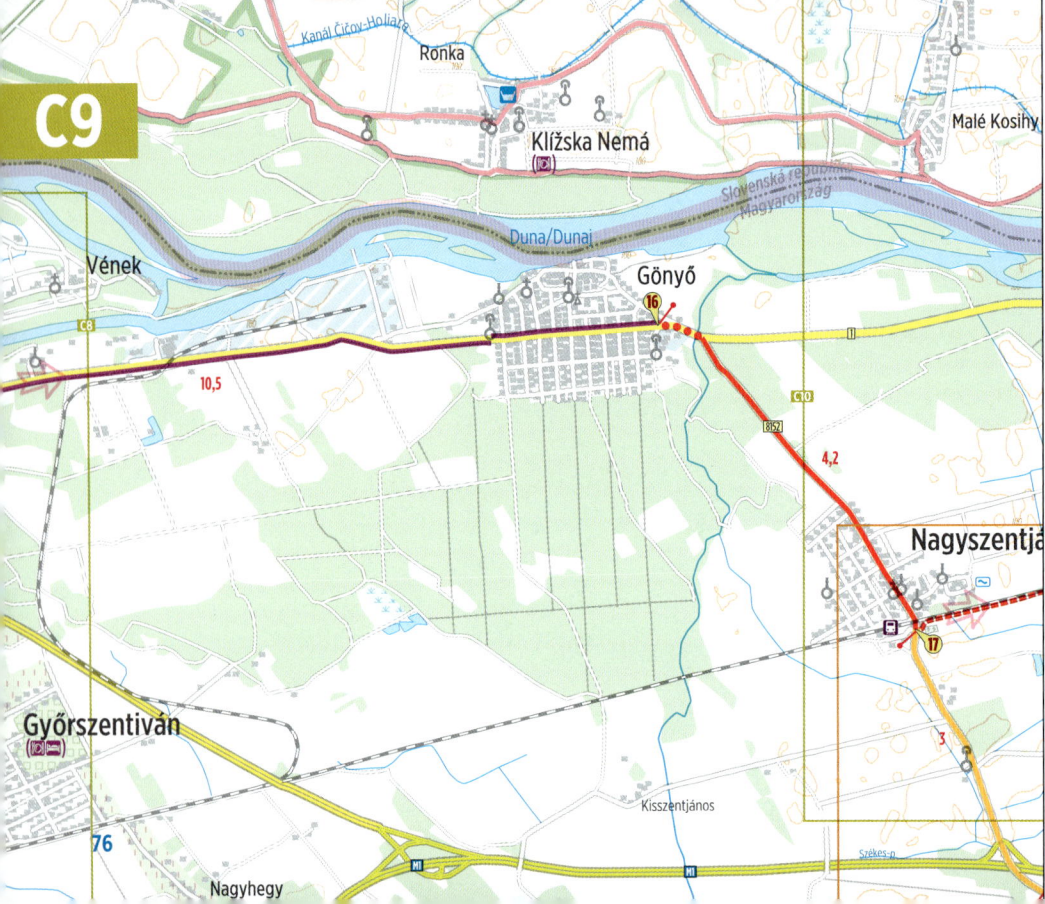

busy road, then turn right onto road no. **8152** to Nagyszentjános.

Nagyszentjános

17 The main route leads to the left after the tracks. Unfortunately, this section of the path is really badly passable. In rainy weather it is most likely impassable. A good alternative is a diversion via Bábolna, where you can additionally visit the Hungarian National Stud.

Alternative via Bábolna 22.1 km

Continue to follow the **8152** road ~ cross the bridge over the motorway ~ at the T-junction turn left towards Bábolna ~ on the main road through the village of Bana ~ after leaving the village follow the right-hand bend of the road.

Bana

Follow the left curve just before the first church ~ turn right in the direction of Tata by the second church ~ a bicycle path begins on the right side just as you reach Bábolna, and ends at the first large intersection.

Bábolna
prefix: 034

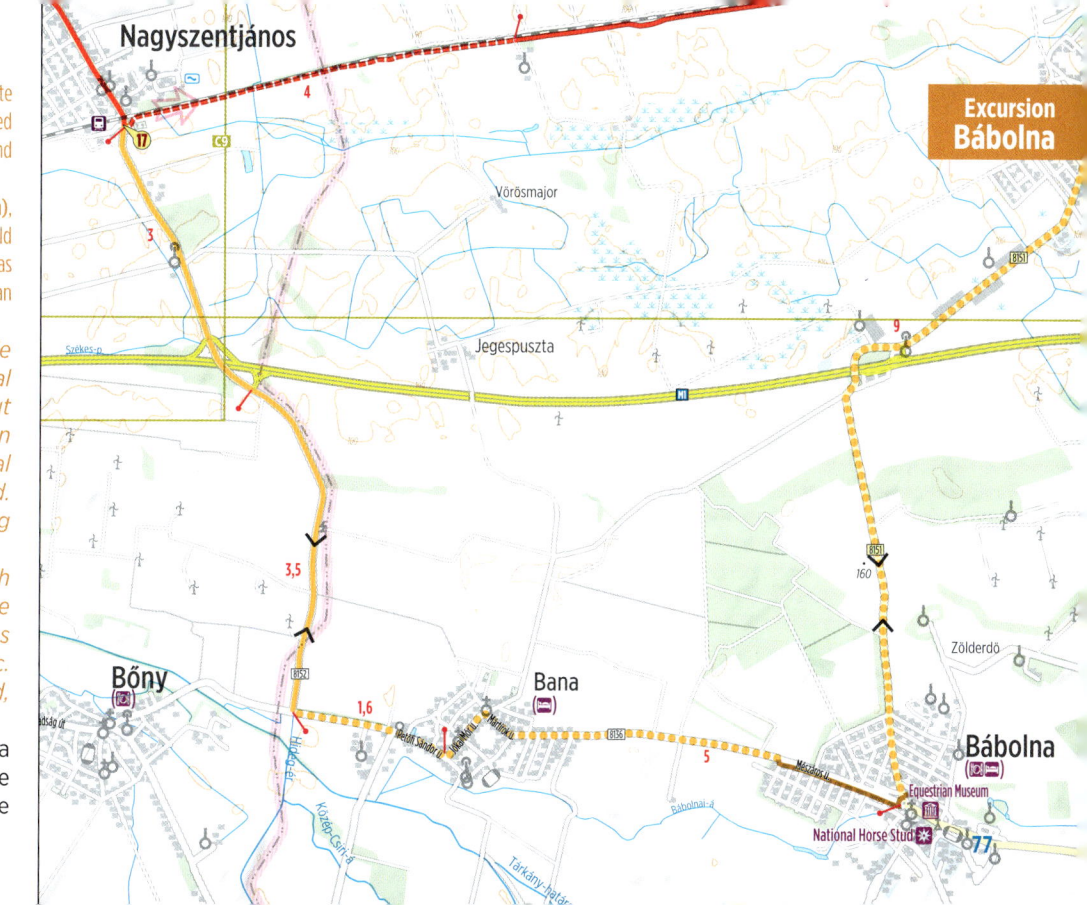

- **Lovas Múzeum (Equestrian Museum)**, Mészáros u. 8, opposite the Studyard, ✆ 569200 🖃 Horse and Coach museum, guided tours of 90 min. through the stables and riding hall, riding and coach rides require advanced booking. @ bed578en
- **Bábolna Nemzeti Ménesbirtok (National Studyard Bábolna)**, Mészáros út 1., ✆ 569200 🖃 Established in 1789, the world famous stud boasts a magnificent interior courtyard as well as a hotel. It is famous for breeding fullblood and Shagya arabian horse. @ tor657en

Bábolna is a tidy and prosperous looking little town, thanks in part to the large agricultural cooperative that built a reputation throughout the former eastern-bloc and the far east. In the centre of the town stands an old imperial building that houses Bábolna's famous stud. This is where Hungary's fastest and best racing thoroughbreds are bred and trained.

To reach the entrance, you cross a park with very old trees, paths and benches. The entire town is built around the stud, which was founded in 1789 and is now open to the public. A rondell has been erected in the courtyard, where horses are shown and sold.

17 On the main route you turn right into a small side road shortly after crossing the railway tracks ⁓ turn left into a path before

Komarom, Elisabeth Bridge

you reach the cemetery ~ follow the track into fields to the left of the cemetery, the track is quite rough and not very wet-weather proof ~ you are now riding to the right of the railway line ~ eventually an asphalt road in poor condition begins, improving as you pass a turnoff to a farm ~ simply continue along the road next to the railway line ~ at the T-intersection keep right and continue along the railway line into Ács ~ by the railway station follow the right bend in the road ~ you pass a sportsfield and restaurant on the left hand side.

Ács

18 Turn left at the main road ~ follow the right-hand curve of the road ~ straight on into **Kossuth Lajos utca**.

ALTERNATIVE On the main route, the first road section after the village is sometimes badly passable, especially in rainy weather. Alternatively, you can take the busy but asphalted road. To do this, turn left at this point, cross the tracks and turn right.

On the main route you pass the last houses and take the unpaved track into the fields ~ you pass through a small forested area ~ the track runs briefly parallel to the main road ~ **19** turn left at the next intersection ~ cross the railway tracks and turn right onto the main road ~ ⚠ after 50 m cross the road and ride into the smaller road leading away to the left ~ turn right and ride between fields into **Koppánymonostor**, a suburb of Komárom ~ at the T-intersection turn right into **Koppány vezér út** ~ follow the street, a bicycle path begins on the right side of the road at the end of the houses ~ you cross railway tracks ~ at the T-intersection cross the main road and turn left ~ continue on the bicycle path, which leads into Komárom on the right side of the road ~ the bicycle path ends after crossing the railway tracks ~ turn right into the first side street ~ then left at the next street ~ and left again at the T-intersection ~ you come back out to the main road, where you turn right onto the two lane bicycle and pedestrian path ~ at the roundabout in the centre of Komárom, continue straight ahead to follow the main route on the Hungarian side of the Danube **20**.

TIP Turning left at the roundabout takes you to the bridge over the Danube and into Slovak Komárno (see p. 52).

Komárom
prefix: 034

- **Tourinform**, Igmándi út 2, ✆ 540590, ✆ 0630/5172068, @ xnx526en
- **Hadtörténeti Kiállítás (Military history exhibition)**, Dunapart 1, at the Monostor Fortress, ✆ 0630/2114166 ⓘ History of Komárom and its fortifications from the 16th century to the Second World War. The museum also displays a model of the Danube bastion. @ mqk323en
- **Klapka György Múzeum (Klapka György Museum)**, Kelemen László u. 22, ✆ 0630/344697 ⓘ Frescoes and other artefacts

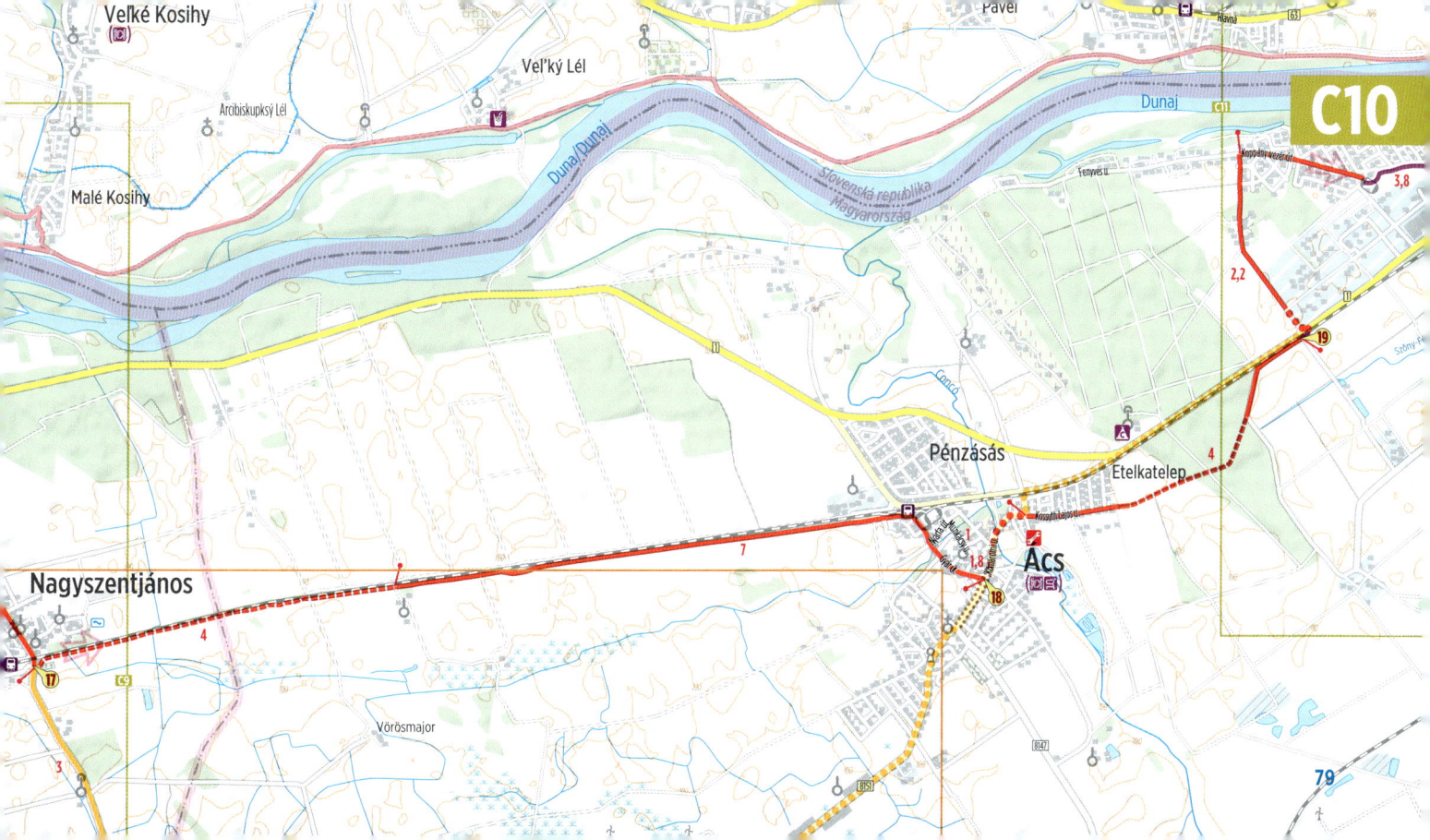

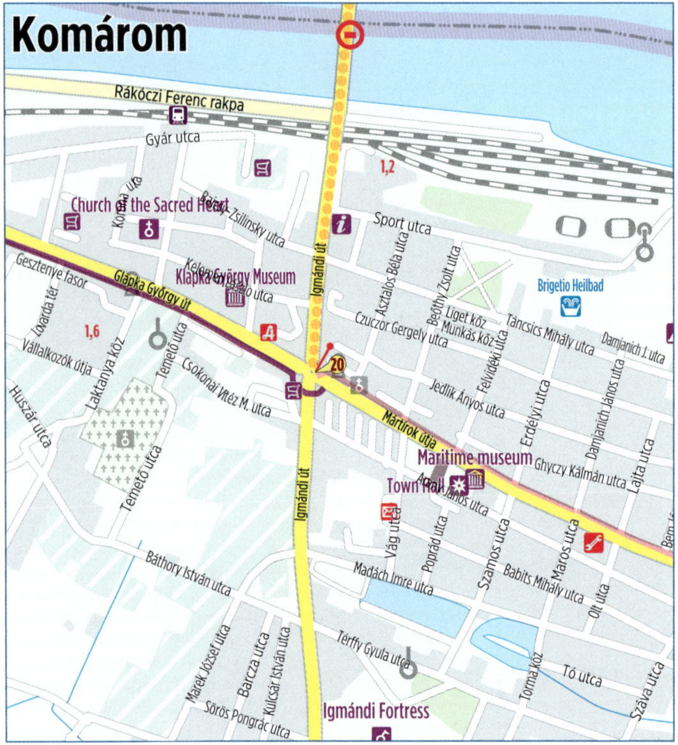

Komárom

Komárom, Monostor Fortress

found at Brigetio, sarcophagi with human remains, gold jewelry and items made of glass and bronze. @ mrw364en

🏛 **Magyar Tengerésztörténeti Gyűjtemény (Hungarian Maritime History Collection)**, Szabadság tér 1, ✆ 541340 History of Hungarian seafaring. The two anchors once belonged to the Danube steamboats "Budapest" and "Szeged". @ our822en

⛪ **Jézus Szíve-templom (Sacred Heart of Jesus church)**, Szent László u. 9, ✆ 340576. The church (1935-37) is a significant example of modern Hungarian church architecture. @ rnu153en

♂ **Igmándi Erőd (Igmánd Fortress)**, Duna part 1, ✆ 540582. Roman Lapidary, exhibits of ancient stone work, inscribed grave stones, plus sarcophagi and altar blocks. @ mcc521en

♂ **Monostori Erőd (Monostor Fortress)**, Dunapart 1., ✆ 540582 Monostor fortress is the largest modern fortification in central Europe and also known as the "Gibraltar of the Danube". Built between 1850 and 1871, it consists of a complex network of fortification walls, moats and underground bunkers. Today it is maintained as a memorial to Hungary's military history. @ oak856en

- **Városháza (Town hall)**, Szabadság tér 1. The neo-Renaissance building was constructed in 1875 on the site of the old town hall. The windows of the tower open daily at 10am, 12pm, 2pm and 4pm to show a hussar playing the trumpet.
- **Brigetio Gyógyfürdő (Brigetio Spa)**, Táncsics Mihály u. 34-36, ✆ 342551, @ qup788en

After WWI, when the border between Slovakia and Hungary was drawn, this city on the Danube was divided into the Slovak Komárno and the Hungarian Komárom. Today they are connected by the "Bridge of Friendship" (Elisabeth Bridge).

In Roman times the Legion Kamp of Brigetium stood where present day Komárom now stands. Excavations have brought numerous objects to light from this period, including sarcophagi and gold coins. These treasures can be viewed in the museum in the Igmándi fortress.

The three city fortifications, Csillag-eröd, Igmándi-eröd and Monostor-eröd, which were of great importance in the Kingdom of Hungary, are still well preserved today. Their strength was proven in 1848, the year of European revolution, when populations across the continent rebelled to demand their freedom and more say in government. The strong fortifications and ample supplies enabled the Habsburg troops to prevent the fortifications from being taken.

Komárno to Esztergom (SK) 56.5 km

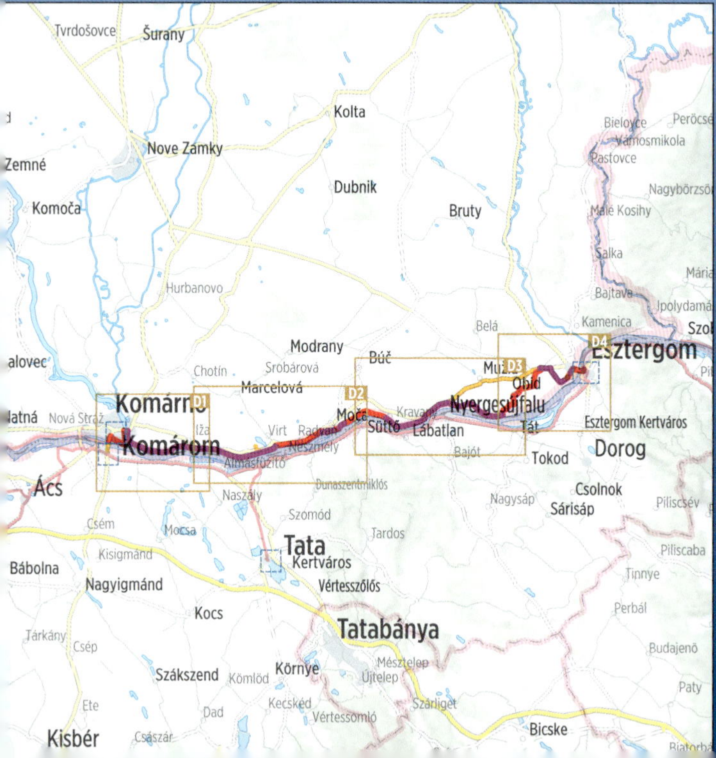

m/km: ↗ 0.4 (22m) ↘ 0.4 (25m) cycle path: 60 % unpaved: 14 % busy road: 10 %

This stage of the ride describes the stretch between Komárno and Esztergom along the Slovak shore of the Danube. The cultural highlights are Komárno, the important archaeological site at "Kelemantia," and certainly Esztergom. The two thermal lakes at Patince are another popular destination. The end destination of this section, as well as its most culturally glamorous part, is Esztergom, the "Rome of Hungary." The massive basilica on top of a hill over the city can be seen from a great distance.

The last section in Slovakia surprises with small, cosy villages and mostly asphalted embankment roads near the Danube. There are only short stretches left on busy roads as well as unpaved paths. The entrance to Štúrovo is on quiet country roads and roadside cycle paths.

Komárno to Iža — 12.6 km

1 At the first intersection after the bridge turn right onto **Leharová** ⇢ follow the right bend ⇢ turn left at the T-intersection, into **Dunajské nábrežie** ⇢ continue straight ahead into **Elektrárenská cestae** ⇢ keep following the riverside road ⇢ turn right onto the bridge across the Váh river ⇢ **2** turn sharply to the right immediately after the bridge and ride along the dyke ⇢ the road takes you through a long left curve to the Danube ⇢ you pass the Kelemantia archaeological site on the dyke road.

Iža 🇸🇰

🏛 **Tábor Kelemantia (Fort Kelemantia)** ㉔ An important archaeological site directly on the main route. Remains of a Roman military camp from the 2nd-4th centuries were discovered here. There were 20 towers and four gates on an area of 175 x 175 m.
@ srs141en

Iža to Moča — 14.6 km

3 To follow the main route continue along the dyke road.

4 *(EXCURSION)* If you turn left here and follow the orange route, you can take a detour to the holiday village of Kúpele Patince with its thermal water lakes.

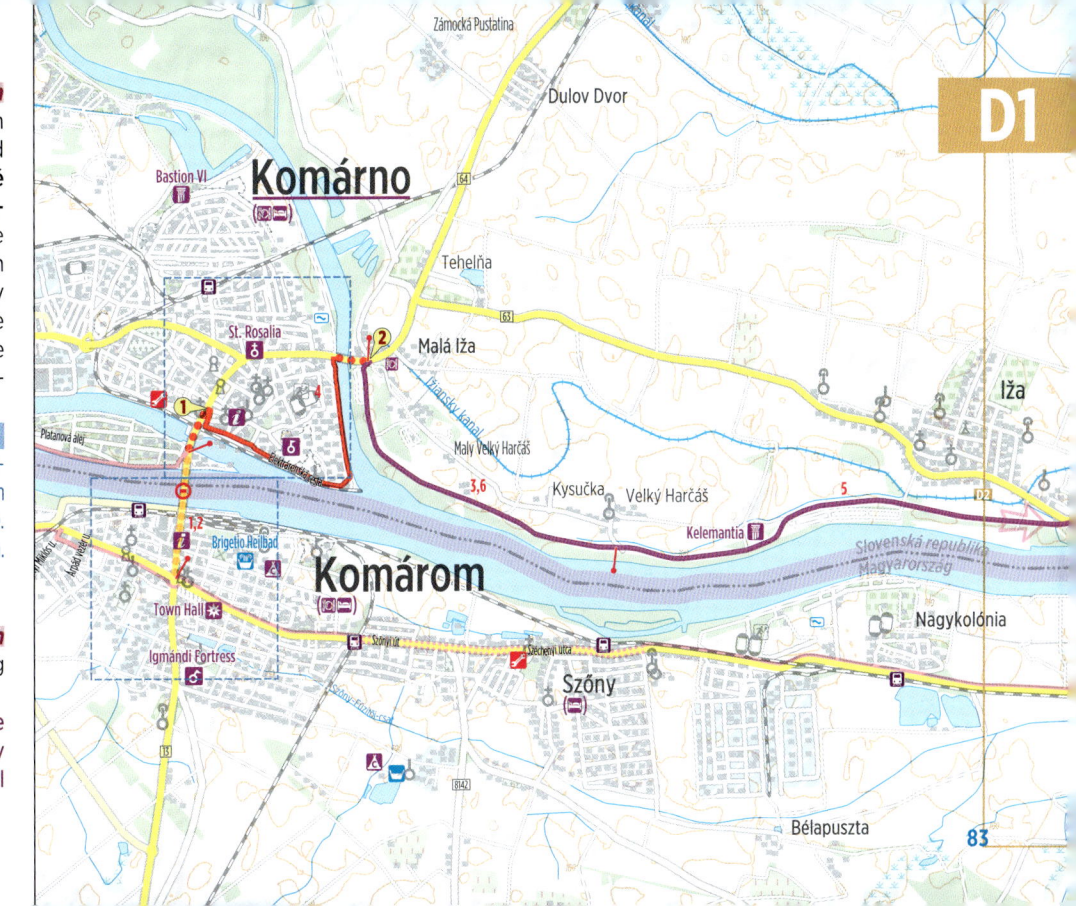

D1

83

Komárno, General Klapka square

Kúpele Patince (Patince) ⓢ
prefix: 035

🛏 **Kúpalisko Patince**, KúpelePatince 147, ✆ 7731444, ✆ 0902/179079, @ lio156en

The main route continues on the dyke until you reach Žitava.

Žitava ⓢ
Leave the embankment cycle path and turn right onto the main road **63** ↝ continue on the moderately busy main road to Radvaň nad Dunajom, a very pretty small town.

Radvaň nad Dunajom ⓢ
5 Just before Moča, turn right and pass the village along the Danube.

Moča ⓢ

Moča to Esztergom   30.5 km
300 m after entering Moča, turn right and leave the main road ↝ follow the left bend and continue along the small street past the church ↝ ride straight between fields as you leave the village ↝ the field road takes you to the right down to the Danube ↝ follow the road along the river bank until you reach Kravany nad Dunajom.

Kravany nad Dunajom ⓢ
You pass a beautiful beach as you reach the village ↝ keep right into the paved path along the river ↝ at the end of the village continue on the small road next to the river ↝ turn right where the dyke road meets the main road **63** follow the main road past the scattered houses of Čenkov.

Čenkov ⓢ
ALTERNATIVE **6** From here you can choose between the main route on the dyke along the river and through the village of Obid, or staying on the main road **63** and riding via Mužla. The dyke path is partly badly passable, especially in rainy weather, but free of traffic. The variant runs along the moderately busy main road.

Alternative route via Mužla   12 km
If you choose the variant, then always cycle straight ahead on the moderately busy main road **63** ↝ after about 6.5 km you will reach the village of Mužla.

Mužla ⓢ
At the intersection keep right towards Štúrovo ↝ after about 5.5 km you will rejoin the main route at the railway station in Štúrovo.

To stay on the main route, **6** turn right at Čenkov after a rest area on the left, ⚠ the turnoff is easy to miss ↝ ride on the track along the dyke, which runs parallel to the main road at first ↝ continue until you reach a pumping station ↝ **7** turn left here and leave the dyke ↝ follow the paved road between the fields, keeping right across the channel ↝ at the T-intersection turn left and ride straight towards Obid.

Obid ⓢ
Turn right at the church into **Kráľa Štefana** and follow the road ↝ **8** turn right into a small

road ⸺ at the T-junction turn left ⸺ along the asphalt road up to the railway tracks ⸺ then continue along a concrete slab path ⸺ turn right and drive along the road **Janka Kráľa** ⸺ then turn left and immediately right again ⸺ along the main road **63** a roadside path continues ⸺ at the big crossroads turn right ⸺ now ride for several kilometres parallel to road 63 to Štúrovo ⸺ at the roundabout straight ahead into **Svätého Štefana** street ⸺ a wide cycle lane begins ⸺ **9** at the cemetery turn right, **Jozefa Bema**.

> **TIP** Before you leave Štúrovo, take the time to explore the city and enjoy the fine views of the basilica at Esztergom, across the river.

Štúrovo
prefix: 036

- **TIK Štúrovo**, Hlavná 8, ✆ 7560199, ✆ 0915/755888, @ aha154en
- **Mestské múzeum (Municipal Museum)**, Pri colnici 2, ✆ 7524002 ⸺ Achaeological and historical exposition focusing on etnography, culture and economics of Štúrova. @ uoq364en
- **Thermal Resort Vadas**, Pri Vadaši 2, ✆ 7560230, @ pik161en

This city is named after the Slovak writer, linguist and nationalist Ľudovít Štúr, who is credited with creating the modern Slovak language. He was also a politician and revolutionary, and died in 1856 at the age of 40 in Modra, north of Bratislava.

Turn right at the main road and after a few metres turn left onto the bridge across the Danube.

> **TIP** On the other bank, at the sandstone house, push left over the zebra crossing and down the ramp.

Straight ahead across the road and the bridge into town **10**.

Esztergom
prefix: 033

- **Irány Esztergom**, Széchenyi tér 5, @ bnd538en
- **Balassa Bálint Múzeuma (Balassa Bálint Museum)**, Mindszenty hercegprímás tere 5, ✆ 500175 ⸺ Overview of the city's 1,000-year history. Archaeology, history and art. @ ovo645en
- **Duna Múzeum (Danube Museum)**, Kölcsey u. 2, ✆ 500250 ⸺ Insights in Hungarian inshore waters, water supply, flood protection, etc. @ dkw427en
- **Főszékesegyházi Kincstár (Cathedral Treasury)**, Szent István tér 1, ✆ 402354 ⸺ Wide collection of ecclesiastical works of art in Hungary, with Byzantine, Hungarian and Italian liturgical requisites. @ gtn626en
- **Keresztény Múzeum (Christian Museum)**, Mindszenty tér 2, ✆ 413880 ⸺ The museum in the former bishops palace holds paintings, sculptures, gobelins, tapestries and porcelain made by important Hungarian, German, Austrian and Italian masters. @ ljd852en
- **Magyar Nemzeti Múzeum Vármúzeuma (Castle museum)**, Szent István tér 1, ✆ 415986, ✆ 0670/5039664 ⸺ Exhibits cover the history of Esztergom castle. @ ipr543en
- **Bazilika (Basilica)**, Szent István tér 1, ✆ 402354, ✆ 0620/2681553 ⸺ The original Adalbert cathedral built by King Stephan was heavily damaged during the Turkish wars. In 1822 construction began on what was to be the largest church in Hungary, commensurate with the importance of the Gran bishopric. The high altar of Carrara marble was designed by Pietro Bonani. The church was consecrated in 1856 in a ceremony for which Franz Liszt wrote his "Gran Mass". @ abh353en
- **Királyi palota (Royal palace)**, Szent István tér 1, ✆ 500095 ⸺ Only a lapidarium remains from the original palace of King Belas III. (1172-96). The palace chapel with its rose window is one of the most beautiful Romanesque structures in Hungary. The upper floor contains renaissance chambers from János Vitéz, humanist and archbishop. @ dqw122en
- **Prímás Pince (Primate Cellar)**, Szent István tér 12, ✆ 541965 ⸺ A paradise for wine lovers with 100 different Hungarian wines, a small museum displays artisan tools of vinification and the relationship between church and wine. @ nyt223en
- **Víziváros (Water city)**, at the foot of the fortress and along the Little Danube. Among the most noteworthy buildings in the old city centre are the 18th c. parish church (Pázmány Péter út), the

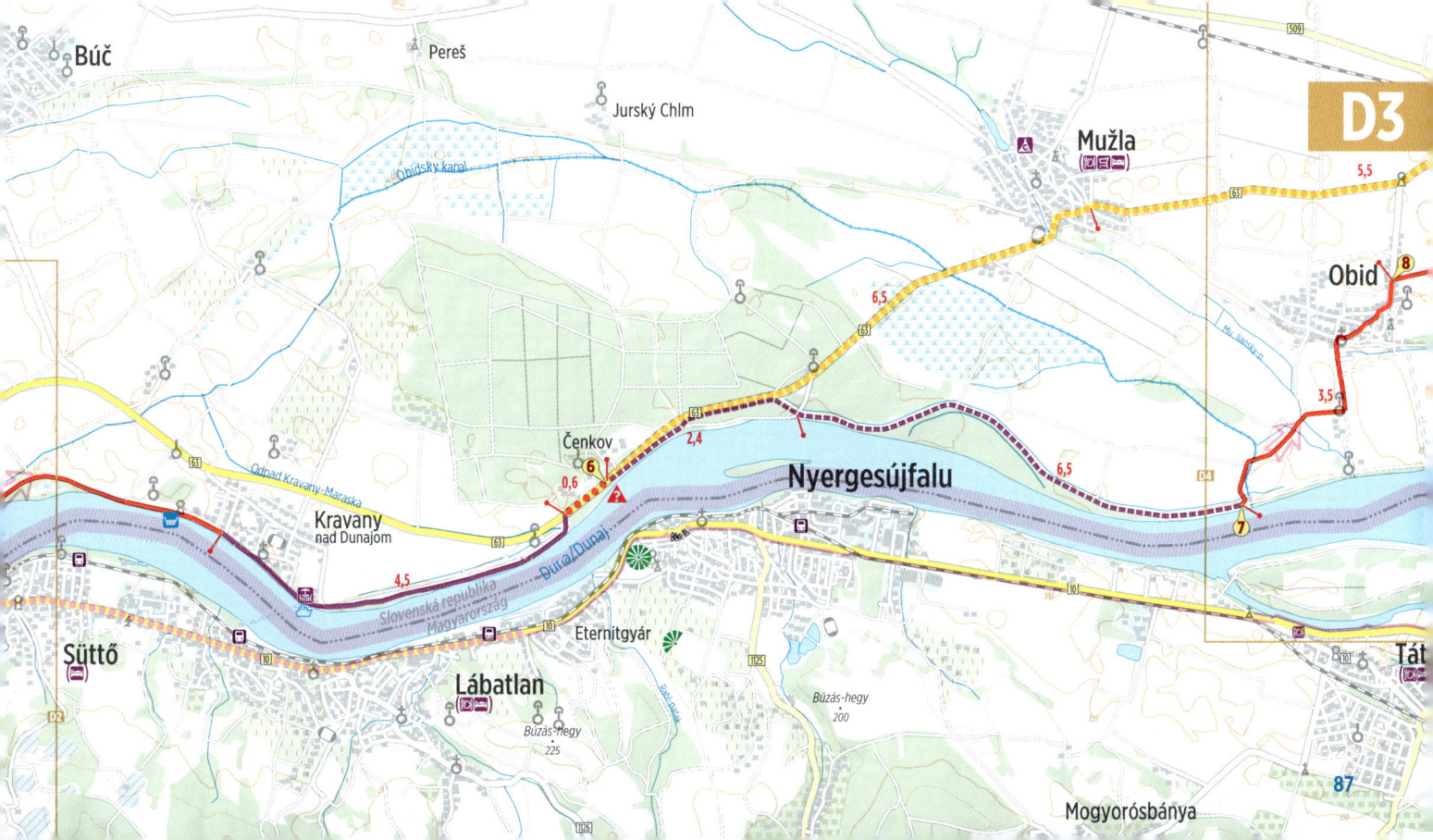

central church (Pór Antal tér), which is one of the prettiest baroque structures in the city (1757-62), and the Greek-orthodox church (Kossuth Lajos u. 60), which is also from the 18th c.

✉ **Szent István Strandfürdő**, Bajcsy-Zsilinszky u. 14., ☏ 312249, @ pcd815en

✉ **Aquasziget**, Táncsics Mihály u. 5, ☏ 030/6123131, @ jxb368en

he Hungarian writer Mihály Babits called Esztergom "Hungary's Rome". Others, like the country's communists, saw Esztergom as the "city of the black reaction". Both views arise from the city's role as the Roman Catholic church's capital in Hungary. The church's highest primate, the Archbishop of Esztergom, has been based here since the 11th century.

Excavations have shown that the castle hill and surroundings were first settled in the Stone Age. The Romans fortified the hill to protect their border. Below, in today's "Water City", lay the civialian centre of Solva Mansio. Esztergom is one of the oldest cities in Hungary. It is even mentioned, as the "Etzelsburg", in the Song of the Nibelungen.

Esztergom

After the Magyars moved into the region in the 10th century, Esztergom became the centre of the Hungarian nation. In the year 1000, Hungary's first king, Stephan the Holy, was crowned here. The city enjoyed its heyday during the reign of King Béla IV. He hired famous foreign architects and artists to design and build his palace and the castle chapel, another of the city's Roman Catholic landmarks. In 1249, after the Mongol invasion, King Béla VI moved his residence from Esztergom to Buda.

The archbishop of Esztergom and other Hungarian clerics then moved into the abandoned royal palace. The city enjoyed a second heyday during the time of János Vitéz, an archbishop during the renaissance. In the 13th century, the city was occupied by the Tartars, and in the 16th century it was the Turks, who remained in Esztergom until 1683. When they were finally driven out, Esztergom was in ruins, with a population of just 400. The city began to recover only after the basilica had been built and the archbishops returned. The current city actually consists of three settlements that were united as a single entity in 1895 under the name Esztergom.

89

Esztergom, interior of the Basilica

The most impressive building in the city is the huge basilica dedicated to St. Adalbert. It is the largest church in Hungary and dominates the views from the surrounding countryside. It was under construction from 1822 to 1869, but was consecrated 13 years before its completion. Franz Liszt composed his well known Gran Mass for the occasion.

The church was heavily damaged during WW II. On the left side as one entres the basilica is the Bakócz Chapel, a precious example of Tuscan Renaissance Architecture. It originally stood in Süttö but was taken apart into 1,600 numbered pieces and brought here to be reconstructed. In the krypt of the basilica is the tomb of the former Hungarian Cardinal Mindszenty. The altar-piece in the choir nave is believed to be the largest of its kind in the world. Painted by the Italian Grigoletti, it measures 13 x 6.5 metres and is based on the Titian painting, "Ascension of Mary", which hangs in the Frari church in Venice.

The dome of the church offers outstanding views. The basilica also houses Hungary's largest collection of church art, while the diocese library is among the best in the country, with over 200,000 volumes, some up to 800 years of age. The library is not open to the public.

The exhibits in the castle museum are mainly drawn from the excavations of the royal palace.

Another impressive structure in the city is the Maria Valeria Bridge across the Danube, built in 1895. It was destroyed in World War II, but not reconstructed until 2001. It forms the border crossing between Hungary and Slovakia and on the Esztergom end is a metal plaque from 1991, with the inscription "The bridge connects".

Komárom to Esztergom (H)   53.2 km

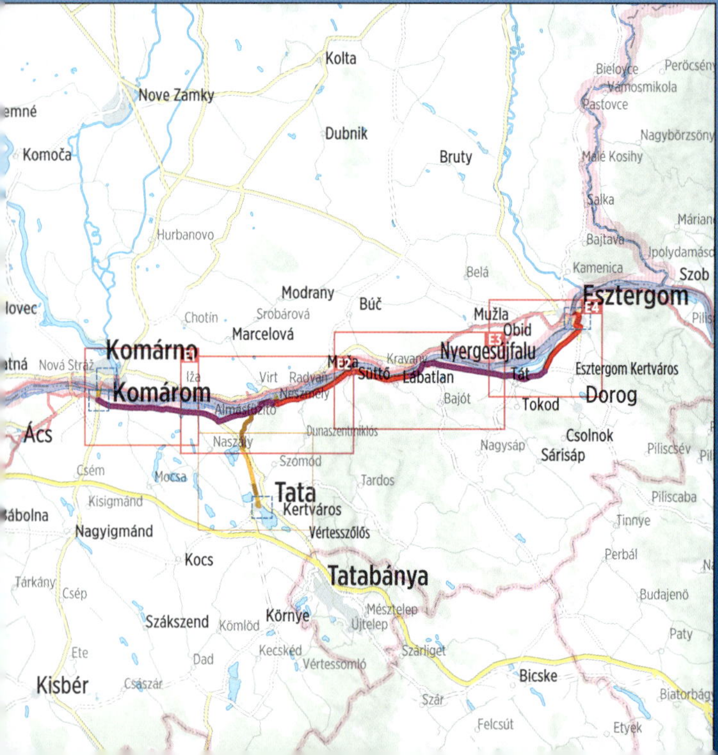

m/km: ↗ 0.3 (15m) ↘ 0.4 (21m)   cycle path: 58 %   unpaved: 0 %   busy road: 42 %

This section of the route follows the flat Danube valley close to the river and takes the rider through different towns and villages and past numerous industrial areas. One often comes to follow the vinyard-clad edge of the hilly hinterland, which can be explored along an alternative route passing by time-honoured town of Tata, at the foot of the Gerecse Mountains. You will finally arrive in the "Rome of Hungary", as Esztergom is also known.

Between Komárom and Esztergom, unfortunately, you still cycle on busy roads for longer stretches. Over time, however, cycle paths will be built along the main roads. Roadside cycle paths exist so far between Komárom and Neszmély as well as from Eternitgyár to shortly before Esztergom. There are no gradients in the Danube valley.

Komárom to Lábatlan — 29.6 km

1 Follow the main road **1** out of Komárom ~ you ride partly on a cycle path, partly on a cycle lane ~ cross the railway tracks and continue on the cycle lane ~ through the village of Szőny.

Szőny (Komárom)

2 Shortly after the railway station, a cycle path begins on the left side of the road ~ continue to follow this path ~ **Nagykolónia** is on the left.

TIP: Shortly before Almásfüzitő, the already narrow but asphalted cycle path turns into an even narrower concrete slab strip. The

Komarom, Monostor Fortress

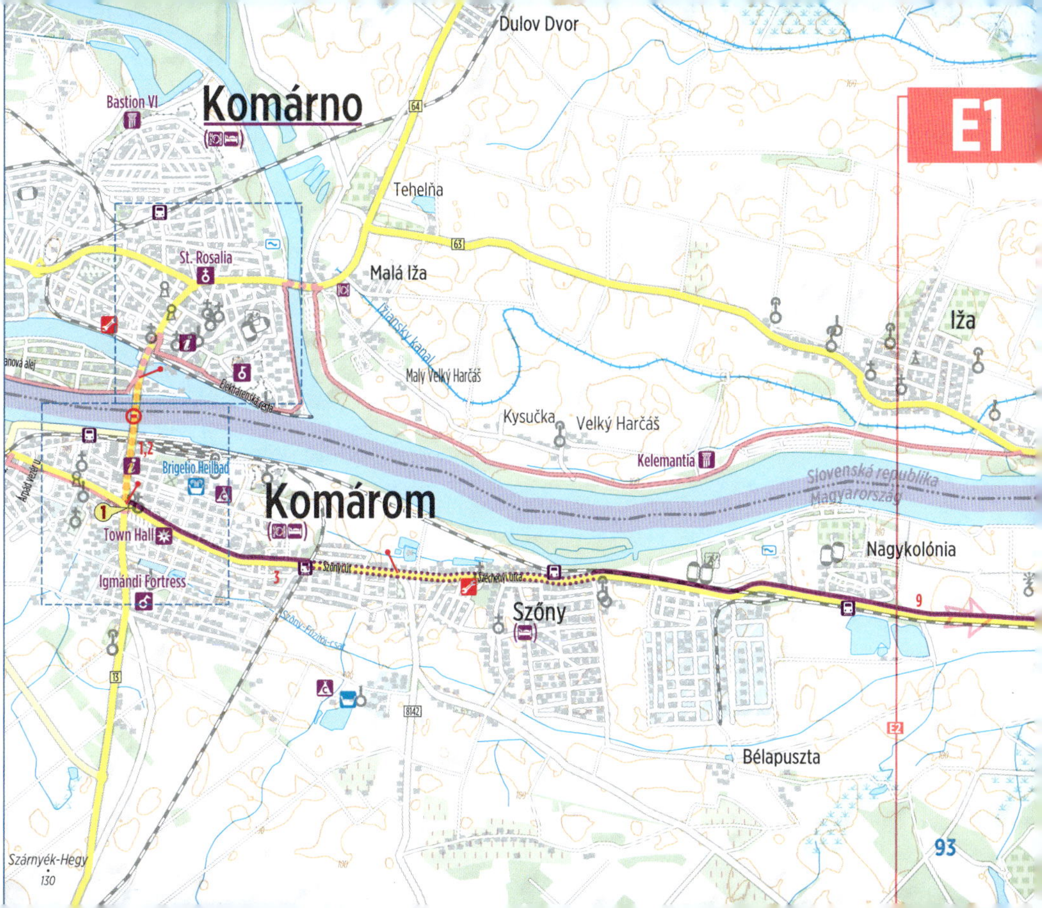

Tata, Calvary hill

road itself, however, is still not allowed for cyclists. Here you have to continue on this narrow path for a good 2 km. At the town exit sign, this path also ends and you continue on the road. On the left, however, a cycle path is already being built.

Almásfüzitő
3 Turn left at the next opportunity ~ there is a cycle path to the right of the road that leads to Dunaalmás.

Dunaalmás
4 To visit the time-honoured town of Tata at the foot of the Gerecse Mountains, turn off the cycle path to the right at a sharp angle and follow the course of the Által-ér brook.
⚠ Take care when crossing the federal road 1!

Excursion to Tata   10.9 km
4 Before the cross road turn right at an acute angle ~ follow the road **Újtelep utca** ~ at the T-junction turn right and left along the cycle path over the small stream Által-ér, which leads you to the B 1 ⚠ carefully cross the main road ~ straight on to the railway tracks and then immediately left ~ the agricultural road is excellently developed and leads dead straight into the centre of Tata ~ the Által-ér stream serves as a good orientation aid.

> **TIP** The Tourinform office in Tata offers various, partly also guided, bicycle tours in and around Tata. Tour information can also be found on the website of the information office.

Tata
prefix: 034

Tourinform, Bercsényi u. 1, ☎ 588633, @ vbc414en

Kuny Domokos Múzeum (Kuny-Domokos museum), Váralja u. 1-3, ☎ 381251. The museum is spread over three floors. The first room houses the products of the faience factory founded in the 18th century. The upper floor of the museum houses various art exhibitions. In the knights' hall on the lower floor you can learn about the history of Tata and its surroundings, from prehistoric times to the 19th century. @ xat768en

Német Nemzetiségi Múzeum (German Ethnic museum), Alkotmány u. 1, ☎ 381251. The museum in the Nepomuk Mill illuminates the history of the Hungarian Germans. The mill, dating from 1758, is a listed building and a reminder of the once very important role of the town's milling industry. The museum highlights the cultural differences between the Germans, the Hungarians and the Slovaks who also live here. These not only concern folk costumes and tools, but also the spiritual traditions of the different ethnics. @ gao715en

Szent Kereszt Plébániatemplom (Holy Cross Parish Church), Kossuth tér 15, ☎ 588163. Late-baroque church built 1751-85 by Anton Pilgram, Jakob Fellner and Josef Großmann. @ kkn812en

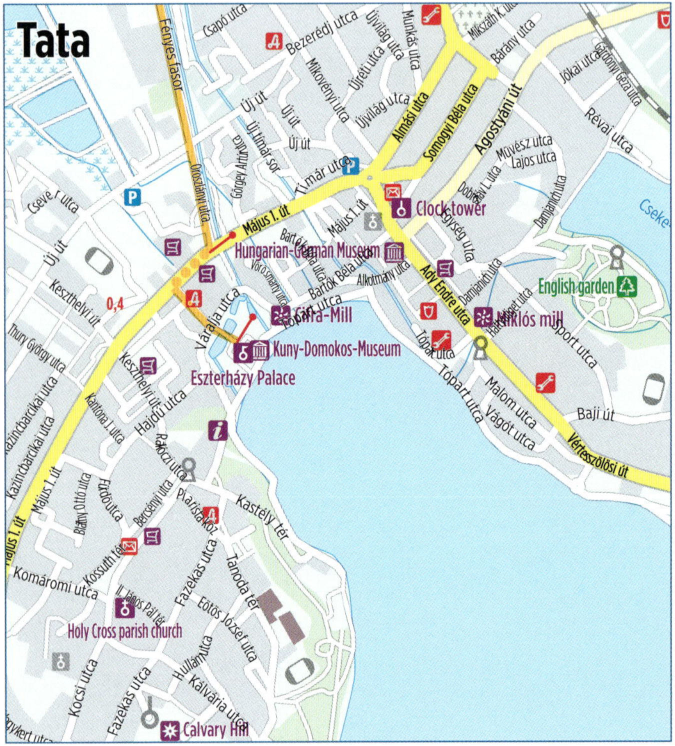

Tata

Tata Castle

- **Esterházy-kastély (Esterhazy palace)**, Hősök tere 9/A, ☎ 0630/7426075. Built in the 18th century in the late rococo style by Jakob Fellner, who worked for the prince's family and helped shape the city's appearance. @ bqr532en
- **Tatai vár (Tata Castle)**, Váralja u. 1-3, ☎ 381251. The original 13th century Gothic structure was expanded in the renaissance style by King Matthias Corvinus (1440-90). Further renovations and additions in the 19th century. @ jsc418en
- **Harangláb (Clock tower)**, Országgyűlés tér. Octagonal wooden tower (1763), formerly the city prison, was built by the master carpenter Josef Eder.
- **Vízimalmok (Water mills)**, Tópart u. The baroque Cifra Mill (1753) is located on the northern shore of the lake, not far from it is the Miklós Mill built by Fellner in 1760.
- **Kálvária-domb (Calvary hill)**. Mount Olivet scene, chapel and observation tower. @ huy338en
- **Angolkert (English garden)**, Erzsébet királyné tér 10, ☎ 0630/8751413. The nature reserve and recreational park date back to an English garden founded by the Eszterházy family in 1782. @ jlo882en
- **Fényes Tanösvény (Fényes nature trail)**, Fényes Fasor, ☎ 0630/5927373. The eco-tourism trail presents the natural treasures of

the spa park in an interactive way on a stretch of 1.5 km.
@ vaj381en
- **Fényes Fürdő**, Fényes fasor, ✆ 588144, @ wjc874en
- **Tatai szabadstrand**, Nyírfa u. 1

Due to its many lakes, natural springs and canals the old city of Tata enjoys a relaxing atmosphere. Tata is centered around the Old Lake (Öreg-tó) and Tata Castle. The region was settled in the Stone Age as evidenced by archaeological finds at Vértesszőlős 5 kilometres distant. The thermal springs that can be found here have since then always been a point of attraction for the people in the region. Hungarians started moving to areas around the lakes in the 10th century. The earliest known official record of the area mentions the existence of a small settlement and a Benedictine abbey in the 11th century. By the 14th century there were two villages named Tata and separated by a low-lying swamp. Since 1397 Tata has been, along with Buda and Visegrád, a favorite residence of the kings.

In the 14th century Hungary's only water-castle was built on the shores of the Öreg-tó. In 1526 the town fell to the Turks during their first invasion, was retaken by the Emperor and then

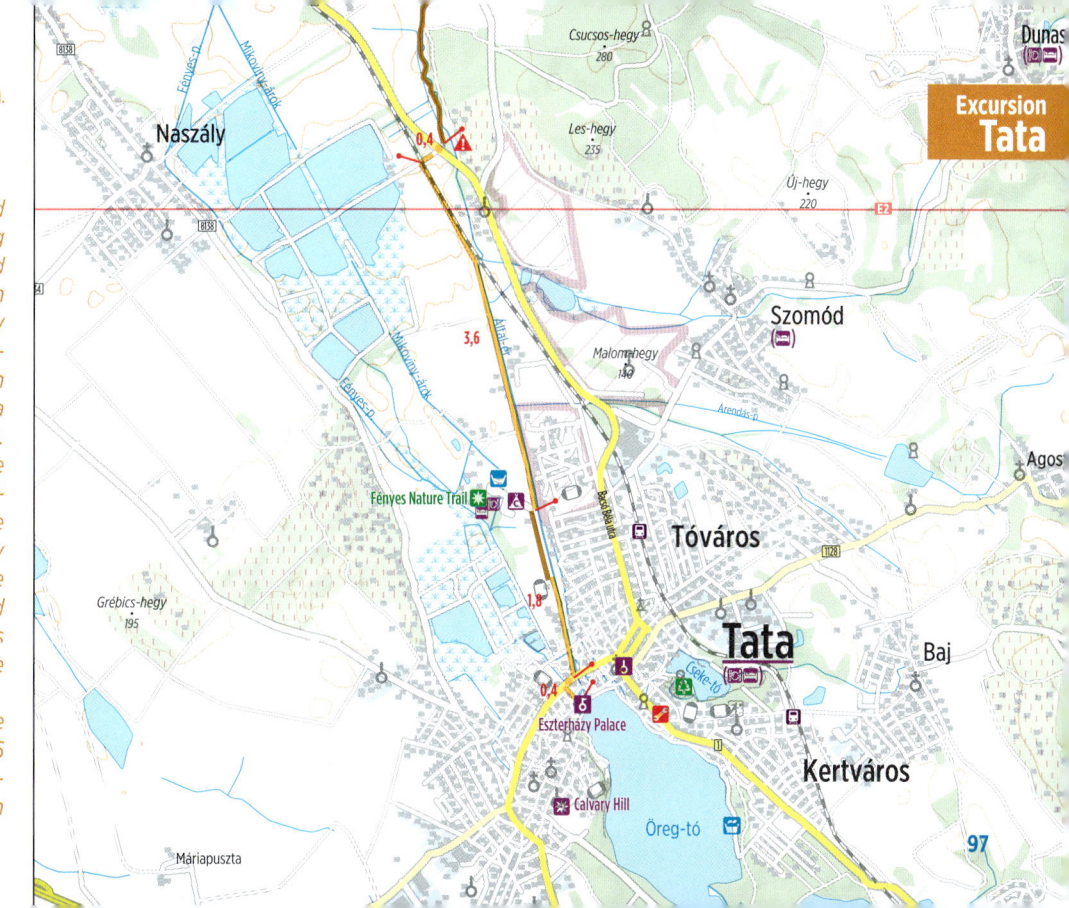

Excursion
Tata

repeatedly recaptured by the Turkish armies. The heavy fighting caused severe damage to the castle as well as the city and its many mills. Towards the end of the 17th century the castle was called the "puszta vár" which means "desolate castle."

After 1727 the town became the property of the Esterházy family. It wished to raze the castle and replace it with a baroque palace, but was unable to finance the project. Instead, the family expanded the castle with a new addition. The Habsburg Kaiser Francis I signed the "Peace of Schönbrunn" while staying here in the fall of 1809.

The castle and the entire grounds remained the property of the Esterházy family until 1945. In 1965 it became the property of the Hungarian Museum. Because the castle moat often served as its garbage dump, excavations on the site have turned up large amounts of weapons, broken armor, cannons and cannonballs as well as boots, shoes and other refuse.

In front of the castle there is a magnificent promenade along the lake through the castle grounds. The promenade is also open to cyclists.

To enter the Kuny Domokos Museum, one walks up the red marble steps to the terrace, there is a café and the museum entrance. The museum stretches over three levels and displays, among other things, the history of Tata, exhibits of art and the products of the 18th century Fayence industry. Fayence are white glased and painted ceramics.

Another interesting museum is the "Hungaro-German Museum" in the Miklós Mill. The mill is designated a historic landmark and recalls the important role that mills played in Tata's development. During and after the Turkish wars, the population of Tata declined severely. Under the Esterházy family many Germans settled in the area.

The museum illuminates the cultural differences between the Germans, the Hungarians and the Slovaks who live in the region. This is not only seen in their costumes and tools, but also in the traditions of the different peoples. On the smaller lake, the Cseke-tó, there is a public park configured as an English garden with small waterfalls and an intricate network of small paths. The mock ruins of a three-nave church were reconstructed in the park using old Roman grave stones and Romanesque blocks from the Vértesszentkereszt Benedictine abbey.

Of the many old water mills, the oldest is believed to be the baroque "Cifra Mill." The octagonal clock-tower on the Országgyűlés tér (parliament square) was built without a single piece of iron hardware by the master carpenter Josef Eder in 1763.

4 Straight ahead across the cross road ~ cross the main road to the left ~ cross the tracks and before the inn turn right into the cycle path ~ continue into the adjacent village of Neszmély.

Neszmély

Komp Neszmély-Radvaň nad Dunajom, Vízimolnár utca

TIP: In Neszmély you come to the new ferry across the Danube. From here you can decide whether to switch to the Slovakian bank or stay on the Hungarian side of the Danube. On the Hungarian side, the cycle path to Esztergom is still under construction. For the time being, however, you have to continue on the busy main road to Labatlan.

Turn right at the crossroad to the ferry.

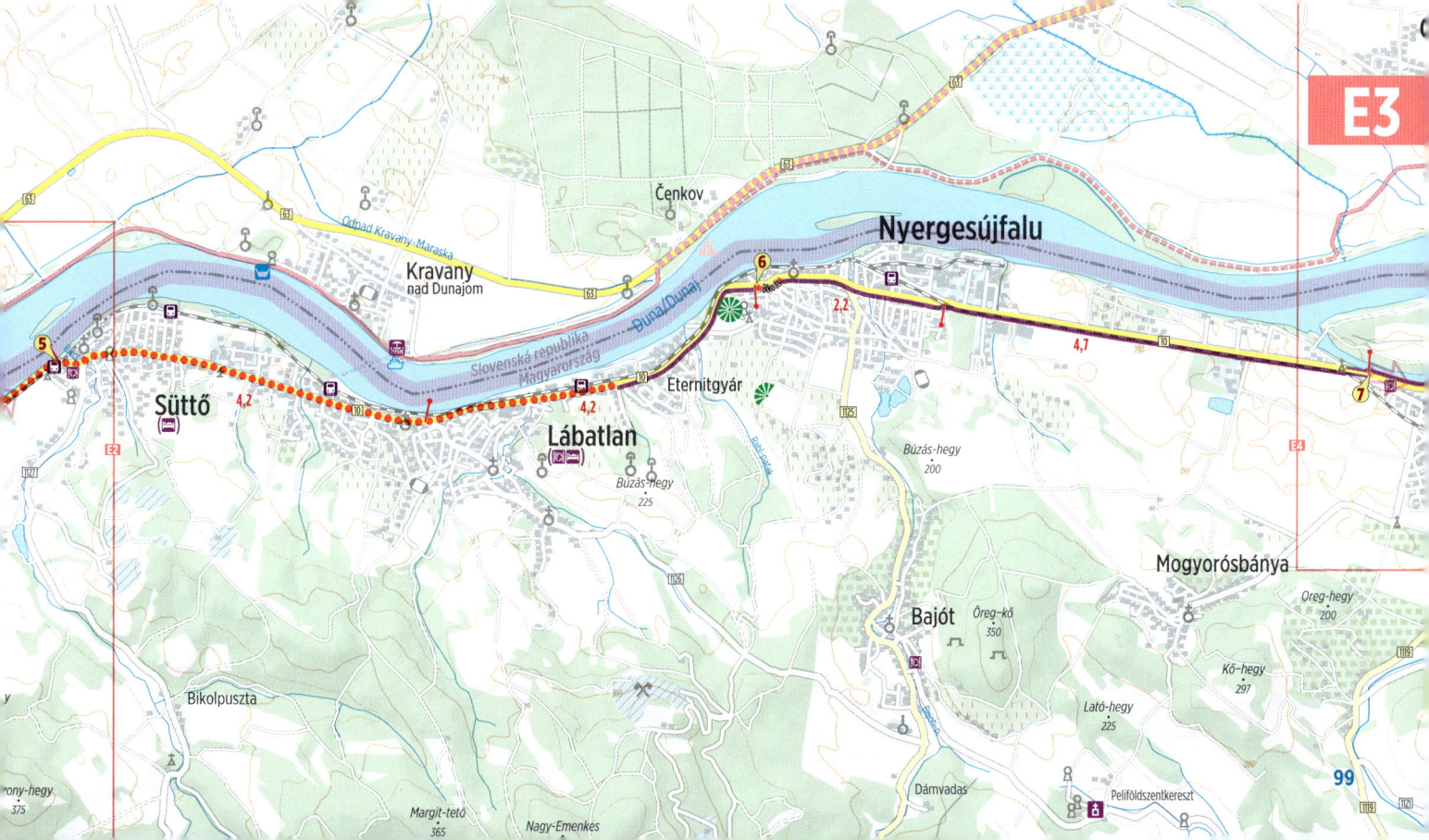

Esztergom, Basilica

TIP: Straight ahead you can already see the cycle path under construction. The date of completion is not known yet.

At the main road turn left ~ shortly before Süttő the busy road leads directly along the mighty Danube ~ **5** a right curve takes you across the railway tracks and into the village.

Süttő

Simply follow the main road through the village ~ you pass a transformer station and industrial buildings before coming into Lábatlan.

Lábatlan

Lábatlan to Esztergom   23.4 km

Continue along the main road through the village ~ after passing the cemetery the road nears the Danube again ~ you ride along the right side of railyards and an industrial area, which continues for almost 3 km between the road and the Danube ~ a bicycle and pedestrian path begins here on the right side of the road ~ the road passes below a steep hill, which can be climbed for a great view, before coming into Nyergesújfalu.

Nyergesújfalu

6 The bicycle and pedestrian path ends by the square with the monument, and riders must turn right into the side street ~ follow the left curve of the street ~ as you reach the main road again, turn right and continue along the bicycle and pedestrian path ~ after crossing railway tracks you leave the town and ride through fields between the road and the railway line ~ **7** upon reaching the houses of Tát, the bicycle path changes to the left side of the road.

Tát

You ride past Tát on the dyke ~ the bicycle path comes to an end at a side road ~ **8** turn left into the narrow and very busy road towards Esztergom ~ continue as far as the roundabout in Esztergom ~ **9** turn left in the roundabout onto **Àrok utca** ~ turn right before the bridge ~ keep left to the **Kis Duna** and ride along the right side of the canal towards the centre of Esztergom ~ cross Lőrinc utca ~ the centre of town is now to the right ~ proceed along the canal to the next bridge, **Kossuth híd**.

Esztergom   see p. 86

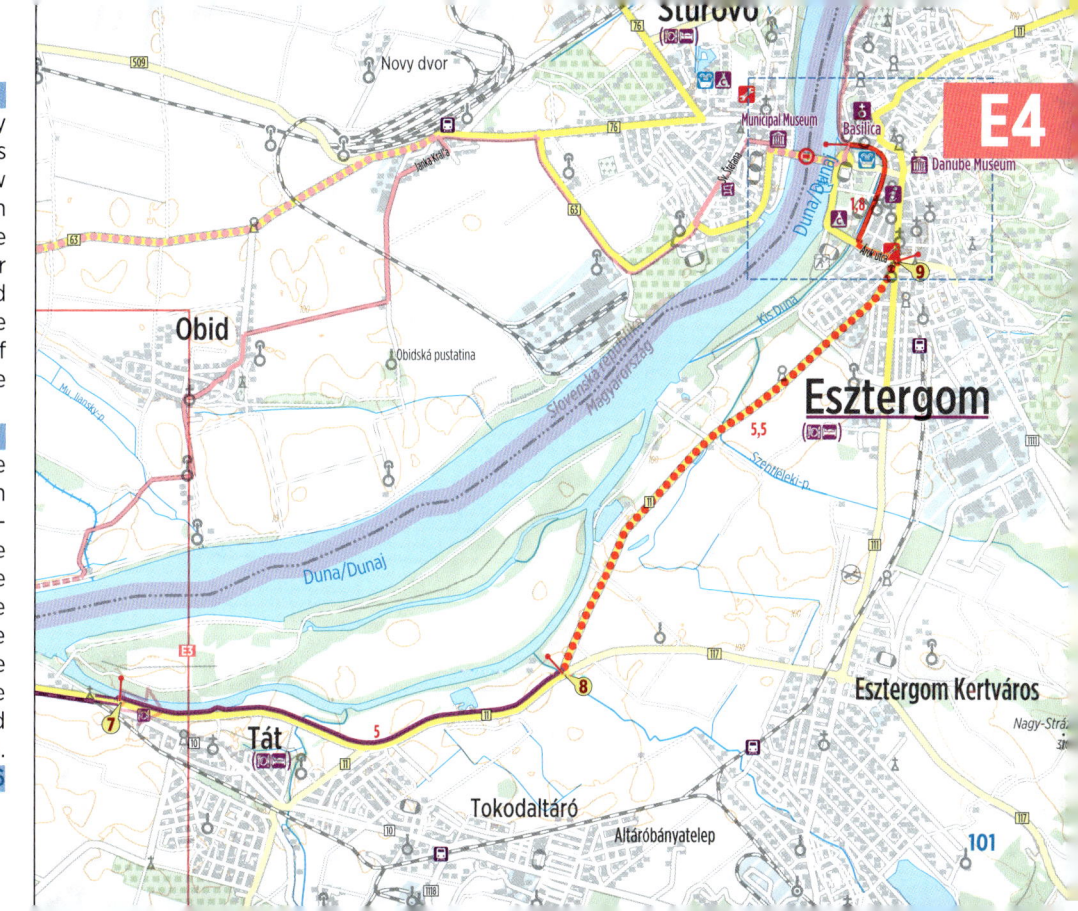

Esztergom to Budapest

81.4 km

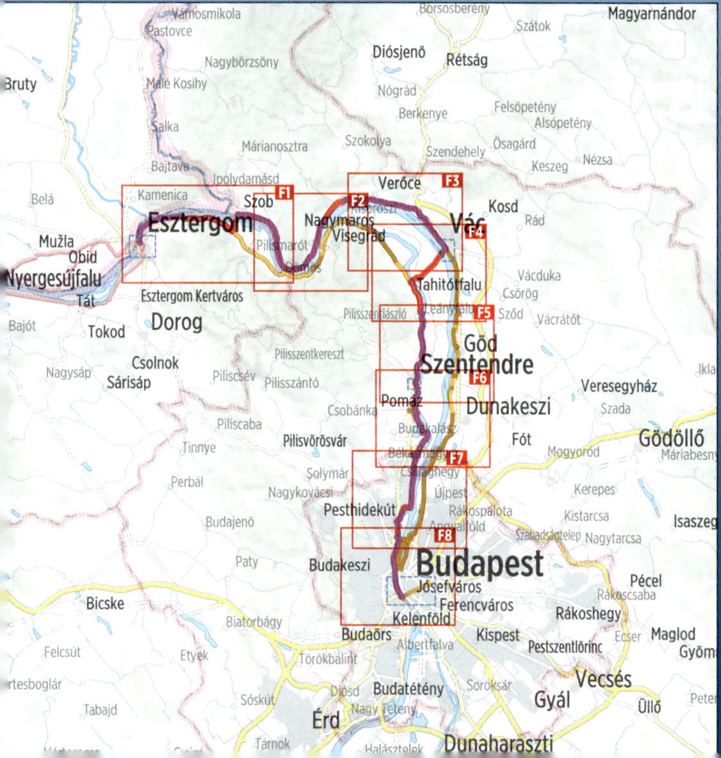

m/km: ↗ 0.8 (62m) ↘ 0.8 (67m)   cycle path: 68 %   unpaved: 0 %   busy road: 12 %

After Esztergom you reach The Danube Bend, one of the most attractive sections of the entire Danube. Here the river winds its way through the Visegrád Mountains and makes an abrupt turn towards the south. Situated on the top of steep hills above the right bank of the Danube, the castle of Visegrád seems to dominate the river and surroundings. Shortly before reaching the end goal, the Hungarian capital and Danube Metropolis of Budapest, the open-air museum and the baroque centre of Szentendre tempt one to linger a little longer.

Many new bicycle paths have been constructed in recent years, yet one is still forced to ride on busy roads along some parts of The Danube Bend. A pleasant surprise is the mostly traffic free ride along quiet side streets and new bicycle paths on the way into the capital Budapest. The only unpaved part along this stretch can easily be avoided.

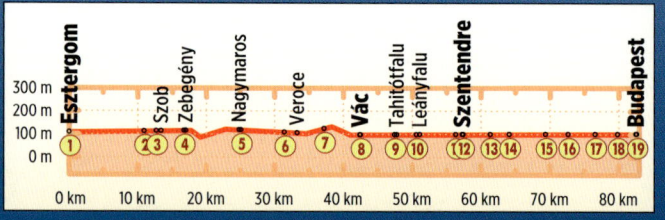

Esztergom to Szob   12.6 km
From the bridge **Kossuth híd 1** there is a nice paved bicycle path for several kilometres down the Danube's shore ⟿ go straight until you come to the B 11 national road ⟿ and continue with traffic on the **B 11**.

TIP 2 It is also possible to continue on the right bank of the Danube to the former royal town of Visegrád. This route has significantly more traffic than the main route however, and it is not well signposted.

Alternative via Visegrád   24.7 km
After about 2.6 km along the national road 11 you come to Pilismarót.

Pilismarót
TIP If you turn left towards the Danube before the church in Pilismarót, then you will reach the beach and a camping ground.

Following the national road again, you will reach the next village.

Dömös
prefix: 033
- Dömösi Galéria és Helytörténeti Kiállítás (Gallery and Local History Museum), Táncsics M. út 2., in the cultural centre, ✆ 507050, ✆ 0630/9444982 ✉ Local history exhibitions and fine arts.

Continue on the **B 11**, which now follows the bank of the Danube closely.

Lepence (Visegrád)
- Lepence Spa, Lepence völgy 2, ✆ 026/801963, @ kcc282en

Shortly after the Thermal Spa, a bicycle path to the left of the main road begins, where you get a good view of the castle at Visegrád ⟿ after another short stretch on the main road you reach a sports field ⟿ turn right onto **Fö út**, which leads straight into Visegrád and past the royal palace.

Visegrád
prefix: 026
- Visegrád INFO, Duna-parti út. 1, ✆ 397188, @ mrf733en
- Visegrád-Nagymaros komp (Ferry Visegrád-Nagymaros), Révkikötő, ✆ 398344, ✆ 0630/9218076. Departures every hour between 6:20 am and 8:45 pm. @ swg367en
- Mátyás-Király-Múzeum (King Matthias Museum), Fö út 23, ✆ 597010 ✉ Archaeological and local history collection. @ hdk566en
- Zugfözde Pálinkamúzeum (Zugfözde Liquor Museum), Rév u. 1, ✆ 0620/9391790 ✉ The museum informs about the history of moonshining in Hungary, where it was illegal to distill brandy until 2010. Other topics are: How to distill brandy and tastings of liquor. @ bnl447en
- Fellegvár (Upper castle), Várhegy, ✆ 398101 ⛳ Built in the 13th c., with a medieval torture chamber. The citadel was the seat of Hungarian kings in the 14th c. @ xsi437en
- Királyi Palota (Royal Palace), Fö utca 29, ✆ 597010 ✉ This large complex on four terraces is 600 m long and 300 m wide. The Lion's fountain of red marble is especially impressive, as is the reconstructed columned courtyard with the Hercules fountain. @ vjc744en
- Salamon torony (Solomon Tower), Salamontorony u. ✉ The rooftop terrace offers fine views of both banks of the Danube. The tower contains local history exhibitions with original finds and objects from 3500 BC to the 17th c. AD. @ ajb734en
- Nyári Bob Pólya (Toboggan track), Mátyás király u. 37, on the Panorama road, ✆ 397397, ✆ 398169 ⛳ Summer and toboggan track and Alpine Coaster, which is accessible throughout the whole year. @ cqk633en
- Ritterspiele (Tournament), in the Salamon tower, ✆ 398081 ⛳ A medieval performance by the St. George order of knights presented several times each week. Starts 12:15. The audience is invited to participate in the presentation. @ rpw727en
- Pilisi Parkerdő (Pilis Park Forest), Mátyás király u. 6, ✆ 598000 ✉ Popular recreational destination with game garden and domestic animal exhibit, forest clubhouse, reconstruction of the upper castle and a thermal spa. @ gdi826en
- Zsitvay-kilátó (Zsitvay look-out tower), Nagyvillám-hegy, ✆ 397099, ✆ 2984739 ✉ From the 378 m high tower (1933),

Visegrad, Upper Castle

visitors can see as far as the Zsámbék Basin, 100 km away, on a clear day. @ yxj116en

Visegrád lies directly on the Danube's "knee" – the narrow gap where the river breaks through the Visegrád mountains and the Börzsöny mountains.

Visegrád has played an important strategic role in the region since the first century after Christ, when the Roman Emperor Trajan began building the "limes", the military fortifications that ran along the right bank of the Danube and marked the border of the Roman province Pannonia. The defenses protected the border as well as roads and rivers that the Romans used.

In the 4th century the Romans built a fortress on the 180-metres high Sibirik Hill. This later became the castle that local lords expanded with an irregular ground-plan, thick walls and horseshoe-shaped towers.

In the 10th century Visegrád emerged as a centre of local government, joining Esztergom and Buda as one of the early bases of royal and church authority.

In medieval times Hungarian rulers extended the fortifications to defend the land against tribes from the east. The lower castle was built in the 13th century during the Mongol invasions. Legend has it that King Salomon was kept prisoner in the lower castle after he attempted for the second time to secure the throne and the crown of his cousin for himself.

In 1246 King Béla IV began construction of the upper castle on the 350 metre high hill-top. The construction was financed by Queen Maria, who sold all her jewels to raise the money. The castle was built to protect surrounding holdings and a convent on what is today known as Margaret Island near Budapest. The island is named after Princess Margaret, who was raised at the convent from the age of four, due to an oath made by her parents.

For many years the king's holy crown was kept in the upper castle. When King Albert of Habsburg died in 1439 after a short reign, his wife, Queen Erzsébet (Elisabeth) ordered the theft of the crown. At the time she was pregnant. Her doctors predicted the child would be a boy, and the queen hoped possession of the crown would strengthen her son's claim to the throne. The crown was not returned to Hungary until 20 years later.

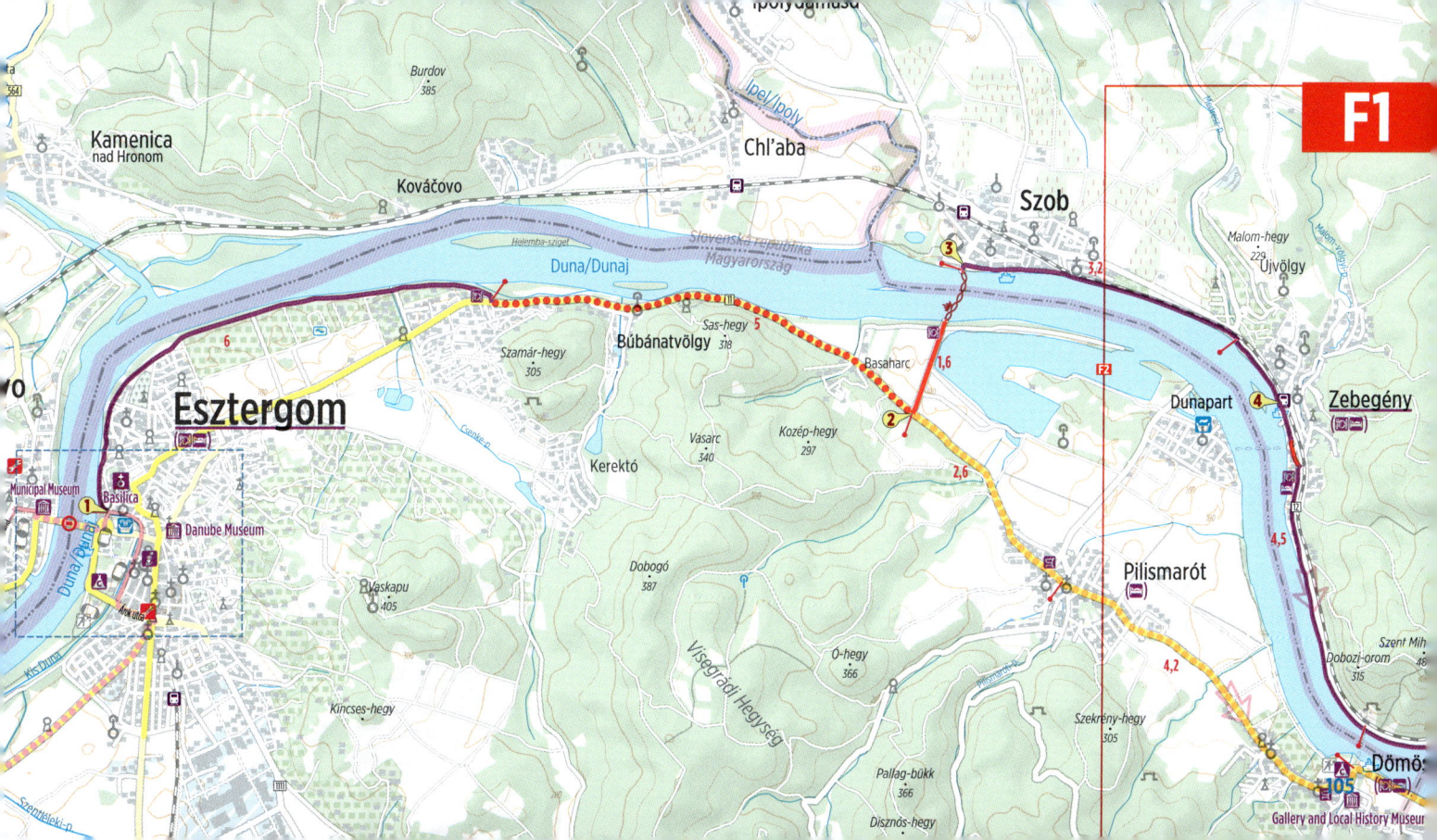

The fortifications were then further improved to include an outer wall which extended from the upper castle to the lower castle and down to the banks of the Danube. Parts of this wall are still intact today

The lower castle was neglected and fell into disrepair after the Turkish occupation. Restoration of the main keep was begun in 1871 in order to convert the castle into a royal hunting lodge. The work was fully completed in 1964, although little effort was put into the project, the outer walls simply being poured in concrete. Today there is a museum in the tower.

In 1323 the royal court from Temesvár (in today's Romania) relocated to Visegrád, which temporarily became the king's residence and the Hungarian capital. Initially members of the royal court lived in the castle until construction of the royal palace began at the foot of the mountain. This residence was built on four terraces carved from the side of the slope, and was intended to be the most magnificent Hungarian architectural accomplishment, a monument to the Hungarian Kings' power and wealth. Even after the royal court moved its capital to Buda, the palace in Visegrád remained an important summer residence. During the renaissance King Matthew Corvinus gave the palace its final touches, which contemporary witnesses richly praised. The inner courtyards were adorned with numerous gothic fountains, only two of which have survived into the present day, one of them the Lions Fountain, built from beautiful red marble.

For many years those testimonials of the palace's beauty were all that remained – it wasn't until 1935 that the ruins of the palace were rediscovered.

Not only the Hungarian kings liked this region. The Turks also remained here for a long period after their 16th century conquests. According to legend, in the year 1570 there was not a single Hungarian person still alive in Visegrád, which was then populated only by Muslims and Greek-Orthodox Bosnians. It was not until 1686 that Visegrád and Buda were liberated from the Turks and the re-population of the region could begin. Many of the new settlers were Germans, who outnumbered Hungarians and Slavs.

Those who wish to visit the numerous attractions in Visegrád will need to put in a bit of effort.

Getting to the Lower Castle (Salomons Tower) is easy enough, simply climbing along the fortification wall or riding the bicycle along the Panorama road. The 5 kilometres to the Upper Castle, however, are another matter, and will require every bit of your strength. But, once there, you are rewarded with a magnificent view which stretches far beyond the Danube; the Danube Knee lies at your feet.

Danube bend

Continue on **Fő út** until you reach the **B 11** again ⇢ turn right onto the main road ⇢ the road curves around a steep hill, following a side-arm of the Danube to Dunabogdány.

Dunabogdány

A sign points the rider across the road to the left, where a wide bicycle path follows the edge of the water almost to the end of the village ⇢ turn right onto the small street ⇢ then left at the main road ⇢ continue along the bicycle path out of Dunabogdány ⇢ at the end of the cycle path, continue on the main road to Tahitótfalu, where you rejoin the main route.

Tahitótfalu

2 To stay on the main route turn left into the side road ⇢ continue to the ferry ("rév") to Szob and cross to the other side of the Danube.

Szob

Komp Pillismarót-Szob (Pillismarót-Szob ferry), Rév utca 12, ✆ 0630/9491833 od. 0630/9487643. Departs hourly. @ oyn624en

Szob to Vác   29.6 km

3 At the ferry landing in Szob turn right on the wide bicycle and pedestrian path along the Danube ⇢ the path crosses a small bridge before taking you between the railway line

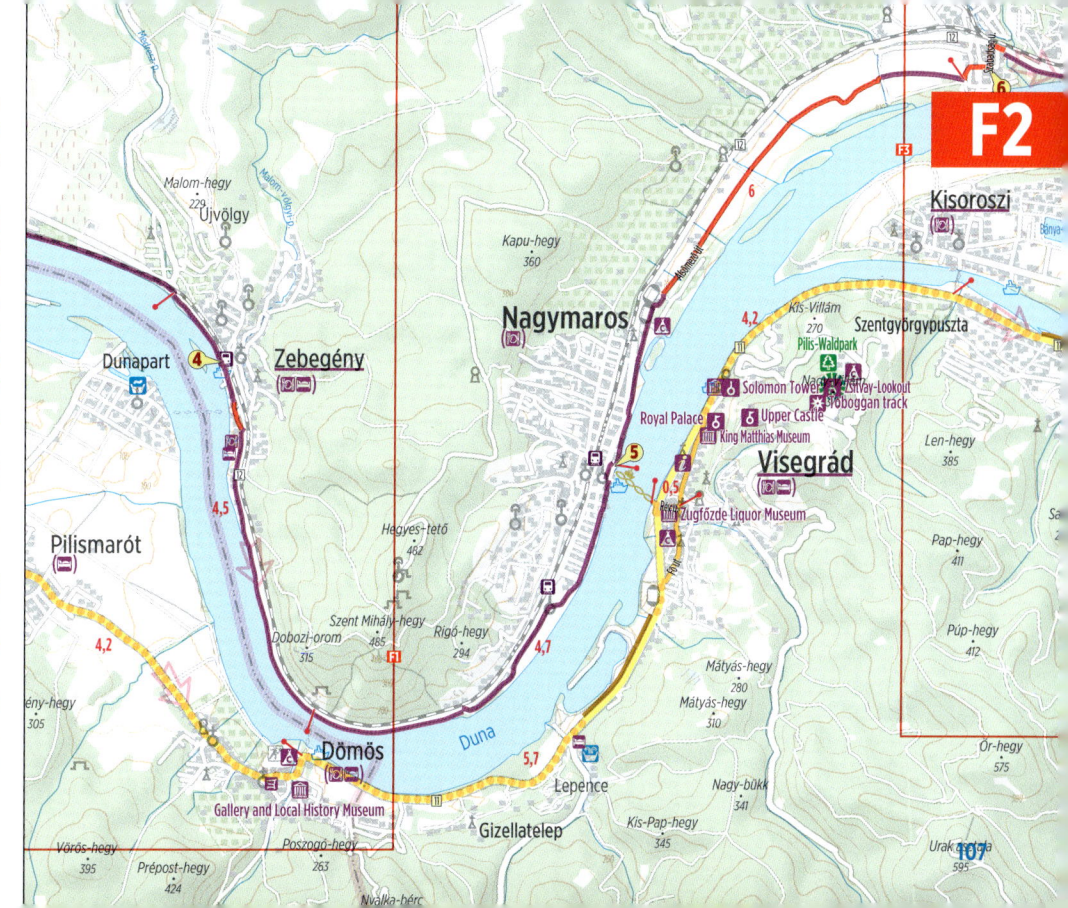

and the river out of Szob ⤳ continue along the path to Zebegény, with its villas.

Zebegény

4 You pass the train station ⤳ follow the bicycle path all the way to Nagymaros.

Nagymaros

Visegrád-Nagymaros komp (Ferry Nagymaros-Visegrád), Révkikötő, ☏ 026/398344, ☏ 070/9305754 🕖 Hourly crossing. @ hdy128en

TIP **5** Here you have the option of taking the ferry to Visegrád and switching to the alternative route on the other side of the Danube.

The Danube bend

The "knee" of the Danube is, along with lake Balaton, one of the most scenic areas of Hungary. Over a distance of about 20 kilometres, the river breaks through steep mountain sides and cliffs, some of which are formed of volcanic rock and soft chalk. The dark slopes and the strangely-formed rocks provide a romantic landscape.

The river curves through a wide bend as it passes through the mountains and then turns southward and divides into two streams as it passes around Szentendre Island (Saint Andrä Island). The main arm of the Danube, also called the Vacer Arm, is used by international shipping. The smaller arm, also called the Szentendre Arm, carries only one third as much water as the main arm.

The right bank is dominated by the Visegrád Mountains and the Pilis Mountains rising into the blue Magyar skies. On the left bank stretch the foothills of the Börzsöny Mountains. Numerous hiking paths criss-cross the region, dotted with rest-areas and picnic-sites. The entire Hungarian highlands make a completely different impression than the wide expanses of the Puszta plains further east. And because this part of the Danube's passage through Hungary played such an important role in the country's history, the area is also rich with historic monuments and sites that reflect its culture and heritage.

In the last century before Christ, Illyrian-Celtic tribes began settling in the area, the Latin name for the city Szentendre was Ulcisia Castra, derived from the Celtic "Ulk".

The Romans were the first to leave lasting marks on the region. Their influence changed the lives of indigenous people and gave the Danube a new importance. During the Roman times, the river formed the Empire's border and defense against barbarian invaders.

5 The bicycle path takes you along the bank of the Danube out of Nagymaros ⤳ you ride on a path made of concrete slabs through fields between the Danube and the main road ⤳ ride up onto the bridge and then take the track on the dyke ⤳ follow the left curve as you come to the village of **Kismaros** ⤳ continue straight into the residential street where the bicycle path ends ⤳ **6** turn left at the next intersection into **Szabadság utca** ⤳ ride up to the main road ⤳ turn right onto the footpath, which quickly becomes a bicycle path ⤳ the bicyclepath ends and

Vác Basilica

you have to drive along the main road through Verőce.

Verőce
At the end of the village, the cycle path starts on the left side of the road ~ **7** it passes underneath the road **B 12** ~ stay to the right of the railway tracks ~ turn right before reaching the main road and follow the bicycle path ~ turn right at the T-intersection ~ follow the left bend in the street ~ continue to another small street and turn right onto a marked bicycle and pedestrian path ~ the path takes you through a cutting ~ by the next street keep left and immediately turn right into the bicycle and pedestrian path which follows a side street ~ the path takes you down to a water body and through a small park ~ at the next street cross to the other side and turn right ~ simply follow the bicycle and pedestrian path along the left side of the street ~ the path takes you down to the Danube and along the very edge of the water all the way to the ferry landing **8**.

Vác
prefix: 027

🛈 **Tourinform**, Március 15 tér 17, ✆ 316160, @ lbt273en

🚢 **Váci Komp (Ferry to Szendendrei Sziget)**, Váci-rév, ☎ 026/386560. Departures between 6 am and 8 pm, every full hour. @ hhh432en

🏛 **Egyházmegyei Múzeum (Diocesan Museum)**, Március 15. tér 4, ☎ 319494 🚇 The museum displays objects from the cathedral's treasury, founded in 1771. The collection includes jewellery, textiles, paintings, sculptures and furniture. @ kxb876en

🏛 **Modern Művészeti Gyűjtemény (Modern Art Collection)**, Káptalan u. 16, ☎ 0630/2580269 🚇 Contemporary art of the last 40 years, with a focus on the 60s and 70s, including works by: Vladimir Szabó, Erik Scholz, János Józsa, Ernő Tóth, Lelly Dombay, Ferenc Sajdik. @ gag852en

🏛 **Tragor Ignác Múzeum (Tragor Ignác Museum)**, Köztársaság út 19, ☎ 200868, ☎ 0630/5557620 🚇 Finds from the former dominican church. The exhibits include mummified corpses and coffins which were uncovered during reconstruction of the church. @ nxe387en

⛪ **Ferences templom (Franciscan Church)**, Géza király tér. Construction of this beautiful baroque church began in 1721 and took 30 years. @ kjg831en

⛪ **Székesegyház (Cathedral)**, Konstantin tér 11 🚇 The pride of the city was built 1763-77 by Isidore Canevale. Frescoes in the choir and dome by Franz Anton Maulbertsch. The crypt has valuable renaissance and baroque wrought iron works. @ srx813en

⛪ **Hegyes torony (Pointed Tower)**, Liszt Ferenc sétány 12. The northernmost tower of the city wall is the only surviving medieval building in the city. @ puw113en

✳ **Diadalív (Triumphal Arch)**, Köztársaság út 65. City residents refer to the monument simply as the "stone arch." Built in 1764 for a visit by Empress Maria Theresa, it is the only arch of its kind in Hungary. @ bku212en

✳ **Főtér (Main square)**, Március 15. tér. The square with its unique elongated triangular shape was built in the early 18th c. as a baroque square on medieval foundations. It was completely redesigned in 2006. Here you can see the uncovered foundations of St. Michael's Church from the 13th c. @ aor482en

✳ **Kőszentes híd (Bridge with the Stone Saints)**, Diadal tér. The bridge was built 1753-57 by order of Bishop Mihály Károly Althann, in honour of St. Nepomuk, the patron saint of bridges and harbours. It is the only baroque bridge still functioning in Hungary. @ klj142en

✉ **Váci Strandfürdő és Uszoda**, Ady Endre sétány 16, ☎ 510400, @ wmc274en

King Stephan I. established a bishopric here in the 11th century and Vác was officially documented for the first time in 1075. Long a residence for the local nobility, the town today is known for its baroque architecture and works of art. For example, Vác's central square in Hungary's only baroque city square. Another equally noteworthy structure is the victory arch at the edge of the upper city (Felsövarós), built to honor a visit by Maria Theresa. The 18th century post-baroque cathedral was designed by the Viennese court architect Isidore Caneval, who was inspired by a neo classical style developed in France.

Vác is a city where old and new stand side-by-side. On the one hand, the old baroque monuments and structures lend the town an air of stately idleness, while on the other hand Vác is also a lively university town, and a cultural and economic centre with a thriving and growing tourism industry.

Vác to Szentendre — 15 km

ALTERNATIVE Before continuing by ferry to Tahitótfalu, you have the opportunity to take the alternative via Göd at the ferry landing in Vác. This leads along the EV6 cycle path near the Danube to Budapest. For some short stretches, you change from the cycle path to quiet residential roads - only in Dunakeszi you ride a short stretch in traffic on the busy national road **2**.

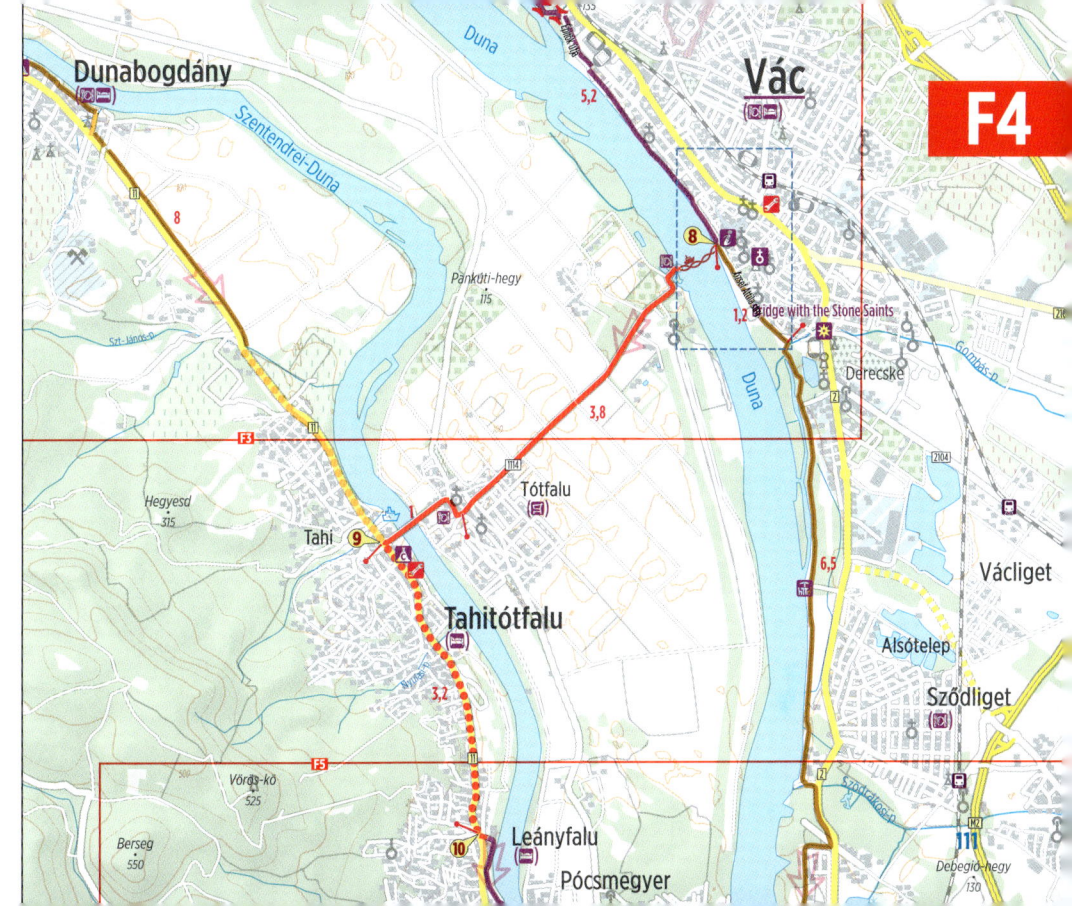

Ethnographic open-air museum "Skanzen"

Alternative via Göd   35.8 km

At the ferry landing in Vác on the cycle path through the Deuil-la-Barre park, following the yellow ground markings ~ then continue to **József Attila sétany**, between the road and the cycle path is a tree-lined avenue ~ steadily slightly downhill you cross a bridge, with a clear view of the Danube ~ past a rest area ~ on the left hand side you find Sződliget.

Sződliget
Continue along the cycle path across a bridge ~ for a short stretch in the settlement area of **Kertváros** change to the road ~ then right again onto the cycle path.

Göd
Huzella Kert (Huzella garden), Jávorka u. 14, 0630/3395671 Botanical garden with several ponds and observation tower. @ ado565en

In Göd and **Alsógöd** follow the cycle path along the settlement road ~ at the end of the settlement area of **Révdülő** continue straight on into the cycle path ~ at the end straight on into **Folyam utca** street ~ at the end turn right and shortly after left into the cycle path, turn left into the centre of Dunakeszi.

Dunakeszi
Cross the B 2 national road and continue along the yellow-marked cycle lane along the **B 2** ~ you pass under the M 0 motorway ~ in **Újpest** the cycle lane changes to the right-hand side of the road ~ after passing under the railway tracks, cycle along the road for a short distance ~ then the route leads away from the road to the Danube.

CONNECTION: At the **Árpád hid** bridge it is possible to change to the other side of the river and to the main route.

After passing under the Árpád hid bridge, follow the cycle path along the **Carl Lutz rkp** road near the Danube.

TIP: With the next bridge you have reached the **Margit hid**, crossing it to return to the main route on the other bank. Shortly before the bridge, follow the cycle path first to the left across the road, then in a right turn around the small park to the bridge across the Danube. At the end of the Margaret Bridge, follow the cycle path to the right again to reach the main route on the banks of the Danube.

8 Take the ferry in Vác to the **Szentendrei Sziget** ~ then continue on a rural road to Tahitótfalu.

Tahitótfalu
Follow the road through the sharp right turn after the square with a monument ~ then through the left bend before you ride over a bridge ~ **9** at the T-intersection with the main road turn left in the direction of Budapest ~ the route along the right bank from Visegrád comes from the right at this T-intersection.

Leányfalu
10 Look for the bicycle route signs pointing you into a small side street ~ a bicycle path begins here and follows the edge of the water closely ~ simply follow this bicycle path into Szentendre ~ you reach a residential street

next to a canal ∾ continue straight ahead past the entrance to a camping area ∾ **11** a bicycle path begins again on the left side before you reach the main road ∾ follow the bicycle path to the left along the main street for a short distance ∾ then ride straight ahead into the side street **Dunakorzó**, where the main road curves to the right ∾ continue along the bicycle path until it ends where you reach the historic town centre of Szentendre **12**.

TIP Travellers who have time may wish to make a side trip to the open-air museum (Skanzen), in which accurate replicas of various kinds of Hungarian villages have been built. The museum is about 3 km outside Szentendre and can be reached by following **Szabadság-Forrás út.** from the main road.

Skanzen

The term "Skanzen" means open-air museum. The name is actually Swedish – the first museum of this kind was built in 1891 in Stockholm, and was named after the district in which it was established. The name was adopted internationally and is now used in many languages. The idea of an open-air Hungarian exhibition

F5

Szentendre

Szentendre

was conceived in 1873 during the Vienna World Fair, where Hungarian houses had been built for an international village. Several years later an ethnographic village was built as part of Hungary's millenium celebrations. Half a year later most of those houses were dismantled. The open-air museum in Szentendre was established in 1967 and is one of five such sites, where rural architecture and lifestyles are preserved and on display.

Original buildings and objects have been used in an attempt to make the replica villages as authentic as possible. A pond and a stream with several bridges complement the exhibition. There is also a cemetery that shows different methods of interment.

The structures are clustered in ten village-like groups, reflecting the origins of the different kinds of buildings and the regions in which they are most common. Since 1972 the museum has been an independent entity and research centre. It also has an extensive ethnographic library with a wealth of materials about Hungarian folk architecture, including drawings, old maps and other documents. This unique museum is well-worth a visit.

Szentendre
prefix: 026

- **Tourinform**, Dumtsa Jenő u. 22, ✆ 317965, @ dkc755en
- **Ferenczy Múzeum (Ferenczy museum)**, Kossuth Lajos u. 5, ✆ 020/7796657 ⊜ Works by members of the Ferenczy family. Károly Ferenczy was a well-known impressionist painter in the late 19th century. His son Béni was a sculptor, daughter Noémi made tapestries. @ uif753en
- **Kmetty Múzeum (Kmetty Museum)**, Fő tér 21, ✆ 0620/7796657 ⊜ The exhibition presents the different creative periods of the artist János Kmetty (1889-1975), who was one of the leading representatives of Hungarian modernism. @ him815en
- **Kovács Margit Kerámiamúzeum (Kovács Margit Ceramics Museum)**, Vastagh György u. 1, ✆ 0620/7796657 ⊜ Baroque residence from 1750 dedicated to artworks by the Szentendre

ceramics maker (1902-77). Her famous figures were often derived from biblical scenes. @ atm247en

- **MűvészetMalom (Art Mill)**, Bogdányi út 32, ✆ 0620/7796657. The former sawmill from the 19th century is a centre for contemporary art. @ pyg355en
- **Szabadtéri Néprajzi Múzeum-Skanzen (Ethnographic open-air museum-Skanzen)**, Sztaravodai út 75, 3 km northwest of town, ✆ 502537 The museum consists of about 300 authentic replicas of buildings illustrating Hungarian rural living and customs from the 18th and 19th centuries. @ mhq254en
- **Szamos Csokoládé Múzeum (Szamos Chocolate Museum)**, Dumtsa Jenő u. 12-14, ✆ 311931 History of cocoa and chocolate, consumption culture of hot chocolate, storage forms of chocolates, tastings and film screenings. @ hkv217en
- **Szentendrei Képtár (Szentendre-Gallery)**, Fő tér 2-5, ✆ 020/7796657 Rotating exhibitions of contemporary art. @ qeh736en
- **Vajda Múzeum (Vajda museum)**, Hunyadi u. 1, ✆ 0620/7796657 The body of works by Lajos Vajda (1908-41) reflect the disillusionment of Hungary between the world wars. Many of the works have been drawn on brown baking paper. @ vsd577en
- **Belgrád székesegyház (Belgrade Cathedral)**, Alkotmány u. Greek-orthodox church built by András Mayerhoffer in 1752 as a Serbian Blagovestenska church. Interior includes a beautiful iconostatis from 1802. @ qqt351en

F6

8 Preobrazsenszka templom (Preobrazienska Church), Bogdányi utca. This Serbian orthodox church was built between 1741 and 1746 and includes a carved icon wall from 1780. @ wro265en

Római Kőtár (Roman Lapidarium), Dunakanyar krt. 1, ✆ 0620/7796657 ℹ The stones left over from the last centuries of the Roman Empire were once used as building material for watchtowers and towns, an early Christian chapel and the gravestones of a contemporary cemetery. @ kvk346en

Fö tér (Main square). The impressive square is lined with 18th century houses in baroque, rococo and late rococo styles.

As in the region around Tata, excavations near Szentendre have also revealed traces of Stone Age settlements that date back about 20,000 years. In the first century BC the Romans established the military camp Ulcisia Castra on the site of the city.

Centuries later it was the Turks who conquered the city and drove the Hungarian population away. After the Turks retreated, many Serbian and Dalmatian immigrants moved to the city, which they called Sveti Andrej (St. Andreas). Since the 1920s Szentendre has been home to an active colony of artists who live and work in the city and are responsible for numerous galleries, exhibitions and cultural events. This artists community and the city's dominant baroque style contribute to Szentendre's special atmosphere.

A popular destination for tourists is Marx tér, the market square, at the centre of which stands a plague column erected in 1763 in gratitude for the end of the deadly epidemic. Here also stands the Serbian-orthodox church from 1752. The square is lined with many fine houses built mostly by Serbian traders in baroque, rococo and late rococo styles of the 17th and 18th centuries. The castle stairs, or Vár-Lépcsö, lead from the square up to Templom tér (church square) on Church Hill where one can enjoy excellent views over the roofs of Szentendre and on down to the Danube. A market is held here during the summer months.

The 15th century church was repeatedly plundered, destroyed and re-built. During renovations after World War II workers discovered Gothic and Romanesque remains, windows and a sun-dial. These historical elements have been painstakingly restored and can be seen in the church today. Today it displays wooden carvings, ikons and old manuscripts.

To explore the historic centre of Szentendre it is best to leave the bicycle and go by foot. Many of the streets are paved with rough cobblestones, and the city is also crowded with tourists, restaurants and souvenir stores. The are numerous small shops and stalls all over and plenty of folk art on sale round the main square.

Szentendre to Budapest   23.8 km

12 From the historic town centre of Szentendre continue along the **Dunakorzó** ~ after a square the route continues against the traffic into a one way street ~ a two lane bicycle and pedestrian path begins on the left side just after a small bridge ~ turn left in front of the car park ~ ride into the park, where the path continues along the top of a dyke ~ simply follow the bicycle and pedestrian path along the top of the dyke ~ the path turns to the right after a sewerage treatment plant ~ and follows the edge of a small creek ~ **13** turn left just before the main road and cross the creek over a cobblestone-paved bridge ~ turn left again directly after the bridge ~ ride onto the unpaved track on the dyke ~ this takes you back along the other side of the small creek ~ at the fork in the track turn left and follow the rough track through the forest ⚬ the track comes back up to the dyke ⚬ after a short distance a paved surface in very poor condition begins ⚬ **14** turn left onto a paved path by the first buildings on the right hand side ⚬ follow the path through the forest ⚬ it takes you back down to the water's edge ⚬ ride straight into the small street ⚬ the bicycle path continues after the houses ⚬ you pass under a large road bridge ⚬ pass houses again ⚬ as you reach a canal, turn right into the street ⚬ follow the street beside the canal for a short distance ⚬ turn left and ride across the bridge over the canal ⚬ turn left onto a small path and ride back along the canal ⚬ this brings you back to the river and onto a wide promenade on top of the dyke ⚬ **15** continue along the pedestrian and bicycle path as it leaves the dyke at the end of the promenade ⚬ the bicycle path proceeds between the river and residential neighborhoods ⚬ past beaches, camping grounds, hotels and inns until you reach a railway embankment leading to a bridge ⚬ **16** turn left across a stream and ride through the underpass under the railway line ⚬ turn right immediately after passing under

F7

the bridge – follow the street as it curves to the left – you come to a somewhat confusing, because crooked, intersection – you turn right for a short distance, then left across the street into **Ángel Sanz Briz út**.

TIP If you turn right at this intersection, ride up to the main road and turn right again, then you reach the Aquincum Museum.

Aquincum Museum

he Romans conquered what is today western Hungary around the time when Christ was born. It became the Province of Pannonia which was split in two in the second century after Christ. The capital of Lower Pannonia was Aquincum, a settlement in what is today Obuda, the northern part of Budapest. The world Aquincum is derived from the Celtic "Ak Ink" which means roughly "plenty of water".

Ruins of this ancient settlement can still be seen along the main road between Budapest and Szentendre. Even by today's standards the Roman homes were relatively comfortable, with running water and a waste-water drainage system.

Initially there was just a small Roman force in Aquincum but by the end of the first century after Christ an entire legion was based here. The first provincial governor to make the city his capital was the future Emperor Hadrian, who moved to Aquincum at the beginning of the second century. Archaeologists have located the governor's palace on the Obudai-sziget. Other ruins of the city, the "municipium" where the civilian population lived, can be seen at the Aquinas museum. In addition to the Roman city, there was a settlement of Avars with a cult centre at the foot of the Gellerthegy. These three communities – the Avar settlement, the Roman military camp, and the civilian Roman city – from what is today known as Aquincum. The city thrived in the 2nd and 3rd centuries, but by the end of the 4th century the Romans' military strength was sapped and Aquincum was vulnerable to attacks by the nomadic tribes moving into Europe from the east. The Romans evacuated the city in the early 5th century, as part of a deal with the invading Huns.

The remains of the city and its treasures were only uncovered when organized excavations were started in the late 19th century. One of the most valuable finds is a small water-organ of a type that Ktesibius the Greek invented about 140 BC. Science had known of this device from ancient descriptions by the Greek mathematician and mechanic Heron of Alexandria and from images preserved on ancient coins but no one had ever heard the instrument's sound. The organ at Aquincum was found in the ruins of a burned house. The 52 bronze whistles produce tones reminiscent of pan-pipes. Among other valuable finds are mosaics in what is known as the Hercules villa.

Continue straight on a bicycle path along the right side of the street – ride past the shopping

Museum Aquincum

centres ⟶ then turn right into **Reményi Ede utca** ⟶ at the next possibility turn left ⟶ at the T-intersection turn right and then left across the street before the bend ⟶ you ride parallel to the railway line ⟶ then cross the tracks at the first possibility and continue along the other side of the railway line ⟶ follow the right bend of the street and immediately left into **Folyamör utca** ⟶ follow the street past the parking area ⟶ continue straight into the bicycle and pedestrian path through a small park ⟶ and straight along the cobblestone street.

You come to a small square with four life-sized bronze figures ⟶ stay to the right on this square ⟶ you quickly come to a larger, more romantic square, the **Fö tér 17** to the left across the square ⟶ through another small square to a bus stop ⟶ stay left and cross the road ⟶ a bicycle path resumes right before the bridge Árpád híd.

ALTERNATIVE Here you have the choice of riding up onto the bridge **Árpád híd** and onto the **Margit Sziget** (Margaret Island). After riding along the island you reach a bridge, the **Margit híd**, at the far end, where you turn right to reach the main route again.

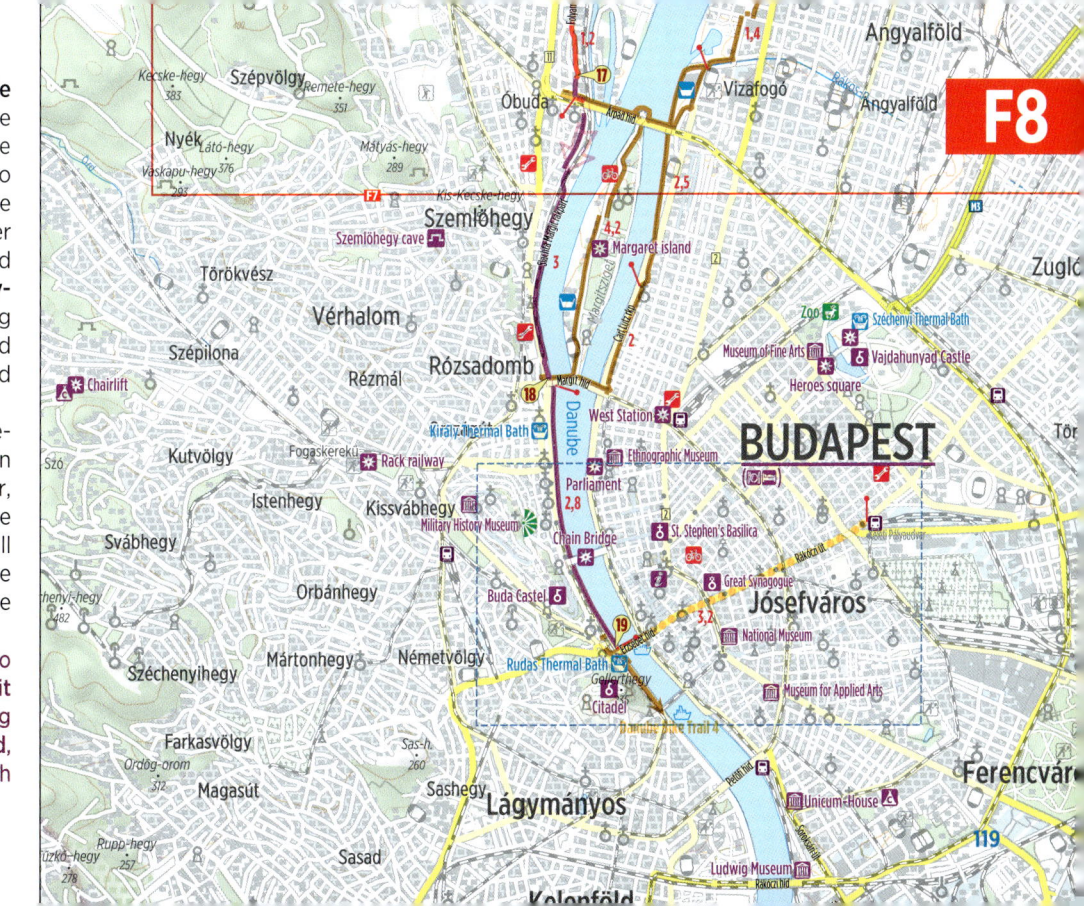

F8

Budapest, Fisherman's Bastion

To stay on the main route, ride under the bridge ⇝ you should see a green bicycle route sign pointing to **Margit híd** 3 km away ⇝ continue along the bicycle path on the right side of the wide road ⇝ ride up onto the bicycle and pedestrian bridge to the other side of the road and railway line ⇝ follow the bicycle path down to and along the Danube until you reach **Margit híd 18** ⇝ after passing under the Margit híd, the route now passes some of the impressive buildings and monuments that distinguish the Hungarian capital ⇝ the **parliament building** can be seen on the other side of the river, then Budapest's imposing **Chain Bridge** comes into view ⇝ to the right are the **Fisherman's Bastion**, the **Matthias Church** and the **castle** above the city, the **Hotel Gellért** and the **citadel** ⇝ continue under the chain bridge and along the bank of the Danube to the **Erzsébet híd 19**.

STATION The easiest and fastest way to Keleti pu. station, from where the main long-distance trains depart in various directions, is via **Erzsébet hid** and **Rákóczy út**. However, there is very heavy traffic here, so it is better to take side streets or push your bike on the pavement.

Budapest
prefix: 01

🛈 **Tourinform**, Sütő utca 2, ☏ 3188718, @ gog253en

⛴ **Mahart Passnave**, Belgárd rakpart, ☏ 4844010. Sightsseing cruises in Budapest. @ dkx584en

🏛 **Aquincumi Múzeum és Régészeti Park (Aquincum Museum and Archaeological Park)**, Szentendrei út 135, ☏ 2501650 The museum presents the remains of the settlement Aquincum (2nd-4th century), which existed in the area of present-day Óbuda during the Roman Empire. The garden of ruins shows the civic centre of Aquincum with public buildings and private houses. @ wbe423en

🏛 **Iparművészeti Múzeum (Museum For Applied Arts)**, Üllői út 33-37, ☏ 4565100. Wide-ranging collection with household and day-to-day items showing the history of design, housed in a handsome art nouveau building. @ rdn822en

🏛 **Ludwig Múzeum (Ludwig Museum)**, Komor Marcell u. 1, ☏ 5553444 Contemporary art collection of Irene and Peter Ludwig, of Cologne, provides an overview of the last 50 years of international art, and the last 10 years of contemporary art in Hungary. @ huc535en

🏛 **Magyar Nemzeti Galéria (Hungarian National Gallery)**, Szent György tér 2, castle palace; wing A, B, C & D, ☏ 2019082,

Your partner for bicycle touring in Budapest
1075 Budapest, Madach Imre ut 12
www.bike-and-relax.com

- Quality Cross- and Touringbike **Rental**
- Delivery/Pick-up in Vienna
- Guided Bicycle Tours
- E-Bikes
- Company- and Familyprograms

Thomas
Bike & Relax Kft
+36 30 300 8 003
info@bike-and-relax.com

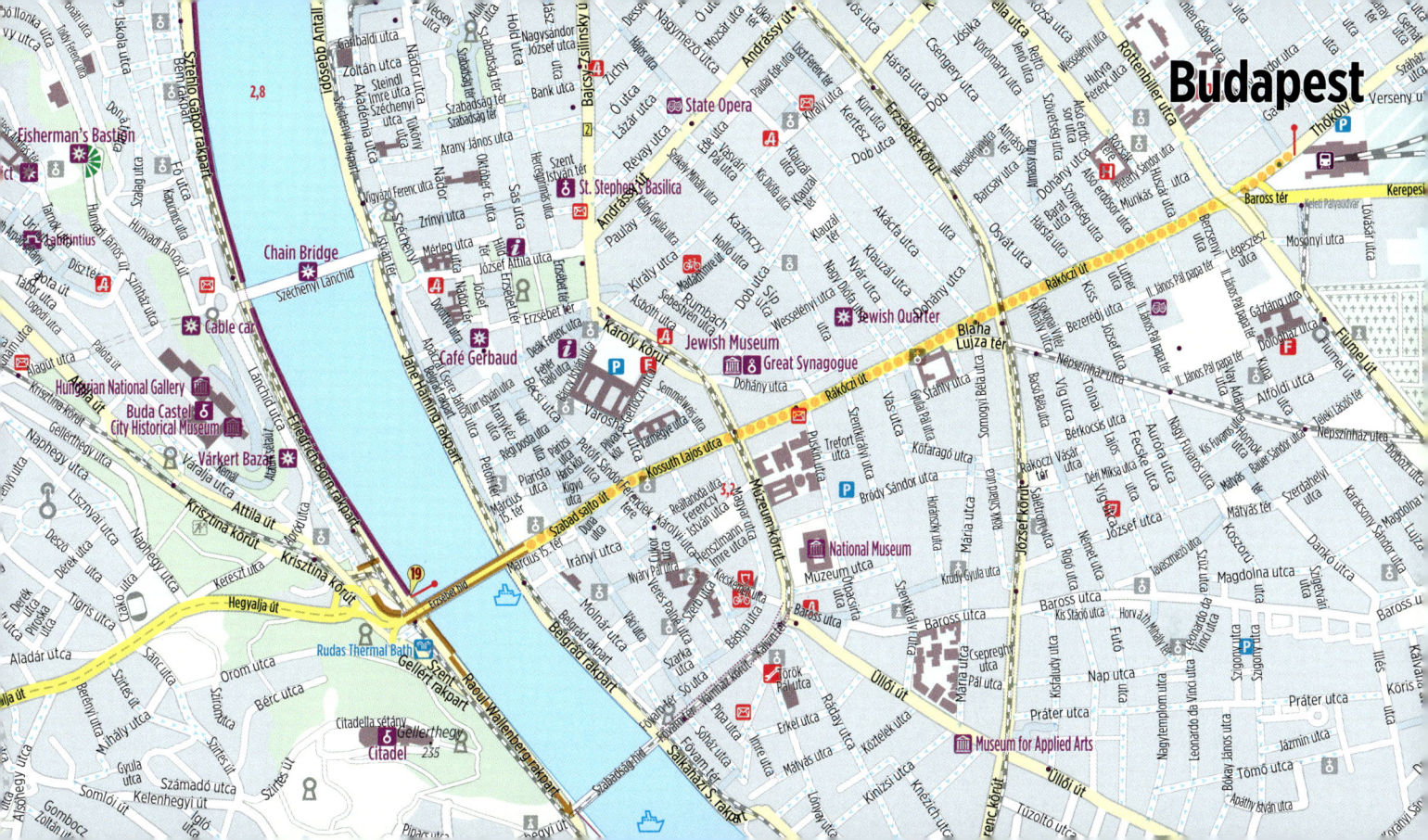

☎ 0620/4397331 @ Collection exhibits works by Hungarian painters from the 15th to 19th c. Noteworthy are the late Gothic altar pieces, portraits and landscapes by the painter Mihály Munkácsy (1844-1900) and the works by Hungarian impressionists, including Pál Szinyei Merse and Kosztka Tivadar Csontváry. @ rho223en

🏛 **Magyar Nemzeti Múzeum (Hungarian National Museum)**, Múzeum krt. 14–16, ☎ 3382122, ☎ 3177806 @ The largest and most prestigious museum in Hungary presents diverse collections about the country's history and people. On display are the Hungarian royal insignia from the year 1000. @ yho521en

🏛 **Néprajzi Múzeum (Ethnographic Museum)**, Kossuth Lajos tér 12, ☎ 4732442, ☎ 0670/4654080 @ Housed in a Neo-Renaissance palace, the exhibitions are centered around the rural lifestyle and include a model of a farmhouse complete with costumes and tools of everyday rural life. @ ldr381en

🏛 **Szépművészeti Múzeum (Fine arts museum)**, Dózsa György út 41, ☎ 4697100 @ The world-famous museum contains the largest collection of Spanish masters (Velazquez, Goya, El Greco) outside Spain. The modern gallery includes works by Monet, Pissarro, Renoir, Cézanne, Gauguin and others. Antiquity collection. @ mqt665en

🏛 **Történeti Múzeum (Historical Museum)**, Szent György tér 2, castle palace; wing-E, ☎ 4878871 @ Exhibits covering Romanesque to renaissance periods – not to be missed by anyone interested in the city's history and especially the castle district. @ cxi264en

🏛 **Unicum Ház (Unicum house)**, Dandár u. 1, ☎ 4762383 @ Here you can learn more about the production of the traditional Hungarian drink and the secrets of the herbs that make it up, as well as the history of the producers, the Zwack family. During the tour you can taste Unicum. @ gtm152en

🏛 **Zsidó Múzeum (Jewish Museum)**, Dohány u. 2, ☎ 4135500 @ Near the large synagogue, collection with valuable objects of Jewish art, information and exhibits about the deportation of Hungarian Jews during the Nazi period and Nazi concentration camps. In 1993 the museum suffered a major art robbery. @ obv387en

⛪ **Mátyás-templom (Matthias Church)**, Szentháromság tér 2, ☎ 4890716 @ Also called the Church of Our Lady, it was built in 1255-69 under King Béla IV. as part of the Buda Castle. Around 1370, King Louis the Great rebuilt the church into a Gothic hall church with three naves. In 1541 the Turks conquered Buda and converted the church into their main mosque, the church was known as Büyük Camii, Great Mosque, for almost 150 years. In the 17th century the church was finally baroqueised. @ kty771en

⛪ **Szent István Bazilika (St. Stephen's Basilica)**, Szent István tér 1, ☎ 3110839 @ Construction of Budapest's largest church began in 1851. In 1868 the dome collapsed. The eclectic church designed by Miklós Ybl was finally consecrated in 1905. @ rkv656en

⛪ **Nagy Zsinagóga (Great Synagogue)**, Dohány u. 2, ☎ 4135584 @ The largest synagogue in Europe, with space for 3,000 people, was built by a student of Otto Wagner. A memorial plaque commemorates Theodor Herzl (born 1860 in Budapest). @ xcf444en

🏰 **Citadella (Citadel)**, Gellérthegy, Gellért-hill. The fortress "guards" the city since 1849, when it was built by the Habsburg rulers in reaction to the Hungarian revolts. Today the hill on which it is built is dominated by the "Liberation Monument," erected in 1947 in memory of the city's liberation by the Soviet army at the end of WWII. Excellent views of the castle and Budapest. @ msi834en

🏰 **Halaszbastya (Fisherman's Bastion)**, Szentháromság tér, ☎ 4583000 @ The bastion was built in 1895-1902 on the site of the old Buda castle wall according to plans by Frigyes Schulek in the neo-Romanesque style; the pointed stone towers symbolise the seven tribal leaders of the Hungarians. The Fisherman's Bastion offers a fantastic view over Budapest. @ nqe112en

🏰🏛 **Vajdahunyad vára (Vajdahunyad castle)**, Vajdahunyad vár, ☎ 4220765 @ Originally constructed of wood for the millennial exhibition in 1896, it was rebuilt in stone and brick between 1896 and 1908. It is in part a copy of the Vajdahunyad castle in Siebenbürgen and was designed by Ignác Alpár in romanic, gothic, renaissance and baroque styles to document the history of Hungarian architecture. @ lak436en

🏛 **Labirintius (Castle Labyrinth)**, Úri u. 9 @ A fascinating presentation of the castle's extensive underground corridors. In the 15th c. Vlad Tepes, also known as Count Dracula, was held prisoner here. Later, the cave system was used as a storeroom, wine cellar and, during the Second World War, as German headquarters. @ ygg217en

- **Szemlő-hegyi-barlang (Szemlöhegy cave)**, Pusztaszeri út 35, ✆ 3256001 🚇 Known as the "underground gardens of Budapest," Eocene cave system with magnificent stalagmites and stalactites. @ nqi188en
- **BudaBike Tours**, Szent István tér 4, ✆ 0670/6711274. Guided sightseeing bike-tours. Meeting point Szent István tér in front of the basilica. @ tib273en
- **Budavári Sikló (Buda Castle Funicular)**, Clark Ádám tér 1, ✆ 2019128 🚇 Built 1870, historic cable car service brings passengers up to the castle in a few minutes. At the base station, near Chain Bridge, is located the "0-kilometre" stone, from which all distances to Budapest are measured. @ etr541en
- **Burgviertel (Castle district)**, Stadtteil Buda, Buda. This was the centre of the medieval city when it was the cultural and political capital of Hungary. After the Turkish occupation, the district was rebuilt in the 18th century.
- **Fogaskerekű Vasút (Rack railway)**, Városmajor, ✆ 2584636 🚇 Built 1874, the 3.5 km train goes through Buda's villa district on its way up to Szechenyi mountain and is one of the highlights of a visit to Budapest. @ hoq725en
- **Földalatti (Old metro)**, Széchenyi fürdő 🚇 The oldest underground railway in Europe, built for the millenium celebrations in 1896, it runs underneath the handsome Andrássy út avenue

Budapest

connecting the central Vörösmarthy tér with the old Zoo in the city park. @ bcw872en
- **Hősök tere (Heroes' square)**, Dózsa György út. Square dominated by the millenium monument, built in 1896 for Hungary's 1,000-year celebrations of their conquest of the country, in honor of Hungarian national heroes. @ tth541en
- **Jüdisches Viertel (Jewish quarter)**, Erzsébetváros, Elizabeth-town, VII. district. Before WW II, about 200,000 Jews lived in Budapest. Today there is little to see of the diverse community life, but the crumbling facades can be of interest to those wanting to discover vestiges of Jewish life and architecture that once flourished here. @ lop546en
- **Kávéház Gerbeaud (Café Gerbaud)**, Vörösmarty tér 7-8, ✆ 4299000 🚇 The Budapest coffeehouse most popular among tourists, worth visiting mainly for its elaborate interior. @ wek634en
- **Magyar Állami Operaház (Hungarian State Opera)**, Andrássy út 22, ✆ 8147100, ✆ 0630/7812630 🚇 The neo-Renaissance style opera house was designed by the famous architect Miklós Ybl and is considered as his masterpiece. @ bwg765en

Budapest, Vajdahunyad-Burg

✳ **Margitsziget (Margaret island)**, XIII. Bezirk, north of the city. The island's more recent history begins in the late 18th c., when vice-king Joseph von Habsburg built a summer residence and a park with exotic plants and trees. In 1867 mineral springs were discovered, leading to the development of a spa resort. Today closed to motorized traffic, the island is a popular recreation site. @ fdd288en

✳ **Nyugati pályaudvar (West Station)**, Nyugati tér 57. Interesting renovated classical terminal train station (1874-77), glass hall by August de Serres and iron construction by Gustave Eiffel, builder of the Eiffel tower in Paris.

✳ **Zugligeti Libegő (Zugliget Chairlift)**, Zugligeti út 97, ✆ 3943764 🚠 The approximately 1 km long railway line runs at an altitude of about 8 m. The ride takes about 15 min. and the view from Johannesberg is dreamlike. @ jtb741en

🦒 **Állatkert (Zoo)**, Állatkerti krt. 6-12, ✆ 2734900 🚠 Opened in 1866, the zoo is one of the world's leading zoos thanks to its historic buildings and its collection of more than 850 animal species and over 2000 plant species. @ piv644en

♨ **Király fürdő (Royal Thermal Bath)**, Fő u. 84, ✆ 2023688. Turkish bath built 1566 by the Pascha Sokoli Mustafa is one of numerous charming bathhouses and spas in the city. Expanded in the 18th century (baroque) and again in 1827 (classical style). The original pools and dome were retained. @ wqr756en

♨ **Rudas fürdő (Rudas Themal Bath)**, Döbrentei tér 9, ✆ 0620/3214568. Site of a bathhouse which predated the Turkish bath built in 1566. Fed by radioactive and sulfur waters. Expanded in the late 19th century by Miklós Ybl. @ awc276en

♨ **Széchenyi Gyógyfürdő (Széchenyi Thermal Bath)**, Állatkerti krt. 9-11, ✆ 0620/4350051, @ hgm311en

Budapest is a city of contrasts and opposites, as well as a young city that has existed in its present form only for just over a century, yet which still exudes the faded glory of its imperial past. As the former sister city to Vienna, and one of the two poles around which the Austro-Hungarian Empire revolved, Budapest today is proud to be at the middle of a nation that was one of the first to cast aside the communist system under which it was governed for most of five decades after WW II.

Budapest is the undisputed queen among Hungarian cities and much more than just its biggest. Much of the Hungarian population has lived in towns that are little more than a formless collection of houses and industrial areas, surrounded by agriculture, or in vast, sparsely populated areas in which urban life in its strictest form could not develop. The young men from the countryside who were brought to the capital by the military in the 19th century, were for the first time to encounter a town hall or market square, not to mention the majestic splendour of this self-affirming city. This is in part still true today, which gives an indication what this magnificent concentration of urbanism must have meant for Hungary in the past. Many regard Budapest to be among the most beautiful cities in the world. Few other cities have so well understood how to wrap themselves in an aura of festiveness and brilliance. The first people were drawn to this fertile land in prehistoric times, attracted by the shimmering waters of the river and the plain spreading eastward from the mountains. Two-thousand years ago the Romans established a city on the west bank. Legally speaking, the city of Budapest was born in 1873, when the towns of Pest, Buda and Obuda were merged. But the roots of Budapest go back to Illyrian-Celtic Avars and the Romans who lived in Aquincum. The Magyars then built the Kurszans castle, their first centre of authority. In 1241 the Mongols destroyed Buda and Pest. In 1247 King Béla IV built the first royal castle on castle hill – it soon became his permanent residence. He awarded city rights to Pest, including the stone quarry and Little Pest on the left bank of the Danube. The name Pest seems to come from the old Slavic word for oven (pesti), referring to the ovens used to burn limestone, and bears witness to the long-time dominance of the Slavik population here.

After the Turks conquered Hungary, Budapest became the provincial capital for a Pasha. Many of the bath-houses left by the Romans were rebuilt in this period as Turkish baths. After the Turks were expelled in the late 17th century, the city began to experience a new economic and cultural boom. By 1848 the traditional main city of Buda had been overtaken by Pest as the spiritual and political centre of the country. During this period the city was seized by the trend toward modernity. In 1896 Budapest became the second city in the world, after London, to open a subway. Many of the city's iron and glass train stations and market buildings were built in this period. The wide and lazy Danube through the centre of the city played a key role in every part of Budapest's history. Today eight magnificent bridges connect the two halves of the city, and the river remains central to Budapest's character, the unifying element that make Buda, Pest and the river's islands into a harmonious whole. Buda is the older part of the city, but its lively centre today is located in Pest. Expansive suburbs have grown around the cramped city centre, radially divided through boulevards with an Parisian imprint of plantan allees and large squares.

Among the many architectural edifices that dot the cityscape with a variety of styles, one of the most distinctive is the Fischer Bastion in the old Castle District. Behind it stands the distinguished old Matthias church and the old city hall with its renaissance windows. The Castle District is a dense maze of small streets and alleys, where handsome baroque city palaces stand next to old patrician houses, some of which are built on Gothic foundations. Above the city on Castle Mountain stands the royal palace. It was heavily damaged by fire when the Ottoman Turks withdrew from the city. Franz A. Hillebrand rebuilt it in the baroque style, and it was later rebuilt by Miklós Ybl. In 1945 it burned again. Visitors to the Castle District should not neglect a visit at Uri utca 9. It is the entrance to a 10-kilometre network of natural caves and man-made connecting tunnels that honeycombs the rock beneath the castle. Many of the tunnels date back to late medieval period.

You have now reached the end of this cycling journey. We hope that you had an enjoyable and experience-rich cycling tour and are happy that you have chosen a bikeline-Cycling Guide to accompany you on your journey.

The bikeline-Team wishes you a safe and enjoyable return trip!

Accommodation and service directory

Accommodation addresses
The following list includes accommodation in the following categories:

Categories
- 🛈 Tourist-Information
- H Hotel
- Hg Hotel garni
- Gh Inn
- P Boarding House, Guesthouse
- Pz Private rooms
- Ho Hostel
- Mo Motel
- NF Friends of Nature House
- AH Aparthotel
- BB Bed and Breakfast
- Fw Holiday Flat (selection)
- Bh Farmf
- B Bungalow
- Hh Hay hotel
- S Other
- Youth hostel
- Camp ground
- Tent site (nature tent site)

We have not attempted to list every possible place where visitors can spend the night, and listings should not be construed as any kind of recommendation. Because we wish to expand this list and keep it up-to-date, we welcome any comments, additions or corrections you may have. There is no charge for a single-line entry, for lack of space we cannot guarantee one.

Identification
I	Price Range	less than € 25,-
II	Price Range	€ 25,- to € 35,-
III	Price Range	€ 35,- to € 50,-
IV	Price Range	€ 50,- to € 70,-
V	Price Range	€ 70,- to € 100,-
VI	Price Range	over € 100,-

- o.F. no breakfast
- HP with breakfast and dinner
- 🛁 only room with shared bathroom
- ⊙ Bed+Bike Accommodation
- 2.5 distance to the route in kilometers

Prices
These categories are based on the price per person in a double room equipped with shower or bath, with breakfast. The indicated price categories correspond to the status of the survey or revision period and may differ from the actual prices. Price fluctuations are possible, especially during trade fairs, due to different room types and not least due to seasonal factors.

Bike Workshops and Rental
- 🔧 Bike workshop
- Bike rental
- E-Bike charging station
- E-Bike rental
- lockable parking facilities

Distance
The blue number (**2.5**) at every accommodation shows the distance to the route in kilometers. Please note that this number refers to the linear distance, the difference in altitude and the actual distance covered is not included.

Updates
For further corrections concerning the overnight accommodation list see the LiveUpdate at www.esterbauer.com

Vienna to Bratislava

Wien (Vienna)
Area Code: 01

- Tourist-Information, Albertinapl./Maysederg., 1. Bezirk (Wien), ✆ 24555 0.5
- Tourist information main station, Am Hauptbahnhof 1, at the infopoint of ÖBB Austrian railways, ✆ 24555 0.5

Wien/1. Bezirk
Area Code: 01

- Tourist-Information, Albertinapl./Maysederg., ✆ 24555 0.5
- Tourist-Information, Albertinapl./Maysederg., ✆ 24555 0.5
- H Alma Boutique Hotel, Hafnersteig 7, ✆ 5332961, IV 0
- H Austria, Am Fleischmarkt 20, Wolfeng. 3, ✆ 51523, II-V 0
- H Das Tigra Hotel, Tiefer Graben 14-20, ✆ 53396410, IV-V 0.5
- H De France, Schottenring 3, ✆ 313260, IV-V 0
- H Domizil, Schulerstr. 14, ✆ 5133199, IV-V 0.5
- H Kaiserin Elisabeth, Weihburgg. 3, ✆ 515260, IV-VI 0.5
- H Kärntnerhof, Grashofg. 4, ✆ 5121923, IV-VI 0.5
- H König von Ungarn, Schulerstr. 10, ✆ 515840, V 0
- H Mailberger Hof, Annag. 7, ✆ 5120641, III-VI 0.5
- H Marc Aurel, Marc-Aurel-Str. 8, ✆ 53336400, ✆ 5335226, IV 0.5
- H Post, Fleischmarkt 24, ✆ 515830, III-V 0.5
- H Royal, Singerstr. 3, ✆ 515680, IV-VI 0.5
- H Schlosshotel Römischer Kaiser, Annag. 16, ✆ 51277510, V-VI 0.5
- H Starlight Suiten Renngasse, Renng. 13, ✆ 5339989, V-VI 0.5
- H Vienna Marriott, Parkring 12a, ✆ 515180, VI 0
- H Zur Wiener Staatsoper, Krugerstr. 11, ✆ 5131274, ✆ 0664/3461840, IV-V 0.5
- H Arenberg Boutique Hotel Zentrum, Stubenring 2, ✆ 51252910, V-VI 0
- BB Dr. Geissler, Postg. 14, ✆ 5332803, III 0
- BB Neuer Markt, Seilerg. 9, ✆ 5122316, III-V 0.5
- BB Opera Suites, Kärntner Str. 47, ✆ 5129310, VI 0.5
- BB Residenz, Ebendorferstr. 10, ✆ 40647860, III-IV 0.5
- BB Riedl, Georg-Coch-Pl. 3/4/10, ✆ 5127919, III-IV 0
- BB Sacher Apartments, Rotenturmstr. 1-3, 7. Stock, ✆ 5333238, ✆ 0676/4451658, OB, IV-V 0.5
- Newton-Bikes, Lobkowitzpl. 3, ✆ 0650/3635346 0.5
- Pedal Power Vienna, Bösendorferstr. 5, ✆ 7297234 0
- Radhaus Singer, Reichsratsstr. 13, ✆ 4062143 0.5
- Trek Bicycle Vienna, Hegelg. 19, ✆ 5130514 0
- Vienna Explorer, Franz-Josefs-Kai 45, ✆ 8909682 0

Wien/2. Bezirk
Area Code: 01

- H Austria Classic Hotel Wien, Praterstr. 72, ✆ 211300, IV-VI 0
- H Henriette Stadthotel, Praterstr. 44-46, ✆ 2148404, IV-V 0
- H Hilton Vienna Danube Waterfront, Handelskai 269, ✆ 72777, V-VI 1
- H Kunsthof, Mühlfeldg. 13, ✆ 2143178, III-IV 0.5
- H Mercure Wien City, Hollandstr. 3, ✆ 213130, IV-V 0.5
- H Odeon, Weintraubeng. 31, ✆ 2142362, ✆ 0650/4720732, IV 0.5
- H Stefanie, Taborstr. 12, ✆ 211500, V 0.5
- H Wilhelmshof, Kleine Stadtgutg. 4, ✆ 21455210, IV-V 0.5
- H ibis Wien Messe, Lassallestr. 7a, ✆ 217700, III-V 1
- Peter Vesecky, Böcklinstr. 64, ✆ 7289311 1
- Radsport Rih, Praterstr. 48, ✆ 2145180 0
- Sator Bike Shop, Böcklinstr. 104, ✆ 7289136 1
- Star Bike, Bruno-Marek-Allee 11, ✆ 2198560 1

Wien/3. Bezirk
Area Code: 01

- H Garten- & Kunsthotel Gabriel, Landstraßer Hauptstr. 165, ✆ 7123205, III-IV 2
- H Mercure Grand Hotel Biedermeier Wien, Landstraßer Hauptstr. 28, ✆ 716710, V-VI 1
- H Urania, Obere Weißgerberstr. 7, ✆ 7131711, III-IV 0.5
- H Vienna Sporthotel, Baumg. 83, ✆ 79882010, IV-V 1.5
- H ibis budget Wien Sankt Marx, Franzosengraben 15, ✆ 7984555, III-IV 2
- BB Bosch, Keilg. 13, ✆ 7986179, III 1
- BB Kibi Rooms, Landstraßer Hauptstr. 33, ✆ 7121068, III 1
- Fahrrad1030, Sechskrügelg. 2, ✆ 0699/17000542 1
- Galaxy Fahrräder, Hintere Zollamtstr. 11, ✆ 0699/11398484 0.5

Wien/4. Bezirk
Area Code: 01

- H Beim Theresianum, Favoritenstr. 52, ✆ 5051606, III 0.5
- H Carlton Opera, Schikanederg. 4, ✆ 5875302, III-VI 0.5
- H Congress, Wiedner Gürtel 34, ✆ 5055506, III 0
- H Drei Kronen, Schleifmühlg. 25, ✆ 5873289, IV 0.5
- H Johann Strauss, Favoritenstr. 12, ✆ 5057624, IV 0.5
- H Kaiserhof Wien, Frankenbergg. 10, ✆ 5051701, IV-VI 0.5
- H Prinz-Eugen, Wiedner Gürtel 14, ✆ 5051741, III-IV 0

127

Wien/5. Bezirk
Area Code: 01

- H Sommerhotel Wieden, Schelleing. 36, ✆ 50152100, III-IV. von Juli bis September geöffnet 0.5
- BB Attaché, Wiedner Hauptstr. 71, ✆ 5032301, III 0.5
- 2rad-shop Gerhardt, Wiedner Hauptstr. 55, ✆ 0676/6850715 0.5
- ARGUS Shop, Frankenbergg. 11, ✆ 5050907 0.5

Wien/5. Bezirk
Area Code: 01

- H Allegro, Matzleinsdorferpl. 1, ✆ 5442743, OB, I-II 1.5
- H Art Hotel Vienna, Brandmayerg. 7-9, ✆ 5445108, IV 1.5
- H Austria Trend Hotel Ananas, Rechte Wienzeile 93-95, Entrance Sonnenhofg. 8-10, ✆ 54620901, III-V 1.5
- H Holiday Inn Wien City, Margaretenstr. 53, ✆ 58850, IV-V 1
- H Ibis Wien City, Schönbrunner Str. 92, ✆ 590070, III-IV 2
- AH Residenz Johann-Strauß, Einsiedlerg. 19, ✆ 5441351, ✆ 0676/5378816, II-IV 2
- MITICO Bikes Vienna, Margaretenstr. 107, ✆ 9072087 1.5
- die radwerkstatt, Margaretengürtel 134, ✆ 5443801 2

Wien/6. Bezirk
Area Code: 01

- H Die Josefine, Esterházyg. 33, ✆ 58870, V-VI 1.5
- H Ibis Wien Mariahilf, Mariahilfer Gürtel 22-24, ✆ 59998, IV 2
- H Leonardo, Matroseng. 6-8, ✆ 599010, ✆ 59901551, IV 2
- H Secession, Getreidemarkt 5, ✆ 588380, V 0.5
- H Terminus, Fillgraderg. 4, ✆ 58773860, III-IV 0.5
- BB Esterhazy, Nelkeng. 3, bei Mariahilfer Str. 67, ✆ 5875159, OB, II-III 1
- BB Haydn, Mariahilfer Str. 57-59, ✆ 58744140, IV 1
- M Kolpinghaus Wien Zentral, Gumpendorferstr. 39, ✆ 58756310, II-IV 1
- M Westend City Hostel, Fügerg. 3, ✆ 5976729, II-III 2
- Bicycle Company, Getreidemarkt 1, ✆ 8901028 0
- Ciclopia, Stiegeng. 20, ✆ 5867633 1
- Cooperative Fahrrad, Gumpendorfer Str. 111, ✆ 5965256 2
- Fahrrad+Skii, Linke Wienzeile 124/128, ✆ 5978288, ✆ 0664/1004659 1.5
- IG Fahrrad, Otto Bauer G. 16, ✆ 5235113, ✆ 0650/3346723 1.5
- Radsport Niesner, Schmalzhofg. 10, ✆ 5970477, ✆ 0664/1810921 1.5

Wien/7. Bezirk
Area Code: 01

- H Admiral, Karl-Schweigerhofer-G. 7, ✆ 521410, III-V 0.5
- H Gilbert, Breite G. 9, ✆ 5231345, IV-VI 0.5
- H Intercityhotel Wien, Mariahilfer Str. 122, ✆ 525850, III-IV 2
- H K & K Maria Theresia, Kirchbergg. 6, ✆ 52123, III-V 0.5
- H Kugel, Siebensterng. 43, ✆ 5233355, V-VI 1
- H Max Brown 7th District, Schottenfeldg. 74, ✆ 3761070, V 1.5
- BB Altstadt Vienna, Kircheng. 41, ✆ 5226666, V-VI 1
- BB Atrium, Burgg. 118, ✆ 0664/3436212, III-IV 1.5
- BB Dormium, Kandlg. 35/7, ✆ 5267340, ✆ 0681/10395390, IV 1.5
- BB Hotel Schani Salon, Mariahilfer Str. 58, ✆ 5240970, V. 1
- BB Urban Stay Columbia, Kochg. 9, ✆ 4056757, III-IV 1
- BB Walzerstadt, Zieglerg. 35, ✆ 5237122, III 1.5
- M JH, Myrtheng. 7, Neustiftg. 85, ✆ 52363160, I 1
- IG Fahrrad, Westbahnstr. 28, ✆ 5235113 1.5
- reanimated-bikes, Westbahnstr. 35, ✆ 5224018 1.5

Wien/8. Bezirk
Area Code: 01

- H Alpha, Buchfeldg. 8, ✆ 4035291, III 0.5
- H Graf Stadion, Buchfeldg. 5, ✆ 4055284, V-IV 0.5

Wien/9. Bezirk

- H Josefshof, Josefsg. 4/8, ✆ 404190, V 0.5
- H Rathaus, Lange G. 13, ✆ 4001122, V 0.5
- BB Adria, Wickenburgg. 23, ✆ 4020238, OB, III 0.5
- BB Andreas, Schlösselg. 11, ✆ 4053488, OB, IV 0.5
- BB Baronesse, Lange G. 61, ✆ 4051061, IV-V 0.5
- BB Excellence, Alser Str. 21, ✆ 4079620, III-IV 0.5
- BB Lehrerhaus, Langeg. 20-22, ✆ 4032358, III 0.5
- BB Zipser, Lange G. 49, ✆ 404540, III-IV 1

Wien/9. Bezirk
Area Code: 01

- H Am Schottenpoint, Währinger Str. 22, ✆ 3108787, IV 0.5
- H Atlanta, Währinger Str. 33, ✆ 4051230, III 1
- H Bleckmann, Währinger Str. 15, ✆ 4080899, III 0.5
- H Gala, Viriotg. 5, ✆ 310083711, III 2
- H Harmonie, Harmonieg. 5-7, ✆ 3176604, V 1
- H Mozart, Nordbergstr. 4, ✆ 3171537, III-IV 1
- H Regina, Rooseveltpl. 15, ✆ 404460, V-VI 0.5
- H Riess City, Türkenstr. 27, ✆ 4022010, ✆ 0660/6241164, OB, III-IV 0.5
- H Strudlhof, Pasteurg. 1, ✆ 3192522, IV 1
- BB Vera, Alser Str. 18, ✆ 4062595, III 1
- AH Pension Huber/Appartements in Wien 9, Sechsschimmelg. 4/17, ✆ 02243/33884, ✆ 0664/1616331, IV 1.5

- Arizona Bike, Nußdorfer Str. 3/3, ☎ 0680/1161575 1.5
- Bikers, Spittelauer Lände 12, bei P+R Spittelau, ☎ 2764960 2
- Enzovelo, Spittelauer Lände 11, ☎ 3100545 1.5
- Mountainbiker, Währinger Gürtel 146/150, ☎ 4707186 2

Wien/10. Bezirk
Area Code: 01
- Bosei, Gutheil-Schoderg. 7B, ☎ 661091096, IV 3.5
- Eitljörg, Filmteichstr. 5, ☎ 6881182, V 4.5
- Kolbeck Zur Linde, Laxenburger Str. 19, ☎ 6041773, II-III 0.5
- Zeitgeist Vienna, Sonnwendg. 15, ☎ 902650, V-VI 0.5
- Arnes, Quellenstr. 120, ☎ 0699/19040580, OB, II-III 1.5
- Puzwidu, Himberger Str. 67-71, ☎ 6882168, ☎ 0664/9821640, III-IV 6
- Rad & Service, Oberlaaer Str. 105, ☎ 0676/6259112 6

Wien/22. Bezirk
Area Code: 01
- ARCOTEL Kaiserwasser, Wagramer Str. 8, ☎ 224040, IV-V 2.5
- Asperner Löwe, Aspernstr. 96, ☎ 2882088, III-IV 3
- Meliá, Donau-City-Str. 7, ☎ 901042003, V-VI 2.5
- NH Danube City, Wagramer Str. 21, ☎ 2675972, ☎ 260200, V-VI 3
- Neue Donau, Am Kleehäufel, ☎ 2024010 0.5
- 2rad-shop Gerhardt, Langobardenstr. 19, ☎ 2825144 2
- Biber Sport, Soldanellenweg 53/2/1, ☎ 972425, ☎ 0699/19472425 3.5
- Bike+More, Agavenweg 21, ☎ 7344401 7
- Bikestore, Erzherzog-Karl Str. 14, ☎ 0660/1112948 3.5
- Copa Beach, Copa Cagrana 1, Reichsbrücke/Donauinsel, ☎ 2635242, ☎ 0664/3458585 2
- DR Bike, Maria-Tusch Str. 9, ☎ 2806986, ☎ 0660/2037104 4.5

Orth an der Donau
Area Code: 02212
- Tourismusinformation, Schlosspl. 1, Schloss Orth, ☎ 3555 0
- Gemeindeamt, Am Markt 26, ☎ 2208 0.5
- Marchfelder Pension, Schwarzeckerweg 4, ☎ 0676/4924490, II 0.5
- Maria, Uferstr. 1, ☎ 2843, ☎ 0699/12374581 0
- Sabine, Wiener Str. 5, ☎ 0664/4644976 0.5

Haslau-Maria Ellend
Area Code: 02232
- Gemeindeamt Maria Ellend, Wienerstr. 11, ☎ 80250 1.5
- Strasser, Bahnhofpl. 1, ☎ 80230, ☎ 0650/2647800 1.5

Scharndorf
- Gemeindeamt, Bodenzeile 1b, ☎ 02163/2303 0

Petronell-Carnuntum
Area Code: 02163
- Donau Niederösterreich Tourismus, Hauptstr. 3, ☎ 355510 0.5
- Gemeindeamt, Kirchenpl. 1, ☎ 2228 0
- Marc-Aurel, Hauptstr. 10, ☎ 2285, ☎ 0650/5611115, III 0.5
- Il Centro, Hauptstr. 21, ☎ 43090, III 0
- Camping Petronell, Bruckerstr. 28, ☎ 0677/62771435 0.5
- nextbike-Station Archäologischer Park Carnuntum, Hauptstr. 1a, ☎ 02742/229901 0.5
- nextbike-Station Bahnhof, Bahnhof, ☎ 02742/229901 0.5

Bad Deutsch-Altenburg
Area Code: 02165
- Marktgemeinde, Erhardg. 2, ☎ 62900 0
- Kurzentrum Ludwigstorff - Parkhotel, Badg. 21, ☎ 626170, V. 79 0
- Stöckl, Hauptpl. 3, ☎ 62337, III-IV 0

- Madle, Badg. 22, ☎ 62763, ☎ 0699/11578335, III 0
- Parkpension Bichler, Badg. 38, ☎ 62977, ☎ 0699/11810141, III 0
- Schön, Neustiftg. 10, ☎ 62753, III 0
- Hofmeister, Badg. 3, ☎ 0676/3538927, II 0
- raditäten, Badg. 24, ☎ 0676/6713040 0
- nextbike-Station, Bahnhof, ☎ 02742/229901 0.5
- nextbike-Station Museum Carnuntium, Badg. 42, ☎ 02742/229901 0

Eckartsau
Area Code: 02214
- Gemeindeamt, Obere Hauptstr. 1, ☎ 22020 0.5
- Kramreiter, Untere Hauptstr. 12, ☎ 2203, II-III 0.5
- Schreiner Maria, Untere Hauptstr. 1, ☎ 0664/73620851 0.5
- Schloss Eckartsau, Schloss 1, ☎ 2240 0

Loimersdorf (Engelhartstetten)
Area Code: 02214
- Pekarek, Ortsstr. 58, ☎ 0680/2070582 4.5

Engelhartstetten
Area Code: 02214
- Gemeindeamt, Obere Hauptstr. 2, ☎ 2292 3
- Privatherberge Ornauer, Untere Hauptstr. 5, ☎ 0676/84972668 3

Hainburg a.d. Donau

Area Code: 02165

- 🛈 Gästeinformation, Ungarstr. 3, ✆ 62111400 ⓞ
- 🛈 Gemeindeamt, Hauptpl. 23, ✆ 621110 ⓞ
- 🏨 Altes Kloster, Fabrikspl. 1a, ✆ 64020, IV-V 🖥 ⓞ
- 🏍 Motel Hainburg, Pressburger Reichsstr. 70, ✆ 64840, ✆ 0676/4895050, III ⓞ
- 🏨 🏍 Pizzeria „el pirata", Pressburger Reichsstr. 72, ✆ 64840, ✆ 0676/4895050, II ⓞ
- 🏨 Zum goldenen Anker, Donaulände 27, ✆ 64810, IV-V 🖥 ⓞ
- 🏨 Nawratil, Ungarstr. 16, ✆ 0699/12641020, II ⓞ
- 🚲 nextbike-Station, Hauptpl. 24, ✆ 02742/229901 ⓞ

Wolfsthal

Area Code: 02165

- 🛈 Gemeindeamt, Hauptpl. 42, ✆ 62676 ⓞ
- 🏨 Fidi, Sportplatzweg 11, ✆ 65120, ✆ 0676/3779504, IV ⓞ
- 🛏 Villa Pannonica, Villag. 9, ✆ 0664/3812074, III-IV ⓞ

Petržalka (Bratislava) ⓢ

Area Code: 02

- 🏨 Miva, Bzovícka 38, ✆ 63822556, II-III 4.5
- 🏨 Incheba Expo, Viedenská cesta 7, ✆ 67272542, ✆ 0911/100725, OB, II 0.5
- 🚲 Chilli's Bike, Šustekova 2690/25, ✆ 62250919 ⓘ

Bratislava ⓢ

Area Code: 02

- 🛈 Bratislava Information Service, Klobučnícka 2, ✆ 16186, ✆ 54419410 ⓘ
- 🏨 Aplend City Perugia, Zelená 5, Staré Mesto, ✆ 0902/411111, IV-V ⓘ
- 🏨 Apollo, Dulovo 1, ✆ 55968922, ✆ 0903/231893, III-V 1.5
- 🏨 Astra, Prievozská 14, ✆ 58238111, OB, II-III 2
- 🏨 Botel Marina Hotelship, Nábrežie armádneho generála Ludvíka Svobodu, ✆ 048/4148753, II-III 0.5
- 🏨 Bratislava, Seberiniho 9, ✆ 20606100, II-III 4
- 🏨 Bôrik, Bôrik 15, ✆ 20925000, III 1.5
- 🏨 Crowne Plaza, Hodžovo nám. 2, ✆ 59348111, IV-V ⓘ
- 🏨 Devín, Riečna 162/4, ✆ 59985111, IV-VI 0.5
- 🏨 Galéria Tachyon, Vančurova 1, ✆ 54777817, III 2.5
- 🏨 Marrol's, Tobrucká 4, ✆ 57784600, IV-VI 0.5
- 🏨 Modena, Vlčie Hrdlo 1/A, ✆ 58597293, ✆ 948/998488, II 4.5
- 🏨 Nivy, Liščie nivy 3, ✆ 55410390, OB, II-III 2.5
- 🏨 No16, Partizánska 16a, ✆ 54411672, ✆ 0903/445900, OB, III 1.5
- 🏨 Plus, Bulharská 1743/72, ✆ 48231920, II-III 1
- 🏨 Radisson Blu Carlton, Hviezdoslavovo nam. 3, ✆ 59390500, V 0.5
- 🏨 Remy, Stará Vajnorská cesta 37a, Nové Mesto, ✆ 44455063, ✆ 0907/408369, OB, I-II 7
- 🏨 Sorea, Kráľovské údolie 6, ✆ 32112870, III ⓘ
- 🏨 Tatra, Námestie 1. mája 5, Staré Mesto, ✆ 59272111, IV-V ⓘ
- 🏨 West, Kamzíkov vrch 3139, Kamzíči vrch, ✆ 54788693, III 5
- 🏨 ibis Centrum, Zamocka 38, ✆ 59292000, III ⓘ
- 🛏 Arcus, Moskovska 5, ✆ 55572522, III 1.5
- 🛏 Gremium, Gorkého 11, ✆ 0911118123, OB, II 0.5
- 🏍 Downtown Bratislava B&B, Panenská 31, ✆ 54641191, ✆ 0902072942, I 🛏 1.5
- 🏍 Svoradov, Svoradova 13, ✆ 54411908, ✆ 0910/842917, OB, I ⓘ
- 🏕 Mladá garda, Račianska 3544/103, ✆ 0918/664020, I 4
- 🏕 ura Hronca Student Home, Bernolákova 2716/1, ✆ 0918/664030, I 2
- ⛺ Camping Zlaté Piesky, Cesta na Senec 2a, ✆ 44257373, ✆ 44450592, I 7

Bratislava to Komárno (SK)

Bratislava ⓢ

see Vienna to Bratislava

Čilistov ⓢ

Area Code: 031

- 🏨 Komárán, Pri hrádzi 33, ✆ 5909100, III 0.5
- 🏨 X-Bionic Sphere, Dubová 33/A, ✆ 3262111, VI 0.5
- 🛏 Lindtner, Lipová 34/7, Hársfa ut. 7, ✆ 5626021, ✆ 0905 517 864 0.5

Šamorín ⓢ

Area Code: 031

- 🏨 Samaria, Bratislavská 100/D, ✆ 0905262092, IV 2
- 🚲 Bike Union, Školská 3, ✆ 0948722822 1.5

Gabčíkovo ⓢ

Area Code: 031

- 🏨 Arpad, Hlavana 1040, ✆ 5595555, ✆ 0903/237951, OB, II 0.5
- 🛏 Hóstád, Hlavná 843/16, ✆ 0905/728919 0.5

Ňárad ⓢ

Area Code: 031

- 🛏 Platan, Ňárad 434, ✆ 5549414, ✆ 0908/188585, III 0.5

Vámosszabadi ⓢ

Area Code: 030

- 🛏 Villa Vamus, Széchenyi u. 5, ✆ 9028451, II-III 1
- 🏨 Intertranscoop Lake House, Szabadi ut. 16/B, ✆ 070/4036003, IV. whole chalet for max. 8 persons 2

Nagybajcs ⓢ

- 🛏 Nagybajcsi Lovaspark és Vendégház, Tómelléki út, ✆ 030/6528006, II-III ⓞ
- 🏨 Körtefa Vendégház, Szabadi út 22, II ⓞ

Čičov ⓢ

Area Code: 035

- 🛏 Jolán, Na priekope 676/37, ✆ 3210100, II 0.5

Veľké Kosihy ⓢ

- 🏨 Countryhouse Kukkónia, Nový rad 134 1.5

Nová Stráž 🇸🇰

- 🏨 Villa Modern house near river Danube, 26 Kostolná, IV-V. whole villa for max. 7 pers. 1̲

Komárno 🇸🇰
Area Code: 035

- ℹ️ Tourist Info, nám. Gen. Klapku 1, ☎ 2851305, ☎ 0948/830202 1̲
- 🏨 Banderium, Nám. M.R. Štefánika 11, ☎ 7730156, II-III 0̲.5̲
- 🏨 Bow Garden, Štúrova 1017/2, ☎ 7732237, OB, I-III 1̲
- 🏨 Litovel, Dunajske nábrežie 10, ☎ 0903/443885, II-III 0̲.5̲
- 🏨 Peklo, Platánová alej 1, ☎ 7740620, IV 0̲.5̲
- 🛏️ Apáli, Mŕtve rameno Váhu č. 50, ☎ 7721721 3̲
- 🛏️ Bella, Jókaiho 9, ☎ 7713028, II 1̲
- 🛏️ Duna, Dunajská 2, ☎ 0911/317730, I-II 0̲.5̲
- 🛏️ Hubert Varga, Jókaiho 19, ☎ 7701787, ☎ 0903/219688, I-II 1̲
- 🛏️ Lehár, Lehárova 10, ☎ 0918/293924, OB, I 0̲.5̲
- 🛏️ Olymp, Lehárova 12, ☎ 0917/871787, II 0̲.5̲
- 🛏️ Szekeres, Svätojánska 12, ☎ 7725927, ☎ 905/431665 1̲
- 🏨 Apartmán Silvia, Kalmana Thalyho 9, ☎ 908/524624, III 1̲
- 🚲 piko bike, Meštianska 3018, ☎ 0948/045115 0̲.5̲

Alzbetin ostrov (Komárno) 🇸🇰
Area Code: 035

- 🛏️ Delta, Malodunajské nábrezie 10, ☎ 7731566, II 0̲.5̲
- 🛏️ Marcipán, Malodunajská cesta 9, ☎ 0915/470877, I 0̲.5̲

Bratislava to Komárom (H)

Bratislava 🇸🇰
see Vienna to Bratislava

Petržalka (Bratislava) 🇸🇰
see Vienna to Bratislava

Rusovce 🇸🇰
Area Code: 02

- 🏨 Ponteo - Activity Park Rusovce, Staroríms-ka 1A, ☎ 20909010, ☎ 0911/445542, III-IV 1.5
- 🏨 Pri Kaštieli, Balkánska 57/86, ☎ 62859112, ☎ 0905/411889, I-II 1̲
- 🏨 Rusovský Penzión, Balkánska 114, ☎ 62859572, ☎ 0902/382139, II 1̲

Čunovo 🇸🇰

- 🅱️ Ubytovanie Cunovo, Novosadná 276/12, ☎ 0918/645426, I 0̲.5̲

Rajka 🇭🇺
Area Code: 096

- 🛏️ Kiserdő Vendégház, Ady Endre út 14., ☎ 030/9161724, OB, I 1̲
- 🛏️ Aranykárász Kemping, Mosoni-Duna part, ☎ 030/2164122 0̲

Dunakiliti 🇭🇺
Area Code: 096

- 🏨 Diamant Hotel, Csölösztői út 1, ☎ 671470, V 1̲
- 🛏️ DuNatura Vendégház, Gyümölcsös ut. 49, ☎ 0620/2366837, I 0̲.5̲
- 🛏️ DunaÁgi Vendégház, Rév u. 14, ☎ 0620/2627988, I 0̲
- 🛏️ Villa Hedi, Gyümölcsös út 62, ☎ 224554, ☎ 0630/4591203, I 1̲
- 🏕️ Vadvíz Kemping, Duzzasztómű, ☎ 0630/4866922 1.5
- 🏕️ Vizpart, Csölösztőszigeti út 1, ☎ 224579, ☎ 0630/2253318 1̲

Feketeerdő 🇭🇺

- 🛏️ Luca Háza, Fő u. 7, ☎ 0620/9353203, III 3̲

Dunasziget 🇭🇺
Area Code: 096

- 🛏️ Családi Kalandok Háza, Park u. 6, ☎ 0620/4769422 0̲
- 🛏️ Zátonyi Csárda, Zátonyi u. 2, ☎ 233505, ☎ 0630/9360520, I 0̲
- 🅱️ Búroki Vendégház, Doborgaz u. 46, ☎ 233137, OB 0̲.5̲
- 🏨 Dunaszigeti Erdei Iskola, Sérfenyő u. 26 / b, ☎ 206887, ☎ 0620/2285220, OB, IV-VI 🐾. Sleeping bags are to be taken 0̲
- 🏨 Karolina Apartmanházak, Cikola u. 39a, ☎ 233060, ☎ 0620/3563585 0̲
- 🏨 Maywald Vendégház, Sérfenyő u. 137, ☎ 233350, ☎ 0620/5997749, I-II 0̲.5̲
- 🏕️ Nagyszigeti Sátorozóhely, Dózsa György utca, ☎ 0620/4428501 0̲.5̲
- 🛏️ Szürke Hód, Doborgaz u. 39, ☎ 0620/3960617 0̲.5̲
- 🏕️ Tündérsziget Ökopark Kemping, Fő ut. 65 0̲.5̲

Cikolasziget (Dunasziget) 🇭🇺

- 🏨 Citellus Apartman, Cikola utca 94, ☎ 0630/3996051, IV 0̲
- 🏨 Cikolaszigeti Kisvesszősi kemping, Duna utca 6, ☎ 0620/3960617, OB, I 🐾 0̲.5̲

Kisbodak 🇭🇺

- 🏕️ Esthajnalcsillag Sátorozóhely, Kisbodak Gátőrház u. 1, ☎ 0620/4319220 0̲.5̲

Dunaremete 🇭🇺
Area Code: 096

- 🏨 Ilona Vendégház, Fő u. 1, ☎ 718005, ☎ 0630/2367362 0̲

Lipót 🇭🇺
Area Code: 096

- 🏨 Orchidea, Rákóczi u. 42-44, ☎ 674042, ☎ 0630/4869537, AI, V 0̲
- 🛏️ Fazekas Vendégház, Kossuth út 27, ☎ 96/721316, ☎ 0630/5922590, I 0̲
- 🛏️ 🏨 Kék Duna, Petőfi S. u. 3, ☎ 674018, ☎ 0670/3866823, OB, I 0̲
- 🛏️ 🏨 Orchidea Panzió és Apartmanházak, Békefa sor 5, ☎ 96/960027, ☎ 0630/3864722, I-II 0̲
- 🏨 Fehér Hattyú, Fő út 80, ☎ 720013, ☎ 0630/5606984, I 0̲
- 🏕️ Lipót Termál és Élményfürdő & Camping, Fő u. 84, ☎ 0630/4737656 0̲.5̲

Mosonmagyaróvár 🇭🇺
Area Code: 096

Halászi

- Ciklámen Tourist, Fő út 8., ☎ 555526 [0.5]
- Tourinform, Magyar u. 9, ☎ 206304 [0.5]
- H ▲ Aqua Hotel Termál & Kemping, Kígyó u. 1, ☎ 579168, HB, IV [0.5]
- H Corvina Szálloda, Mosonyi Mihály út 2, ☎ 218131, ☎ 576065, II-III [2]
- H Engler Hotel, Partos u. 14, ☎ 566425, I [2.5]
- H Flexum Thermal Superior, Kolbai Károly u. 10, ☎ 206871, IV [0.5]
- H Fészek Fogadó, Kígyó u. 22, ☎ 211599, ☎ 0620/9823224 od. 0620/2216299, I [0.5]
- H BB Hotel Latja Park, Kórház Str. 6, ☎ 207088, III [0.5]
- H Panoráma, Gulyás Lajos u. 21, ☎ 216167, II [1]
- H Simbad Hotel, Kolbai Károly u. 4, ☎ 0630/6462520, III-IV [0.5]
- Mo ▲ Kis-Duna Motel & Kemping, Gabonarakpart 6, ☎ 216433, I [4]
- Mo Motelnet T, Kölcsey u. 4, ☎ 576796, I [2.5]
- BB Czinger Vendégszobák, Csillag u. 24, ☎ 219807, ☎ 0630/2156948, OB, I [0.5]
- BB Nimród, Királyhidai út 59, ☎ 211141, II [1]
- BB Oroszlán Panzió, Gorkij u. 48, ☎ 213540, ☎ 0630/2590939 [0.5]
- BB Vitalitás panzió, Kereszt u. 5, ☎ 576754, ☎ 0620/3721775, II [0]
- B Kovács, Zurányi u. 9, ☎ 212135, ☎ 213020, ☎ 0630/2984337, I [1]
- AH Erdős Vendégház és Apartman, Horgász u. 7, ☎ 579197, ☎ 0630/5168752, I [2.5]
- ▲ Körkerékpár Szaküzlet, Kolbai Károly u. 23, ☎ 576013, ☎ 0670/4330410 [0.5]

Halászi

Area Code: 096
- BB Regia, Kossuth u. 102, ☎ 210684, ☎ 0620/3128676, I [0]
- AH Radek Vendégház, Kossuth u. 21, ☎ 830314, ☎ 0620/3712060, I [0]
- AH UGO Babos-Major, Kőhídi utca 11, ☎ 210-303, ☎ 0620/9513116, III [0.5]
- ▲ Party Csárda, Duna stny, ☎ 573036, ☎ 0630/2729015 [0.5]

Hédervár

Area Code: 096
- BB Barokk Vendégház, Rózsa F. u. 61, ☎ 0630/4549485, I [0.5]
- BB Hédervári Lovasklub Vendégház, Vámkerék u. 2, ☎ 0630/6304471, I-II [1]
- BB Kont, Kossuth Lajos u. 19, ☎ 571001, ☎ 0630/9792902, OB, III [0]
- BB Park Panzió, Fő út 41, ☎ 204974, ☎ 0630/6227090, I [0]
- AH Kék Apartman, Kossuth L. u. 13, ☎ 215430, ☎ 0630/3742426, I [0]

Kimle

Area Code: 96
- BB Dunahaus Vendégház, Béke u. 59, ☎ 096/228644, ☎ 0630/2707450, OB, I [4]

Novákpuszta (Kimle)

Area Code: 96
- ▲ BB Szigetköz Camping & Vendégház, Iskola u. 2/1, ☎ 096/228068, ☎ 0630/9050500 [3]

Ásványráró

Area Code: 096
- AH Horgásztanya, Petőfi u. 45, ☎ 524988 [2]
- AH Lali Vendégház, Lipóti u. 13, ☎ 0630/9081363, V [1.5]
- ▲ Part Camping, Kikötő u. 51, ☎ 0670/6254881 [2]

Mecsér

Area Code: 096
- BB Dunaparti, Ady E. u. 45, ☎ 213386, ☎ 0620/9495789, OB, I [1.5]

Dunaszentpál

- BB Lovas Panzió, Magyar utca 4, ☎ 096/352291 [2]

Dunaszeg

Area Code: 096
- B Horváth, Fő u. 32, ☎ 602460 [0.5]
- B Pércsi, Rákóczi u. 11, ☎ 352137, ☎ 0620/9648331, I [0]
- B Zöld Vendégház, Szechenyi u. 8, ☎ 602276, ☎ 0620/2003068 [0.5]
- BB La Curia, Somosalja u. 1, ☎ 0630/6485244, III [0]

Győrzámoly

Area Code: 096
- AH Klauz-ház, Szent István u. 5, ☎ 0630/3551484 [0]

Győr

Area Code: 096
- Tourinform Győr, Árpád u. 32, ☎ 311771, ☎ 336817 [0]
- H Alfa, Tihanyi Árpád u. 23, ☎ 316846, II [1]
- H Amarillis Hotel, Királyszék u. 25, ☎ 447261, ☎ 0630/6227241, OB, I [5]
- H Amstel Hattyú Fogadó, Töltésszer u. 18, ☎ 518423, II-III [0.5]
- H Arany Szarvas Fogadó, Radó sétány 1, ☎ 517452, ☎ 0620/2783229, II-III [0.5]
- H Baross, Baross Gábor u. 69, ☎ 516290, ☎ 516300, I [1]
- H Bolero Hotel, Fehérvári u. 75, ☎ 526400, II [1.5]
- H Capitulum, Király u. 3/b, ☎ 512350, III-IV [0.5]
- H Corvin Hotel, Corvin u. 17-19, ☎ 515490, ☎ 312171, II [0.5]
- H Famulus Hotel, Budai u. 4-6, ☎ 547770, IV [0]
- H Fonte Hotel, Kisfaludy u. 38, ☎ 513810, III-IV [0]
- H Fortunátus Szabadidő Klub, Kandó K. u. 15b, ☎ 311206, ☎ 0620/9353940, I [0.5]
- H Golden Ball Club, Szent István u. 4, ☎ 618100, IV [0.5]
- H Ibis Győr, Szent István út 10/b, ☎ 509700, III [0]
- H Isabell, Lakatos u. 15, ☎ 528020, III [1]
- H Klastrom, Zechmeister ut 1, ☎ 516910, III [0.5]
- H Konferencia, Apor Vilmos püspök tére 3, ☎ 511450, III [0]
- H Kálvária, Kálvária u. 22D, ☎ 510800, ☎ 0620/2587211, II-III [1]
- H Lévai, Schweidel u. 23, ☎ 317685, ☎ 335572 [0]

- H Rába, Árpád út 34, ✆ 889400, II-III 0̲
- H Rákóczi, Rákóczi u. 41, ✆ 524703, ✆ 312717, I 0.5̲
- H Révész, Hédervári u. 22-24, ✆ 320667, ✆ 0670/3623279, III 0̲
- H Smaragd Hotel, Eörsy u. 19, ✆ 519283 1.5̲
- H Weldi, Pesti út 35-37, ✆ 529540, III 0̲
- H Wesselényi, Wesselényi u. 3, ✆ 510040, III-IV 0̲
- BB Csendes Éj, Szabadság u. 52, ✆ 333100, ✆ 0670/3899595, I 0.5̲
- BB Duna, Vörösmarty u. 5, ✆ 329084, ✆ 0620/9261778, II-III 0.5̲
- BB Família Panzió, Szt. Imre u. 131/b, ✆ 436961, ✆ 0670/5519999, I 3.5̲
- BB Fantázia Panzió, Banai u. 56/b, ✆ 411819 2̲
- BB Fehér Hajó, Kiss Ernő u. 4, ✆ 317608, ✆ 0670/8812253, I 0.5̲
- BB Gróf Cziráky, Bécsi kapu tér 8, ✆ 528466, ✆ 310688, ✆ 0670/3778707, I-II 0.5̲
- BB Hummel, Kálvária u. 57, ✆ 412599, ✆ 823301, OB, I 1.5̲
- BB Hunyadi, Hunyadi u. 10, ✆ 329162, II 0.5̲
- BB Katalinkert Panzió, Sarkantyú köz 3, ✆ 542087, ✆ 542088, ✆ 0630/2775592, I 0.5̲
- BB Kertész, Iskola u. 11, ✆ 317461, III 0̲
- BB Kiskút, Kiskúti út 41/A, ✆ 0670/8815673, II 0.5̲
- BB AH Kuckó Panzio, Arany János u. 33, ✆ 316260, ✆ 0620/9321941, OB, I 0̲
- BB A Pihenő, 1-es főúton, HRSZ 0681/4,

- ✆ 0670/4536330, I 0̲
- BB RQ Boutique & Unique Hotel, Híd u. 12, ✆ 310408, III 0.5̲
- BB Relax, Rába u. 60, ✆ 315584, II-III 1.5̲
- BB AH Soho Panzió, Kenyér köz 7, ✆ 550465, ✆ 0630/7582181, I-II 0̲
- BB Szederfa Panzió, Hédervári u. 16, ✆ 0620/4283871, OB, I 0̲
- BB Szenti Panzió, Fehérvári u. 155, ✆ 0620/4283871, I-II 2.5̲
- BB Teátrum, Schweidel u. 7, ✆ 310640, II 0̲
- B A City Camping & Bungalow & Apartman, Hédervári út 56, ✆ 325223, OB, I-II 0̲
- 🍴 Blaskovics, Tihanyi Á. út 58., ✆ 421194 1.5̲
- 🍴 Blaskovics, Baross G. út 61-63, ✆ 438174 1̲
- 🍴 George Sport, Szent István út 39., ✆ 0620/3114244 0̲
- 🍴 Peppe, Nagy Imre út 91., ✆ 419507, ✆ 0620/2046685 2.5̲
- 🍴 Álmos Vezér, Corvin u. 44., ✆ 335567, ✆ 0620/2180072 1̲
- ⚡ Charging station, Jókai u. 8, in der Parking Garage Györszol 0.5̲

Bábolna (H)
Area Code: 034
- B Gémesi Család Vendégháza, Jégeri u. 23, ✆ 369087, ✆ 0670/5239729, OB 0.5̲
- B Török, Csikótelepi u. 19, ✆ 369317, ✆ 0670/3752257, I 0.5̲

Ács (H)
Area Code: 034
- AH Akácvirág Vendégház, Akácfa u. 45, ✆ 0630/4573498, I. whole cottage for max. 6 pers. 2.5̲
- A Natura Camping, Fö út 1, ✆ 0630/9467361 0̲
- 🚴 Turcsan Tekerde Kerékpár Centrum, Bartók Béla utca 44, ✆ 0620/7770520 0.5̲

Komárom (H)
Area Code: 034
- ℹ Tourinform, Igmándi út 2, ✆ 540590, ✆ 0630/5172068 0.5̲
- H Aqua, Táncsics M. u. 34, ✆ 342190, II-III 1̲
- H Carrier, Varga József u. 9, ✆ 526445, ✆ 030/5710631, OB, II 0̲ 6̲
- H Forrás, Táncsics Mihály u. 34, ✆ 540177, III 1̲
- H Karát, Czuczor Gergely u. 54, ✆ 342222, ✆ 0620/3320180, I 1̲
- H A Thermál Hotel & Camping, Tancsics M. u. 38, ✆ 341222, III. Admission to the spa included in the hotel price 1̲
- H Tulipán, Kelemen Laszlo u. 1, ✆ 342604, II 0.5̲
- BB Aranytál, Szent László u. 1, ✆ 030/5658599, II 0̲
- BB Kocsis, Táncsics Mihály u. 79, ✆ 342400, I 1̲
- BB Vasmacska/ Pension Anker, Erzsébet tér 2, ✆ 341342, I 0.5̲
- AH Hét Vezér, Táncsics Mihály u. 34, ✆ 540720, III-IV 1̲
- AH Czanek, Táncsics M. u. 47, ✆ 343339,

- ✆ 0620/8244872, III 0.5̲
- AH Ilona, Czuczor utca 47, ✆ 0620/4246411, I 0̲
- A Solaris Camping, Táncsics M. u. 34-36, ✆ 342551 1̲
- A WF Szabadidöpark, Puskaporosi u. 24, ✆ 540448, ✆ 030/6649227, I 3̲
- 🚴 Komfront Kft., Mártírok u. 47, ✆ 344443 1̲

Komárno to Esztergom (SK)

Komárno (SK)
see Bratislava to Komárno (SK)

Alzbetin ostrov (Komárno) (SK)
see Bratislava to Komárno (SK)

Kúpele Patince (Patince) (SK)
Area Code: 035
- H Hotel Wellness Patince, Patince 431, ✆ 0918/886715, IV 0.5̲
- H Olive Family Resort, Patince-kúpele 292, ✆ 7731444, ✆ 0902/179079, II-III 0.5̲
- Hg Harmonia, Areal TK 143, ✆ 0911/187870, III 0.5̲
- BB Bonaparte, Patince kúpele 292, ✆ 7731444, ✆ 0903/444834 0̲

Patince (SK)
Area Code: 035
- AH Paddi Aparmán, Hlavná ulica 11, ✆ 0905/132138 0.5̲

Radvaň nad Dunajom (SK)
- AH Mlyn, Nr. 213, ✆ 0905/717104, II-III 0̲

133

Moča (SK)
Area Code: 035
- **BB** Helén, Hlavná 779, ✆ 7777971, ✆ 0903/231864, I 0.5

Mužla (SK)
Area Code: 0036
- **H** Montanara, Mužla 713, ✆ 7583200, ✆ 0917/519104 0

Štúrovo (SK)
Area Code: 036
- **i** TIK Štúrovo, Hlavná 8, ✆ 7560199, ✆ 0915/755888, III 0.5
- **H AH** Guest Centre, Hlavná 78, ✆ 7511023, ✆ 0908/130079, II-III 0.5
- **H** Hotel Thermal, Pri Vadaši 2, ✆ 7560101, IV-V 0.5
- **H** Zahovay, Námestie Slobody 10, ✆ 7511137, ✆ 0907/432150, OB, I 0
- **BB** Mika, Bocskaiho 29, ✆ 0911/811711, OB, I 0.5
- **BB AH** Penzión Kormoš, Komenského 8, ✆ 7522890, ✆ 0905/513732, I-II 0
- **BB** St. Florian, Széchenyiho 6a, ✆ 7520060, ✆ 0908/796202, ✆ 0908/796202, II-III 0
- **BB** Welya, Pri starej pošte 1, ✆ 7511614, ✆ 0911/667884, OB, III 0.5
- **Ho** Hostel Dunaj, Ostrihomská 6, ✆ 7511036, ✆ 0948/124711, OB, I 🚫 0
- **▲** Campsite ATC Vadaš termálne kúpalisko, Vadašská, ✆ 7560122, ✆ 7560121 0.5
- **▲** Mihálko, Hasičská 3, ✆ 0907/980547 0.5

Esztergom (H)
Area Code: 033
- **i** Irány Esztergom, Széchenyi tér 5 0.5
- **H** St. Adalbert, Dózsa György tér 10, ✆ 541972, ✆ 541900, ✆ 0620/7704528, II 0.5
- **Mo** Grante, Dorogi út 5–7, ✆ 435272, ✆ 0630/9691742, II 4.5
- **BB AH** Alabardos, Bajcsy-Zsilinszky u. 49, ✆ 312640, ✆ 0620/5774061, II 0.5
- **BB** Decsi, Babits Mihály út 12, ✆ 400811, ✆ 0630/5003350, I-II 1
- **BB** El Greco, Pázmány Péter utca 15, ✆ 33/631064, ✆ 0630/9140595, I 0.5
- **BB** Márta Panzió, Bocskoroskúti út 1, ✆ 311983, ✆ 0630/9528016, I 1.5
- **BB** Ria Panzio, Batthyány u. 11-13, ✆ 313115, ✆ 401-428, ✆ 0620/9383091, III 0.5
- **BB** St. Kristóf, Dobozi Mihály u. 11, ✆ 416255, OB, II 1
- **BB** Szalma, Nagy Duna sétány 2, ✆ 315336, ✆ 0630/9549138, I 1
- **BB** Szent György, Andrássy út. 21, ✆ 502180, ✆ 0620/2064587, II 1
- **▲ M** Gran Camping, Nagy Duna stny 3, ✆ 402513, ✆ 0620/9795259 0.5
- **🚴** Altrix Sport Bolt, Kossuth Lajos u. 65, ✆ 502175, ✆ 0620/5307946 1
- **🚴** Neuzer, Mátyás király u. 45, ✆ 500580 4

Komárom to Esztergom (H)

Komárom (H)
see Bratislava to Komárom (H)

Tata (H)
Area Code: 034
- **i** Tourinform, Bercsényi u. 1, ✆ 588633 0.5
- **i** Arnold, Erzsébet királyné tér 8/a, ✆ 588028, ✆ 588130, II 1
- **H** Casablanca, Tópart stny. 3, ✆ 489586, II 1.5
- **H** Gottwald, Fekete ut 1, ✆ 586114, ✆ 0630/1323779, III 🚫 3
- **H** Kalóz Fregatt, Almási u. 2, ✆ 382382, ✆ 0670/3211234, I 0.5
- **H** Kiss, Bacsó B. u. 54, ✆ 586888, II-III 1
- **H** Kristály, Ady Endre út. 22, ✆ 026/383614, III-IV 🚫 0.5
- **H** Penta Lux, Boróka u. 10, ✆ 588140, ✆ 0630/8301491, III 2.5
- **H Ho** Öreg-tó, Fáklya u. 4, ✆ 487960, ✆ 0630/7566116, III 2.5
- **BB** Parti, Boroka u. 6-8, ✆ 487864, I-II 2.5
- **▲** Fényes Fürdö Kemping, Fényes fürdö, ✆ 0630/4300180 0.5
- **🚴** Kerékpár centrum, Bacsó Béla u. 18, ✆ 382610 1
- **🚴** TOM Kerékpár Szaküzlet és Szerviz, Ady Endre u. 48, ✆ 070/5008576 1
- **🚴** Tóparti Kerékpárbolt, Tópart u 18, ✆ 0630/4336738 0.5

Szomód (H)
Area Code: 34
- **BB** Gleichauf Panzió, Tatai u. 20, ✆ 034/491178, ✆ 0630/4392457, I 2.5

Dunaszentmiklós (H)
Area Code: 034
- **BB** Molnár Porta, Petőfi u. 68, ✆ 0620/9753667, I-II 4
- **BB** Rozsa, Uj u. 4, ✆ 491923, ✆ 0620/5607390, II 3.5

Dunaalmás (H)
Area Code: 034
- **BB** Vadvirág, Lilla u. 51, ✆ 450227, ✆ 0630/3618025, I 0.5

Neszmély (H)
Area Code: 034
- **H** Hilltop Neszmely Winehotel, Meleges-hegy Pf. 4, ✆ 550440, ✆ 0670/7746663, III 1.5
- **BB** Szabó Vendégház, Fő u. 144, ✆ 451934, ✆ 0630/4931944 0
- **▲** Duna Büfé és Camping, Vízimolnár u. 2, ✆ 0630/4170628 0
- **▲** Éden, Str Nr. 10, ✆ 0633/474183 0

Nyergesújfalu (H)
Area Code: 033
- **BB** Bali Butique Rooms, Bartók B u 20, ✆ 0620/9528360, II-III 0.5
- **AH** Paskom Aparmanház, Paskom utca 33, ✆ 0630/1437170, III 0.5

Tát
- Fontana, Béke Tér 39, ☎ 0670/5564109, II `1`

Esztergom
siehe Komárno to Esztergom (SK)

Esztergom to Budapest

Esztergom
see Komárno to Esztergom (SK)

Pilismarót
Area Code: 033
- Kishíd Vendégház, Kishíd utca 4, ☎ 0630/9057266, II `0.5`
- Villa Pilis Dunakanyar, Táncsics Mihály u. 9a, ☎ 0620/3245569 `0.5`

Dömös
Area Code: 033
- Dunazug Apartment, Alsórét utca 10, ☎ 0630/5154671, II `0.5`
- Dömös Camping, Dunapart 1, ☎ 482319 `0`

Lepence (Visegrád)
- Thermal Hotel Visegrád, Lepence völgy 2, ☎ 026/801900, ☎ 026/801910, HB, V-VI `0`

Visegrád
Area Code: 026
- Visegrád INFO, Duna-parti út. 1, ☎ 397188 `0`
- Butikhotel, Mátyás király út 61, ☎ 0620/3880676, III-IV `1`
- Honti & Autokamping Kék Duna, Fő u. 66, ☎ 398120, II-III `0`
- Mr Görgey Art Hotel, Fő u. 9, ☎ 01/2279614, ☎ 0630/1394749, HB, IV-V `0`
- Mátyás Tanya, Fő u. 47, ☎ 398309, I `0`
- Royal Club Hotel, Fő u. 92, ☎ 597100, HB, V-VI `0.5`
- Silvanus, Panoráma út 2, ☎ 398311, HB, V `1`
- Visegrád, Rév u. 15, ☎ 397034, HB, IV `0.5`
- Elte, Fő út 117, ☎ 398165, I-II `0`
- Fekete Holló Panzió, Rév u. 12, ☎ 397290, ☎ 0630/8272255, OB, I `0.5`
- Patak Fogadó, Mátyás király u. 92, ☎ 397486, ☎ 0630/9153995, III. For adults only `1.5`
- Villa Harmónia, Mátyás király u. 28, ☎ 0630/1546660, II `0.5`
- Jurta Camping, Mogyoró-hegy, Mátyás király út 4., ☎ 398227, ☎ 020/3997002, ☎ 20/9846052, I `1`

Dunabogdány
Area Code: 026
- Irene Vendégház, Erzsébet Királyné u. 36, ☎ 390170, ☎ 3788039, ☎ 0630/3788039, OB, I `0`

Szob
Area Code: 020
- Malomvölgyi Tabor & Kemping, Malomvölgy telep 1, ☎ 0670/6225709 `4.5`

Zebegény
Area Code: 027
- Hubertus, János Hegy 7, ☎ 373227, ☎ 0630/9522165, II `0`

- Natura Hill, Szarvas utca 76, ☎ 030/5995732, V `1`
- Almáskert, Almáskert u. 13, ☎ 373037, ☎ 030/9494200, III `1.5`
- Malomkerék, Malom u. 21, ☎ 373010, ☎ 0630/9764472, I `1`

Nagymaros
Area Code: 027
- Törökmezői turistaház, Törökmező 013/2 hrsz., ☎ 350063, ☎ 0630/4844684, OB `3.5`
- Camping Nagymaros, Sólyomszigeti út 67., ☎ 355575, ☎ 0630/3688688 `0`

Verőce
Area Code: 027
- Fehér Hattyú, Árpád u. 60, ☎ 350057, ☎ 0630/3261244, I `0`
- Magyarkút, Magyarkúti út 5, ☎ 380587, ☎ 020/5604961, ☎ 0620/5618716, I `3`
- Csobogó Vendégház, Zentai u. 52, ☎ 0670/3683341, III `1`
- Ilona Prémium Vendégház, Szokolyai út 40, ☎ 0620/3982020, II-III `0.5`
- ODU House, Meredek köz 3, ☎ 0630/5877072 `0.5`

Vác
Area Code: 027
- Tourinform, Március 15 tér 17, ☎ 316160 `0`
- Camelot Club, HRSZ 07, at the main street 12 between Veroce and Vac, ☎ 308310, ☎ 0620/6658170, II `0`

- Vörössipka, Honvéd u. 14, ☎ 501055, I `1`
- Csillag, Balassagyarmati út 8, ☎ 316421, II `0.5`
- Napsugár, Papp Béla ut 15, ☎ 316490, I `0.5`
- Zeke, Zeke u. 5, ☎ 313206, ☎ 30 525 4046, I `1`
- Alt-Tabán Guesthouse, Tabán u. 25, ☎ 316860, ☎ 030/9103428, I `0`
- Szivárvány, Újhegyi u. 106, ☎ 315831, ☎ 0620/5395291, OB, III `1`
- Fónagy & Walter, Budapesti főút 36, ☎ 310682, ☎ 0630/9615116, II `0.5`
- Lujza & Koriander, Ady Endre sétány 5, ☎ 0630/190664, II `0`
- Göncöl, Ilona u. 3, ☎ /020/7727982, ☎ 0620/7727970, OB, I `0`
- DZ Bike, Galcsek u. 8-10, ☎ 310554 `1`

Szigetmonostor
Area Code: 026
- Rezeda Resort, Rezeda út 27, ☎ 0630/7436287 od. 0630/4455711 `1`
- Regatta, Parti u. 16, ☎ 0670/3702002, II `1`

Dunakeszi
- Kikelet Panzió, Kikelet utca 1, ☎ 0670/2215544, II-III `0.5`
- Part Cafe Pension, Duna sor 20, ☎ 027/349225, ☎ 0630/505/611, I `0`

Budapest/Káposztásmegyer
- Aquaworld, Íves út 16, ☎ 01/2313600, IV-V `1.5`

Budapest/XV. kerület
Area Code: 01
- Pólus, Szentmihályi út 131, ☎ 4109600, I `5`

Accommodation and service directory
Budapest/XIII. kerület – Budapest/I. kerület

Budapest/XIII. kerület
Area Code: 01
- Danubius Hotel Helia, Kárpát utca 62-64, ✆ 8895800, IV-V
- Ensana Grand Margaret Island, Margitsziget, ✆ 8894752, ✆ 01/8894700, IV 0.5
- Fortuna Boat, Szt. István park, alsó rakpart, ✆ 7001854, ✆ 0670/3894305, II
- Island Hostel, Sirály Csónakház, Margitsziget, ✆ 0630/5877079, I-II 0.5
- Apartment4you Budapest, Victor Hugo u. 25, ✆ 0630/9147606, II 0.5

Budapest/XXII. kerület
Area Code: 01
- Belle Fleur, Bencés u. 32, ✆ 2282374, II-III 6

Tahitótfalu
Area Code: 026
- Garden Étterem Kávézó, Visegrádi út 58, ✆ 385025, ✆ 0620/3282047, OB, II 0
- Boglárka Üdülőház, Pacsirta u. 34, ✆ 35310543, OB 0.5
- Duna Camping Panzió, Kamping u., ✆ 385216, ✆ 0670/3677830 0

Leányfalu
Area Code: 026
- Kati Pihenőház, Temető u. 6, ✆ 380278, ✆ 0621/3251040, OB, II 1
- Villa Székely, Mókus u. 5, ✆ 0670/3272162, ✆ 0630/3857252, I-II 0.5
- Dunakanyar Kemping, Alszeghy tér 1,

✆ 383154, ✆ 0670/7718311 0

Szentendre
Area Code: 026
- Tourinform, Dumtsa Jenő u. 22, ✆ 317965 0
- All Waterfront Hotel, Dunakorzó 5, Yacht Club, ✆ 500478, ✆ 0670/3258925, I-II 0.5
- Bükkös, Bükköspart 16, ✆ 501360, IV 0.5
- Centrum, Bogdányi u. 15, Dunakorzó, ✆ 302500, OB, II-III 0
- Panzió 100, Ady Endre u. 100, ✆ 310661, II-III 0.5
- Róz, Pannónia u. 6/b, ✆ 311737, ✆ 0620/9995660, III 0
- Cola, Dunakanyar krt. 50, ✆ 310410, I 0.5
- Corner, Dunakorzó 4, ✆ 300027, ✆ 0670/3277195, OB, I-II 0
- Erika Vendégház, Levendula u. 7, ✆ 313633, ✆ 0620/3339701, OB, I 0.5
- Horváth Fogadó, Darupiac 2, ✆ 313950, ✆ 0620/9710036, II 0.5
- Ilona, Rákóczi F. u. 11, ✆ 313599, ✆ 0620/5629841, I 0.5
- Mathias Rex, Kossuth u. 16, ✆ 505570, II-III 0.5
- Szent Andrea, Egres ú. 22, ✆ 311989, ✆ 311989, ✆ 0630/9007821, I 0.5
- Vadrózsa, Vadrózsa u. 5-7, ✆ 314849, II 1.5
- Zita, Örtorony u. 16, ✆ 313866, I 0.5
- Jesztrebszki Tiborné, Levendula u. 10, ✆ 313636 0.5

- Jászai Tibor Lászlóné, Céh u. 3, ✆ 310657, ✆ 0630/3138731, I☏ 0.5
- Főtér, Futó u. 3, ✆ 0630/4733128, III 0
- Pap-Szigeti Camping & Pension Paprika, Pap Sziget, ✆ 310697, ✆ 310909 0.5
- Balázs Kerékpárbolt, Előd u. 2/a, ✆ 312111, ✆ 0620/2031246 0.5

Pomáz
Area Code: 026
- Tutti Panzió, Budakalászi u. 14, ✆ 325888, ✆ 0630/3612160, OB, I 3

Budakalász
Area Code: 026
- Jármy, Fürj u. 13, ✆ 342700, ✆ 0204350487, I 2.5
- Müller-Fogadó, Pomázi u. 42, ✆ 342733, ✆ 0630/3906982, I 3
- Cuki, Budai u. 39, ✆ 341238 2
- Lupa, Tó u. 1, ✆ 0670/3807129 0.5

Üröm
Area Code: 026
- Kőhegy Fogado, Kőhegy u. 73/14, II 4

Budapest
Area Code: 01
- Tourinform, Sütő utca 2, Deák tér, ✆ 3188718 1
- Bike & Relax Kft, Madach Imre ut 12, ✆ 0043 664 402 1691, ✆ 0630/3008003 1.5
- Bar-Ker, Cserhát u. 16, ✆ 3522395 3
- Bringangyal, Balzac u. 48a,

✆ 0620/5553884 0.5
- Duna, Katona József u. 3, ✆ 0670/4515526 0.5
- K2 Bike, Pacsirtamező u. 16, ✆ 4530818, ✆ 0630/9952728 0.5
- Wilker, Árpád fejedelem út 8, ✆ 3263646 0
- Bringóhintó, Hajós Alfréd sétány 1, Margitsziget, ✆ 3292073, ✆ 0620/4234600. Pedal car rental 0.5
- Dynamo Bike and Bake, Képíró u. 6, ✆ 0630/8681107 1

Budapest/I. kerület
Area Code: 01
- Aquincum, Árpád fejedelem útja 94, ✆ 4364159, V 0
- Art'otel, Bem rakpart 16-19, ✆ 4879487, V 0
- Benczúr, Benczúr utca 35, ✆ 4795650, II-III 2
- Budapest Marriott, Apáczai Cserer János utca 4, ✆ 4865000, VI 0.5
- Carlton Hotel, Apor Péter utca 3, ✆ 2240999, III-V 0
- Hilton Budapest, Hess András tér 1-3, ✆ 8896600, V-VI 0.5
- Mercure Buda, Krisztina körút 41-43, ✆ 4888100, IV 1
- Novotel Centrum, Rákóczi út 43-45, ✆ 4696103608, I 2
- Orion, Döbrentei utca 13, ✆ 3568583, III-IV 1
- Victoria, Bem rakpart 11, ✆ 4578080, IV-V 0

Budapest/II. kerület
Area Code: 01
- [H] Beatrix, Széher út 3, ☎ 2750550, III 4
- [H] Tiliana, Hárshegyi út 1-3, ☎ 3910027, III-IV 5
- [B&B] Mohácsi, Bimbó út 25/A, ☎ 3267741, ☎ 0620/3233154, I-II 1
- [Ho] Grand Hostel, Hűvösvölgyi út 69, Versec sor 1, ☎ 2741111, I-II ⚤ 4

Budapest/III. kerület
Area Code: 01
- [H] Alfa Art, Királyok útja 205, Kossuth Lajos üdülőpart 102, ☎ 4530060, ☎ 4530062, ☎ 0620/3967555, III-IV 0
- [H] Attila Hotel, Attila u. 20, ☎ 2403373, II-III 1.5
- [H] Bed-Breakfast, Rozália utca 76-78, ☎ 4541610, I 1.5
- [B&B] Alfred, Vasút sor 20, ☎ 4369316, ☎ 0630/5255832, II 1.5

Budapest/V. kerület
Area Code: 01
- [H] Danubius Hotel Astoria, Kossuth Lajos utca 19-21, ☎ 8896000, IV-VI 1
- [H] Danubius Hotel Erzsébet City Center, Károlyi Mihály utca 11-15, ☎ 8893700, V-VI 1
- [H] InterContinental, Apáczai Csere J. u. 12-14, ☎ 3276333, V-VI 0.5
- [H] Kempinski Corvinus, Erzsébét tér 7-8, ☎ 4293777, VI[⚤] 1
- [H] Mercure Budapest City Center, Váci utca 20, ☎ 4853100, IV 0.5
- [H] Mercure Budapest Korona, Kecskeméti utca 14, ☎ 4868800, IV 1
- [H] Parlament, Kálmán Imre u. 19, ☎ 3746000, IV-VI 1
- [B&B] Old Monarchia Hotel, Váci utca 79, ☎ 266-6479, ☎ 0620/4358875, I 1
- [Ho] Domino Top Hostel, Váci u. 44, ☎ 2350492, ☎ 0620/4627287, I ⚤ 0.5
- [Ho] Maverick, Ferenciek tere 2, ☎ 2673166, OB, I-II 0.5

Budapest/VI. kerület
Area Code: 01
- [H] Cortile, Dessewffy u. 14, ☎ 6049339, IV-V 1
- [H] Ibis Budapest Heroes Square, Dózsa György út 106, ☎ 2695300, II-III 2
- [H] Medosz, Jókai tér 9, ☎ 3743000, III 1.5
- [H] Radisson Blu Béke, Teréz körút 43, ☎ 8893900, IV-V 1
- [Ho] Home Made, Teréz krt. 22, ☎ 3022103, ☎ 030/2004546, I 1.5

Budapest/VII. kerület
Area Code: 01
- [H] Baross City Hotel, Baross tér 15, ☎ 4613010, III-IV 3
- [H] Hungaria City Center, Rákoczi ut 90, ☎ 8894400, III-VI 2.5
- [H] Ibis Budapest City, Akácfa utca 1-3, ☎ 4783050, III-IV 2
- [H] Ibis Styles Budapest Center, Rákóczi út 58, ☎ 4628100, III-IV 2

Budapest/VIII. kerület
Area Code: 01
- [H] Museum, Trefort u. 2, ☎ 4851080, III-V 1.5
- [H] The Three Corners Hotel Anna, Gyulai Pál u. 14, ☎ 9009071, III-IV 1.5
- [Ho] Budapest, Könyves Kálmán körút 64, ☎ 2100816, I ⚤ 4.5

Budapest/IX. kerület
Area Code: 01
- [H] Actor, Viola u. 10-14, ☎ 7092423, ☎ 3230027, III-IV 2.5
- [H] Ibis Budapest Aero, Ferde utca 1-3, ☎ 3479700, III 7
- [H] Ibis Budapest Centrum, Ráday utca 6, ☎ 4564100, III-IV 1.5
- [B&B] Boulevard City Pension, Angyal utca 13, ☎ 2152169, ☎ 30 9217 673 2
- [Ho] Barocco, Lónyay u. 9/1/5, ☎ 9520089, I 1
- [Ho] Violet Premium Hostel, Lónyay u. 25, ☎ 0630/2901357, I 1.5
- [C] Haller Camping, Haller utca 27, ☎ 0630/2310923 3.5

Budapest/X. kerület
Area Code: 01
- [H] Expo Congress Hotel, Expo tér 2, ☎ 2636800, IV-V 6
- [C/B&B] Arena Camping Budapest, Pilisi ucta 7, ☎ 0630/2969129, I 8

Budapest/XI. kerület
Area Code: 01
- [H] Bara, Hegyalja u. 36-36, ☎ 3853445, ☎ 2094905, I-III 1.5
- [H] Luna, Vegyész utca 17, ☎ 2046868, ☎ 0620/3604112, III 5
- [H] Rubin Wellness & Conference Hotel, Dayka Gábor utca 3, ☎ 5053600, III-IV 3
- [H] Ventura, Fehérvári út 179, ☎ 2081232, III-IV 4
- [B&B] Korona, Sasadi út 123, ☎ 3191255, OB, I-III 3.5

[AH] Agape, Akácfa ucta 12, ☎ 7004102, ☎ 0620/9327260, OB, II-IV 2

English-Hungarian-Slovak dictionary

English	Hungarian	Slovak
Numbers		
zero	nulla	nula
one	egy	jeden
two	kettő, két	dve
three	három	tri
four	négy	štyri
five	öt	päť
six	hat	šesť
seven	hét	sedem
eight	nyolc	osem
nine	kilenc	deväť
ten	tíz	desať
Greetings		
Good morning!	Jó reggelt!	Dobré ráno!
Good day!	Jó napot!	Dobrý deň!
Good evening!	Jó estét!	Dobrý večer!
Good night!	Jó éjszakát!	dobrú noc!
Goodbye!	Viszontlátásra!	do videnia!
Thank you!	Köszönöm!	dakujem

English	Hungarian	Slovak
Help!	Segítség!	pomoc
please	kérem, tessék	prosim
yes	igen	áno
no	nem	nie
Weekdays		
monday	hétfő	pondelok
tuesday	kedd	utorok
wednesday	szerda	streda
thursday	csütörtök	štvrtok
friday	péntek	piatok
saturday	szombat	sobota
sunday	vasárnap	nedela
tomorrow	holnap	zajtra
yesterday	tegnap	včera
today	ma	dnes
midday	délben	na obed
holiday	ünnep(nap)	sviatok

English	Hungarian	Slovak
Directions		
straight	egyenesen	priamo
left	bal, balra	dolava
right	jobb, jobbra	doprava
downhill	lefelé	nadol
uphill	felfelé	do kopca
back	vissza	späť
centre	központ	centrum
railway station	pályaudvar	železničná stanica
railway stop	állomás	železničná zastávka
hospital	kórház	nemocnica
doctor	orvos	lekár
time	idő	doba
bridge	híd	most
lake	tó	jazero
river	folyó	rieka
mountain	hegy	hora
church	templom	kostol
city/town	város	mesto
village	falu	dedina

English	Hungarian	Slovak
square	tér	námestie
street	utca, út	ulica, cesta
pool	fürdö	bazén
toilet	vécé, toalett	toaleta
room	szoba	izba

Shopping

English	Hungarian	Slovak
money change	pénzt váltani	vymeniť pe niaze
pharmacy	gyógyszertár	lekáreň
service	kiszolgálás	služba
shop	üzlet	obchod
open	nyitva	otvorený
closed	zárva/szünnap	zatvorený
pay	fizet, kifizet	zaplatiť
market	piac	trh
groceries	élelmiszer	potraviny

Eating

English	Hungarian	Slovak
eat	Enni	jesť
inn	vendéglö	hostinec
occupied	foglalt	obsadený
available	szabad	voľne
order	rendelni	objednať
menu	étlap	jedálny listok
breakfast	reggeli	raňajky
lunch	ebéd	obed
dinner	vacsora	večera
beer	sör	pivo
bread	kenyér	chlieb
butter	vaj	maslo
eggs	tojás	vajce
fish	hal	ryba
red meat	hús	mäso
poultry	szárnyas	hydina
vegetables	zöldség	zelenina
coffee	kávé	káva
potatoes	burgonya	zemiak
cheese	sajt	syr
milk	tej	mlieko
rice	rízs	ryža
salad	saláta	salát
soup	leves	polievka
water	víz	voda
wine	bor	vino
saussage	kolbász	klobása, saláma

Bicycle

English	Hungarian	Slovak
bicycle	kerékpár	bicykel
bicycle lock	zár	zámka
air	levegö	vzduch, po vetrie
tools	szerszám	nástroj, náradie
screw	csavar	skrutka
tire	abroncs	bicyklová pneumatika

Location index

Page numbers from page 126 refer to the list of accommodations

A
Ács	78, 133
Almásfüzitő	94
Alzbetin ostrov	131, 133
Ásványráró	68, 132

B
Bábolna	76, 133
Bad Deutsch-Altenburg	35, 129
Baka	49
Bana	76
Bezenye	63
Bratislava	40, 130, 131
Budakalász	136
Budapest	120, 136

C
Čenkov	84
Číčov	52, 130
Cikolasziget	62, 131
Čilistov	46, 130
Čunovo	57, 131

D
Dömös	103, 135
Dunaalmás	94, 134
Dunabogdány	107, 135
Dunakeszi	112, 135
Dunakiliti	61, 131
Dunaremete	131
Dunaszeg	68, 132
Dunaszentmiklós	134
Dunaszentpál	132
Dunasziget	62, 131

E
Eckartsau	34, 129
Engelhartstetten	129
Esztergom	86, 134, 135

F
Feketeerdő	131

G
Gabčíkovo	50, 130
Göd	112
Gönyű	75
Győr	70, 132
Győrzámoly	132

H
Hainburg a.d. Donau	36, 130
Halászi	68, 132
Haslau-Maria Ellend	30, 129
Hédervár	63, 68, 132

I
Iža	83

K
Káposztásmegyer	136
Kimle	132
Kisbodak	131
Klížska Nemá	52
Kľúčovec	52
Komárno	54, 131, 133
Komárom	78, 133, 134
Kravany nad Dunajom	84
Kúpele Patince	84, 133
Kyselica	49

L
Lábatlan	100
Leányfalu	112, 136
Lepence	103, 135
Lipót	63, 131
Loimersdorf	129

M
Malé Kosihy	52
Mecsér	132
Medveďov	52
Moča	84, 134
Mosonmagyaróvár	64, 132
Mužla	84, 134

N
Nagybajcs	130
Nagymaros	108, 135
Nagyszentjános	76
Ňárad	130
Neszmély	98, 134
Novákpuszta	132
Nová Stráž	131
Nyergesújfalu	101, 134

O
Obid	84
Orth an der Donau	30, 129

P
Patince	134
Petronell-Carnuntum	32, 129
Petržalka	130, 131
Pilismarót	103, 135
Pomáz	136
Püski	62

R
Radvaň nad Dunajom	84, 134
Ragendorf	58
Rajka	58, 131
Rusovce	131

S
Šamorín	130
Scharndorf	30, 129
Schönau an der Donau	29
Stopfenreuth	34
Štúrovo	86, 134
Süttő	100
Szentendre	114, 136
Szigetmonostor	135
Szob	107, 135
Sződliget	112
Szomód	134
Szőny	93

T
Tahitótfalu	107, 112, 136
Tát	101, 135
Tata	94, 134

U
Üröm	136

V
Vác	109, 135
Vámosszabadi	130
Veľké Kosihy	131
Verőce	109, 135
Visegrád	103, 135

W
Wien	20, 127
Wolfsthal	38, 130

Z
Zebegény	108, 135
Žitava	84